The Fate of the
Revolution

The Fate of the Revolution

INTERPRETATIONS OF
SOVIET HISTORY
FROM 1917 TO THE PRESENT

Revised and Updated

by
Walter Laqueur

CHARLES SCRIBNER'S SONS

NEW YORK

Copyright © 1967, 1987 by Walter Laqueur

Charles Scribner's Sons
Macmillan Publishing Company
866 Third Avenue, New York, N.Y. 10022

Library of Congress Cataloging-in-Publication Data

Laqueur, Walter, 1921–
  The fate of the Revolution.

  Bibliography: p.
  Includes index.
  1. Soviet Union—History—Revolution, 1917–1921—
Historiography. I. Title.
DK265.A553L37 1987   947.084′1′072   87-7783
ISBN 0-684-18903-8

10 9 8 7 6 5 4 3 2 1

Printed in the United States of America

Contents

CONTENTS

Preface (1987)

Seventy years have passed since the uprising in Petrograd, twenty years since this study of the interpretations of the October revolution and the course of Soviet history was first published. The issues that were hotly discussed in the 1950s and 60s – the causes of the revolution, the place of Lenin and Stalin in history, the question of inevitability, and other problems are still as much debated as they were at the time. When the present book first appeared the Brezhnev era had just dawned, de-Stalinization was frozen like much else in the Soviet Union. The resolutions of the 20th and 22nd party congresses (1956 and 1962), which were to serve as 'milestones for generations to come', became non-events as were the admonitions to 'fully restore historical truth' (Resolutions of the 22nd congress).

The following years witnessed the opening of new institutes and the launching of new journals in Moscow and other Soviet centers, as well as the publication of many books. But compared with the (modest) liberalization that had been inaugurated by Khrushchev, the subsequent two decades were a period of retreat on the 'historical front'.

In 1987 we witness the dawn of yet another era, the *perestroika* (restructuring) of Soviet society. As these lines are written, it is as yet uncertain how far and how fast the reform will go, whether, and to what extent, it will affect the 'ideological superstructure', which includes the writing of history; whether, in other words, it is yet another false dawn, or whether changes of real substance may take place. Historical issues that were taboo for twenty years are again mentioned in novels and movies. Will a similar license be given to historians?

New histories of the Communist party and the Soviet Union were announced in 1986. The amazing Mr. Mints, aged ninety-one, a member of the Academy and doyen of Soviet historians who had been involved in the writing of all Communist party histories since Stalin's days, made it known that the guiding principles of these new histories would be 'democratism, openness, bold and candid judgment, and a critical approach'.* He also said that while it would be naive to hope that reorganization in the field of history would proceed at a rapid rate, historians would begin to take a calmer view of many facts and developments without blinkers and dogmatism – 'in a word, more honestly'. This meant, no doubt, a more positive attitude towards the NEP (the era of the New Economic Policy initiated by Lenin in 1921) that became something like a model in the early Gorbachev years. It also implied a more critical approach toward the collectivization of agriculture as well as the partial rehabilitation of Khrushchev, who is now regarded as a well-meaning, if bumbling and erratic, leader who genuinely wanted to break with the negative heritage of the past. Soviet publications in the early Gorbachev period reveal a conflicting pattern: While some criticized Stalin and his system, others defended him. Nor was it clear whether such dissonances were to become a lasting feature or whether they were only manifestations of confusion, a transitional period in the emergence of a new party line. In 1956, under Khrushchev, the historians had moved more quickly towards a more liberal approach, only to retreat a few years later.

When Gorbachev met a group of leading Soviet writers in June 1986 he told them that one of the aspects still off limits to *glasnost* (openness) was the Soviet past: 'If we start to deal with the past, we'll lose all our energy. It would be like hitting the people over the head. We'll have to go forward. Eventually we'll sort out the past and put everything in its place. But right now we have to put our energy forward'.

But can one go forward without having confronted the past? By February 1987 Gorbachev seemed to have reached the conclusion that the historians, too, needed some more *glasnost*. In a speech to leading representatives of the Soviet mass media he said, 'There should be no forgotten names or blanks either in history or literature', and later on, 'those who made the revolution must not be pushed in the background. . . . It is immoral to forget or pass

---

* *Tass* interview, March 4, 1987. Another, more detailed, interview with Mints was published in *Ogonyok*, February 1987.

over in silence large periods in the life of the people.' It remains to be seen whether this refers only to Bukharin and Rykov, the forefathers of the 'communism with a human face' school of thought, who were almost rehabilitated in 1956, or whether Trotsky, too, will benefit from the new spirit. How will the Mensheviks, Social Revolutionaries, and Anarchists fare? What about the place in history of those who opposed the revolution? Will there be a change in the party line or will historians be permitted – within reasonable limits – to write the historical truth as they see it, even if it should not coincide with the official histories?

At best these changes will not come overnight, and, as in other fields, they will face resistance. In the meantime the controversies about Russia's past and present continue in the West. These changes to a certain extent reflect the general climate. If, as the radicals claimed, Western historiography of the 1950s had been influenced by the Cold War, the radicalism of the 1970s was determined by Vietnam and Watergate.

Nevertheless, there is a danger of exaggerating the *Zeitgeist*. On historical studies of value and importance it always had some influence but seldom a decisive impact. There never was a party line in Soviet studies in the West. Most of the important work was done by individuals following their own convictions and predilections rather than by intellectual fashions and constraints.

In the twenty years since this book was first published, many hundreds of studies on recent Soviet history were published in various languages. But since it was never my intention to provide a full review of the literature, I have not singled out even all the most important among them. I tried to concentrate on issues, on the main bones of contention and I am grateful for the advice of several colleagues whose service in the cause of Soviet studies has been more constant than mine. I would like to thank Peter O'Brien, Michael Uster, and Pamela Rein, who assisted me in my research. The original version of "Totalitarianism" first appeared in *Commentary* (October 1985), but I have enlarged the chapter and made changes in light of the debate which followed, and as the result of further thinking on the subject.

March 1987
Washington, D.C.

Preface (1967)

This is a study of the problems which have faced historians of the Soviet Union, and a discussion of their interpretations. It is meant to be an introduction to the Soviet period of Russian history, but in itself it is neither a history nor a bibliography. I was aware before I started – and I am even more painfully aware now – of the difficulties involved in writing a book of this sort. The gulf between the professional and the general student of history is steadily widening, as in all other fields of learning, and it is increasingly difficult to bridge it and re-establish communication. There are other obstacles. Professor Geyl's *Napoleon: For and Against* was in many ways my model, but it was clear to me from the beginning that in this book the approach would have to be different. I have tried to reproduce or to summarize fairly views and arguments that are not my own. All other problems apart, the writer about Russia faces greater methodological difficulties than his colleagues who tackle the French Revolution or Napoleon. The literature is far more extensive, and he has to be more selective, more critical, more arbitrary, and this of course makes him more vulnerable to criticism.

If this were a survey of historical writing about the Soviet Union it would clearly be indefensible to comment on certain writers at considerable length, while devoting only a few lines to others of equal merit. But the problems facing the historian often emerge more clearly from controversial books than from straight scholarly ones. If I were to rewrite this book now, perhaps I would exclude some writers and schools of thought and include others, but there is no ideal solution to satisfy everyone, a work many times this size would be needed, which would defeat its purpose. As Voltaire wrote in a letter to Bertin de Rocheret: The man who ventures to write contemporary history must expect to be attacked both for everything he has said and for everything he has not said.

I have not tried to break fresh ground in this book as far as source material is concerned, nor have I attempted an historical synthesis. The aim was less ambitious. I wanted to provide a guide for the non-expert, to stimulate further study and critical thought rather than offer my own answers to the many questions posed. I felt that in a book of this kind the personal note should not be too strong. Such restraint has certain disadvantages, and it may above all create the impression of a false symmetry. The fact that apologists for Stalin are discussed, as well as critics, may lead some to the mistaken conclusion that historical truth is likely to be somewhere in the middle between the two extremes.

This book has grown partly out of a series of lectures at Brandeis University; sections of the first two chapters were originally published in *Survey*. I am grateful to several friends who read the manuscript and provided detailed criticism. Mrs Annette Pringle helped me to obtain many publications, and with reading the proofs. I am grateful for Mr Zeev Ben Shlomo's assistance in the research on some chapters and for Mrs Mary Michaelides' and Mrs Meriel Wyndham Baker's help in typing and retyping the manuscript.

The Fate of the
Revolution

« I »

Russia and the West

It is difficult to think of any great historical event on which there is unanimity of opinion. A recent historian of the French Revolution has noted that while there is universal agreement on the main events such as the meeting of the States General, the fall of the monarchy, or the execution of Robespierre, there continues to be controversy about all the wider issues, whether it was a revolution of poverty or prosperity, whether it was a bourgeois revolution that overthrew feudalism or a national struggle for liberty and democracy. There continues to be a controversy not only about its 'class character', political significance and ultimate achievement, but even about such questions as when it began, when it ended, and what were its most significant landmarks.[1]

If debates of this character continue about the French Revolution (or about the causes of the English Civil War, or the origins of the American Civil War), the fact that there is more than one interpretation of the Russian Revolution of 1917 and of Soviet history since that date, will not come as a surprise. The Russian Revolution is not only that much nearer to us in time; its impact has been far more universal than any of the events mentioned so far. On that at least there is full agreement among those who have provided conflicting explanations in other respects. There is much dispute as to whether the second uprising that took place in Russia in 1917 was a *coup* engineered by a militant minority, or a revolution that had the backing of the masses. There are conflicting views about almost every major phase of Soviet history, whether Stalinism was inherent already in the régime established by Lenin, whether Stalin was really necessary, whether his policy of rapid industrialization and forced collectivization was the only possible one. Hardly anyone will now dispute the historical importance of Lenin, or defend the purges and

---

[1] G. Rudé, *Interpretations of the French Revolution*, London, 1961, p. 3.

1

trials of the nineteen-thirties. But on how many other events, or persons, or policies is there similar agreement? Certainly not on Western policies *vis-à-vis* Russia, or the Russo-German pact of 1939; neither on the significance of the October revolution, nor on the achievements of five decades of Soviet rule. There is no agreement on whether Leninism is a legitimate offspring of Marxism, or to what extent ideology shaped Soviet policy in the past, and matters now. We have had the long debates about totalitarianism, and more recently about a possible convergence between the Soviet Union and the West. Few are willing to try answering the question whether the revolution is finished, or whether it still continues. Frequently these are quarrels between communists and their critics. But if that were the only dividing line our task would be a much easier one. There are, however, many different views within the non-communist camp. One need only study a few successive editions of Soviet history books to realize how often and how radically official interpretations have changed there.

The present work is an attempt to review and to compare some of these interpretations. One of the questions that has intrigued the author is whether the historical experience of five decades offers present-day observers any lessons or guidance. I use the term 'lesson' with some hesitation; eighty years ago, historians were more sanguine in this respect than they are now. Henry Adams, in a famous address to the American Historical Association, spoke of a generation which felt that it was on the verge of some discovery that would do for history what Darwin had done for nature. That discovery, alas, has not yet been made, and most historians now would rather agree with Lucien Febvre, who wrote that the only thing history teaches us is that there are no historical lessons – '*elle renseigne rigoureusement rien*', as Paul Valéry said. If so, what value is there in reviewing and reassessing the work of past historians? For if each historical situation is unique and unrepeatable, if all historical explanation is a fabric riddled with innumerable holes, what can the insights and mistakes of historians of past generations teach us? These are legitimate questions, although they arise more suitably at the end of this essay than at the beginning.

The literature on the Russian Revolution and the history of the Soviet Union is immense and many volumes this size would be needed to cover so extensive a bibliography. I have chosen such books as seemed to be of particular interest in the context of the present study; this was the sole criterion. I have interpreted 'contemporary history' in the widest sense, to include the writing of philosophers, journalists, social and political scientists. Contemporary history is a wide-open field; historians have often shied away from dealing with unfinished trends and processes, with topics on which few reliable sources are available. Non-professionals have not been hampered by these inhibitions, and the results have sometimes been disastrous. But it is also true that of the most important contributions to the study of the Soviet Union, many have been made by outsiders or, at any rate, latecomers to the groves of academe. Professional historians may have a rigorous training and special techniques, but they have a monopoly neither of detachment, nor of wisdom and insight; to limit our discussion to their works would have been impossible.

One more preliminary note: there is in the nature of this topic a strong temptation not only to take sides but to award marks, ranging the writers of the twenties and thirties in order of merit. I have attempted to give a fair account of diametrically opposed writers and schools of thought, but I do not think that objectivity, detachment and impartiality are necessarily synonyms. Detachment is of course the great, permanent, if for ever elusive ideal. But is it not also true that the superhuman efforts made by some historians to stand *au dessus de la mêlée* often have had unfortunate effects? I agree with Stuart Hughes that what results from this kind of bloodless history, inspired by antiquarian curiosity rather than deep personal concern, often has no clear focus and is shot through with metaphysical and moral assumptions that are all the more insidious for being artfully concealed. But this does not give us the right to write partisan history with a good conscience. The philosophical discussions on whether there is historical truth and what constitute historical facts are likely to continue for ever. There is a danger of too much sociology of knowledge, just as there is a danger of too little. A political philosophy is not like a taste for ice-cream, in the sense that there is no point in arguing, and that one can only state one's taste and depart. The idea that each *Weltanschauung* is somehow *unmittelbar zu Gott*, that (to mention but one example) the interpretation of the Russian Revolution given by the late Alfred Rosenberg ought to be taken as seriously as the views of, say, Messrs E. H. Carr and Seton-Watson, strikes me as somewhat fanciful. There is no need to bother with statements about Russia's

3

development that are manifestly wrong. If someone says that fifty years hence the Soviet Union will be the richest and freest country in the world, this can be neither proven nor refuted. If he says it is now, or has been all along, there is no reason to take him seriously. I would like to give one more example: the industrial production of the Soviet Union, in particular heavy industry, has made considerable headway over the last thirty-five years. It can be argued that these advances were achieved at the price of great sacrifices, material and other, but any interpretation of Soviet history that denies this, or considers Soviet economic progress irrelevant, is not worthy of serious consideration.

Lastly, some words in defence of contemporary history against its detractors. There are two main arguments against contemporary history: the one is that the source material is usually not available to provide the necessary information about events and trends in the recent past. (*Pas de documents, pas d'histoire,* as a famous history textbook said.) This is unfortunately correct as far as Soviet history is concerned, though it applies to a much lesser extent to other aspects of contemporary history. The historian of the French Revolution has long had a great deal of documentation at his disposal; the position of the historian of the Soviet Union is rather less fortunate. He does know what happened, but often not how and why. This is a serious drawback, but it does not make the writing of Soviet history impossible; the search for motives is not the only task of the historian.

The other main argument against contemporary history brings us back to the question of detachment; it says that human passions are too closely involved, when we are dealing with events that happened in our own time and had a direct impact on our lives, to make fair and objective judgment possible. It is no doubt true that distance in time often helps us to see historical events in a wider perspective, thus adding an important dimension to understanding. With these considerations in mind, many historians two or three generations ago decided that one should refrain from discussing unresolved problems of current politics, and some still do so today. Their assumption is, of course, that it is possible to deal with a distant period in an objective, detached, scientific spirit, whereas such an approach is wellnigh impossible with reference to the very recent past.

These are weighty arguments, but they are not irrefutable, and the

4

pendulum of historical opinion has swung back in recent decades. Historians are now on the whole less optimistic about the scientific validity of their conclusions even if their subject is a very remote one. Indeed, many have realized that all history is, in fact, contemporary history. It is all very well to decide to refrain from dealing with unresolved problems that are still making their political impact, but if so can we really comment on the French Revolution or the English Revolution of the seventeenth century? The more important an historical event, the more likely it is to provoke controversy; there are exceptions, but not many. One philosopher has argued that if a man has read Herodotus, then, from a philosophical point of view, he has studied enough history. Others have said that, again from a philosophical point of view, the differences between important and unimportant periods are irrelevant, that it does not matter whether a man studies the history of Kidderminster, or of some Afghan village, or the French Revolution.

But historians, both amateur and professional, have usually shown a tendency to concentrate on places and periods that seemed to them of particular importance. From Thucydides onwards, there have been very few great historians who have not at one time or another written on the history of their own time. Even those who, like Burckhardt, have said that insight came only from calm observation from a greater distance, have done so. Even those who have not written contemporary history have been strongly influenced by it – Niebuhr by the revolution of 1830, Ranke, Thiers, Guizot and others by 1848, Mommsen by the era of Bismarck and Wilhelm II; could any historian writing in the nineteen-thirties or forties about dictatorship in antiquity have failed to be influenced in his judgment by what was going on in the world around him?

Temptations and pitfalls no doubt loom larger in contemporary history than in any other field of historical study. The dividing line between history and political journalism, moreover, is not always readily obvious: a history of the revolution by a trained historian – say Milyukov – is not necessarily superior to a book on the same subject by one who had no professional training – say Trotsky. Burke and Paine wrote political journalism, but no one could safely ignore their books when writing about the French Revolution. There has been much chaff, but this is as true for books of unblemished academic character. Meanwhile, contemporary history has been written, is being written, and will continue to be written with

5

undiminished enthusiasm. The Soviet Union is an obvious case in point and no further apology seems necessary.

Russia is one of the countries to which students of political metaphysics have attributed a historical mission and a manifest destiny. This goes back to the days when the idea of a Third Rome was first conceived; there was a special emotion about the direction in which the country was moving; in a famous passage, Gogol compared Russia to a troika in full gallop, of which nobody knew the destination. Some native sons and a few foreigners regarded Russia alternatively as the scourge of the West and its saviour. Outside Russia, speculation about the country's historical role goes back to the seventeenth century; it occupied poets and pamphleteers in Britain, diplomats and essayists in France, and in Germany it became in the nineteenth century something like a popular national sport. Did Russia belong to the West or the East?

> *Britain and Russia differ but in name*
> *In nature's sense all nations are the same*

Aaron Hill wrote in a poem in 1718 dedicated to Peter I, who was, however, called by another contemporary, Jean Jacques Rousseau, *'le plus barbare de tous les hommes'*.

In the nineteenth century Russia was the great bogy of most European democrats and liberals, though there were some dissenting voices: Heine regarded Tsarist absolutism as the best ally of the European revolution in its struggle against the old order – something in the nature of Hegel's 'cunning of reason'. The Frenchman, Ernest Coeurderoy, wrote a remarkable pamphlet in 1854, *Hourra ou la révolution par les Cosaques*, in which he welcomed the 'proletarians from the North' as allies in the struggle against the decayed culture of the West. Some recently rediscovered nineteenth-century philosophers of history, such as Vollgraf and Lasaulx, developed most detailed theories about the decline of the West and the rise of the East, anticipating much that has been said more recently by Spengler and Toynbee.

In most of these writings there was a strong element of speculation about the future of Russia. Much of it was erroneous and has rightly been forgotten by all but the professional historian of ideas. Speculating about the future of one particular country or the world at large is a risky pastime in which few reputations are made and many undone. Political (and metapolitical) prediction is hazardous in days of peace and calm; it becomes even more difficult in times of unrest and revolution. And yet it is precisely in times of revolution, when people are most acutely confronted with the great issues of the day, that they become most passionately involved in politics and wish to know most fervently what the future holds in store.

The French Revolution is the classic example; nobody in Europe could stay aloof. Eloquent witnesses have told us how it appeared to the enthusiasts – and what decent man was not an enthusiast in that blissful dawn? Klopstock, no less sympathetic than Wordsworth, spoke for the majority of German *Dichter und Denker* when he wrote

> *Frankreich schuf sich frei. Des Jahrhunderts*
> *edelste Tat hub sich da zum Olympus empor.*

In Britain, the French Revolution in its early days was immensely popular, and not only in literary and artistic circles. It seemed to mark the end of medieval obscurantism, the destruction of despots in Church and State, the prospect of an era in which human personality, freed from the shackles of the past, could achieve a new fulfilment.[2] For two generations of Russian revolutionaries, the French Revolution served as what would now be called a political model, and even after 1917 there was much talk about a Russian Robespierre, a Soviet Gironde and Vendée, about Bonapartism and a new Napoleon. Whether these constant references and analogies, which have only recently begun to disappear, did more to clear up or to becloud the issues at stake is a moot point. But the discussions and controversies about the French Revolution in England and Germany in the seventeen-nineties bear a certain resemblance to the debate on Soviet communism in the nineteen-twenties and thirties. Burke, it seems in retrospect, had as little feeling and understanding as some twentieth-century conservatives for the existence of a revolutionary situation, and attributed all that happened to individual wickedness. The Declaration of the Rights of Man was a great historical event and Thomas Paine was right in saying so, but it came to mean little under the Committee of Public Safety and under Napoleon. The Stalin Constitution was probably the most democratic of its kind, as its sponsor claimed, but there were few people naïve enough to accept it at its face value.

2 J. H. Plumb, *England in the Eighteenth Century*, London, 1950, p. 155.

7

The French Revolution was welcomed by public opinion in Europe in its overwhelming majority; but by 1792 most of its early wellwishers had had second thoughts. Was it because it then entered its more radical phase, that all the 'wishy-washy liberals' fell by the wayside? An analogy with the Russian Revolution should make one cautious: the Russian Revolution was hailed in 1917–19 by a minority only. It became respectable and indeed won enthusiastic support only much later, under Stalin, in the 'popular front' period and during the second world war.

The contribution of the professional students of Russia towards our understanding of the revolution will be discussed elsewhere. Suffice it to say here that in 1917 the Russian experts were quite unprepared to explain to the non-Russian public the meaning of the events in Petersburg and Moscow. Pares, Hoetzsch, and the other experts had been accustomed to dealing with a Russia that bore hardly more resemblance to the new Soviet Russia than did China to Brazil; the fact that the new rulers spoke the same language as the old was about the only helpful feature in an otherwise chaotic situation in which all the familiar landmarks had disappeared.

Yet the public clamoured for explanations and these were provided by newspapermen, politicians, travellers and anyone with a claim to Russian or revolutionary expertise. Most of what was said and written at the time makes strange reading – there is no denying that the Soviet Union was much sinned against in those early days. 'Among the Bolsheviks we see nothing but servants of Germany', Pertinax wrote on 9 November 1917 in *l'Echo de Paris*. The very first editorial on the revolution in the London *Morning Post* was headed 'Revolution made in Germany'; many other contemporary observers commented in a similar vein. The same paper blamed 'Russian Jews of German extraction' for the upheaval; later on, in the summer of 1920, it published a long series of articles purporting to reveal the truth of the revolution in Russia and the cause of the world's unrest in general – these were the 'Protocols of the Elders of Zion'. A typical headline in *The Times* between 1917 and 1920 would read: 'LENIN THE TERRIBLE', 'OUTRAGES ON SCHOOL GIRLS', 'BOLSHEVIST BLOOD LUST', 'HORRORS OF HEATHEN ROME REVIVED', and so on. There would be detailed accounts of the nationalization of women – the original report, it should be added, had been published by another London paper, and it had also been mentioned in a White Paper on Bolshevism published by the Foreign

Office. There would be stories about human fingers swimming in the broth served in the communal kitchens in Petrograd and about monuments that had been consecrated by Sovietdom to Judas Iscariot, one of its main heroes. *The Times* also believed for a while in the 'Protocols' – the Russian people had nothing at all to do with a revolution inspired and carried out by German-Jewish invaders. What had the Jews to say in reply to these terrible and scandalous revelations?

American attitudes towards the Soviet régime were different during the initial period of its existence. It was generally assumed that Bolshevism, if left alone, would become moderate. The Bolshevik leaders were regarded as utopians, impractical dreamers rather than fanatical extremists, as Christopher Lasch has shown in an interesting monograph. There was considerable sympathy for them, not only among liberals. It was hoped that the realities of life would lead the Bolsheviks away from the rigour of formula and theory. The turning point came after Brest Litovsk; yet it was not the fear of socialism that inspired hostility, but the unwillingness of the new Russian leaders to defend themselves against what seemed to most Americans the overriding menace: German militarism.

After the hope had been dispelled that Russia would stay on in the war, reports in the American press became much less friendly. Nor were they particularly well-informed. The *New York Times*, to give but a few random examples, reported on 20 February 1918 from Finland via London, that Lenin had fled. A few days later it announced that Lenin had dismissed Trotsky. On 29 June of that year, the Bolshevik leaders were again said to have escaped from the capital. The headline of 12 August said that

LENIN MAY SEEK REFUGE IN BERLIN: PREPARES FOR FLIGHT
WITH TROTSKY AS RED RÉGIME TOTTERS

and, on the next day:

RED LEADERS FLEE: REACH KRONSTADT: ENTIRE BOLSHEVIST
GOVERNMENT ESCAPING FROM MOSCOW

On 15 August yet another report about their flight. On 26 October Lenin is reported in prison. On 9 December – RED LEADERS READY TO FLEE TO SWEDEN. A week later – LENIN READY TO GIVE UP. On 9 January 1919 – LENIN HAS BEEN LOCKED UP AND TROTSKY PROCLAIMED DICTATOR. A week later Lenin was reported to have

9

reached Barcelona. On 28 May the Politburo was again in flight, and so it went on for quite a while. There were dispatches about the systematic attempts to corrupt and deprave Russian children by the new masters in order to obtain a lasting hold over them: 'The atmosphere of the Bolshevist schools is impregnated with precocious criminal instincts and bestial jealousy. All the children's time is taken up with flirtation and dancing lessons' (*New York Times*, 11 June 1919). Women were nationalized (though the State Department had denied it in February 1919), children were socialized (*Christian Science Monitor*, 6 November 1918), and the Chinese hangmen who performed executions on behalf of Lenin and Trotsky at 50 rubles a head sold the flesh of their victims for human consumption, passing it off as veal at fabulous prices (letter to *The Times*).

A gradual change in Western public opinion took place in the middle twenties; more reliable news was now available about Soviet affairs, more diplomats and newspapermen were now stationed in the Soviet capital, whereas most information in the early days had emanated from Riga, Prague, and Helsinki. True, there was still much misinformation about Russian affairs and ignorance of the elementary principles of Bolshevism, and above all a great lack of political imagination. The Soviet experiment, the economists agreed, could not possibly work. Communism in Russia was doomed economically, *The Times* wrote on 28 June 1921, the manoeuvres of the Bolshevik leaders could not prevent the restoration of capitalism, the current was irresistible. The city editor of the London *Daily News* (not a very hostile paper) returned from Moscow in June 1924 and reported that 'Communism fails because it is an impractical ideal'. Similar arguments recurred time and time again up to the early thirties: communism was bound to fail because it was too egalitarian, everybody earned the same, there was no incentive to produce, planned economy was a chimera. At one time it was believed that the Soviet government would soon orientate itself towards the new NEP bourgeoisie. Meditating in front of the Kremlin in 1927, M Alfred Fabre Luce reported that Stalin was regarded as '*le roi des kulaks*'.

The contemporary public image of the Bolsheviks was fairly accurately depicted in some of the novels of John Buchan and Sapper's *Bulldog Drummond*. Communism was a synonym for destruction, anarchism, a conspiracy to throw the whole world into chaos. There was an international clearing-house of crime inspired and controlled by Moscow – its members were moral imbeciles, fanatics, sadists, negating all traditional values, purely destructive in character, willing to sacrifice everything, including their lives, for the realization of a mad ideal.

If this was the attitude of comparatively restrained commentators in England, France, and the United States during the first decade after the revolution, there is no need to present in detail Nazi comments on Bolshevism. Bolshevism, they declared, was a conspiracy of the racial underworld to overthrow Aryanism, all that was valuable, creative, pure. It was a government of gangsters, bloodsuckers, enemies of mankind which, if not nipped in the bud, would conquer the world as completely as Christianity had. (Thus Hitler in 1932 – ten years before he had talked contemptuously about the chaos and utter weakness of 'Soviet Judaea'.) Whether Hitler was really that much afraid of Bolshevism is doubtful; this is not the place to discuss to what extent his anti-Bolshevism was a strategem to gain the support of the frightened middle classes both in Germany and in other European countries. The enmity towards Bolshevism, the lack of any serious attempt to understand its sources and what it stood for, was coupled with the traditional German feelings of superiority towards Russia and the Slavs.

The early period of blind hate and know-nothingism did not last in the West – outside some right-wing extremist groups – beyond the middle twenties. As time passed and the 'Soviet experiment' became a new reality, as it achieved some spectacular economic and military successes, as it was realized that Russia was neither a paradise of free love nor a heaven for the anarchists, the pendulum swung to the other extreme; the inclination grew to dismiss criticism of Russia and Soviet communism altogether. As a result, the Soviet Union under Stalin began to attract more support than it did under Lenin.

Such boundless admiration could already be found among some of the very earliest visitors to Russia after the revolution, even if these were by temperament and conviction anything but Bolsheviks. George Lansbury, one of the first British visitors, was essentially a Tolstoyan who believed no evil and tried to think good of all men. It was an attractive attitude but it made it difficult for him to find his way in this evil world of power politics. Ultimately, after a visit to Germany, it induced Lansbury to believe in Hitler's pacifism and his essential goodwill towards mankind. In Russia in the early days Lansbury found that Lenin was both a gentle man and more devoted to the cause of humanity than any he had ever known. Like Tom Paine, 'to do good was his religion'. Lansbury regarded the Russian Revolution as a triumph for pacifism – 'when peace is restored', he wrote, 'the secret police will be abolished'.

The belief that the Bolsheviks were the spiritual heirs of Tolstoy died hard among contemporary British radicals; Maxim Litvinov was introduced to the British public by the *Manchester Guardian* in 1918 as a Bolshevik by party affiliation but essentially a Tolstoyan ...

The Webbs, on the other hand, were not Tolstoyans but hard-headed realists who had no time for sentimental idealism; they believed in socialism because it seemed to them the most rational social order. Yet they came to persuade themselves in the early thirties that the USSR was the 'most inclusive and equalized democracy in the world' and that Stalin had less power than President Roosevelt. They reported that free criticism, however hostile, was not only permitted but actively encouraged in the Soviet Union, and that elections, too, were free. Of the political police they said that when it struck its case was practically watertight. The idolization of Stalin had largely ceased, they asserted, he was elected strictly according to the constitutional procedure of a political democracy; he was, like any other leader, ultimately dependent on the votes of the people. The attitude of the great 'bourgeois' newspapers of the Western European capitals also began to change. Sometimes the very same people who had been the chief purveyors of misinformation in the early days of Soviet rule came now to adopt Stalin's policies, hook line and sinker. Mr Walter Duranty, for many years *New York Times* correspondent in Moscow, had began his career as a Russian expert with the usual horror stories about mass executions by the Soviets' Chinese henchmen, impaling their victims alive on wooden stakes, torturing, burning, and mutilating them in a fashion too hideous to relate (*New York Times*, 24 February 1919). Ten years later he was firmly installed in Moscow, sending out party-line editorials disguised as news stories. The transition of *The Times* from the nationalization of women and the 'Elders of Zion' to the eulogies of the nineteen-forties took longer and was more subtle. Yet basically it was part of the same trend; the Soviet Union had come to stay, it was a powerful country and Stalin a mighty ruler. And power, as we all know, confers respectability.

The fascination exerted on so many Western intellectuals by Stalin, and by Russia under Stalin, is a complex phenomenon which cannot be explained by any single formula; different people were attracted by different aspects. Lion Feuchtwanger, a sensitive writer and the author of a number of eminently readable historical novels, was not a communist, certainly not a Stalinist, before he went to Moscow in 1937. What did he see, how was he impressed at the height of the purges?

'The whole big city of Moscow breathed satisfaction and agreement, more than that, happiness', Feuchtwanger wrote. And again: 'Whoever has eyes to see and ears to hear, to differentiate between the genuine and the spurious, feels at every step that the phrases about "the happy life" are no mere idle talk.'

What about Stalin and the Stalin cult? 'The people feel the urge to express their gratitude to Stalin, their boundless admiration.' Not that Stalin really wanted so much adulation: 'He is particularly reserved ... It manifestly annoys Stalin to be deified.' How to explain the purges and the show trials?

Some of my friends, otherwise not unreasonable people, find the trials from beginning to end, in both their content and their form, tragi-comic, barbaric, incredible, and monstrous ... But when I attended the second trial in Moscow my doubts dissolved like salt in water under the impression of what Radek and his friends said. If these were lies, or somehow prearranged, then I don't know what is truth.

To those Western intellectuals who persevered nevertheless in their doubts and maintained that Stalin's despotism and terror were the expression of his lust for power, Feuchtwanger said reprovingly:

Such rigmorole shows ignorance of the human soul and lack of judgment. One need only look at any book, any speech by Stalin, one need only recall any specific step he has taken in connection with the reconstruction of the USSR, and it emerges beyond any shadow of doubt that this wise, superior man cannot possibly have committed the colossal stupidity of staging such a clumsy comedy with the help of countless collaborators.[3]

Lion Feuchtwanger was not the most extreme case; there were many like him in Paris, London, and New York willing to give Stalin not

[3] Lion Feuchtwanger, *Moskau*, London, 1937, pp. 14, 20, 77, 82, 141.

merely the benefit of the doubt but the most enthusiastic support. Harold Laski (to name but one) was a highly intelligent man, and, in contrast to Feuchtwanger the litterateur, he had made a lifelong study of politics, national and international. And yet he reported after a visit to Stalin's Russia in the middle thirties:

Basically I did not observe much difference between the general character of a trial in Russia and in this country.

The Soviet courts, he thought, were much more concerned with prevention and cure than with deterrence and punishment. Nobody was more concerned with the prevention of crime than Mr Vyshinsky, with whom Professor Laski had a long and amicable conversation:

I was predisposed to think of him essentially in his capacity as prosecutor ... I found him a man whose passion was law reform. No one I met was more open about the weaknesses of the system, no one more clear about the steps he wanted to take for their improvement. He was doing what an ideal Minister of Justice would do if we had such a person in Great Britain – forcing his colleagues to consider what is meant by actual experience of the law in action. He brought to the study of the law in operation an energy which we have not seen in this country since the days of Jeremy Bentham.[4]

Vyshinsky-Bentham as the ideal Minister of Justice in Great Britain – it was a daring and original suggestion, but no more so than many of the statements of the Webbs and Professor G.D.H. Cole and many others in the West at the time.

These were the intellectuals, who in the name of progress and idealism declared their support for Josef Stalin. But there were others who were neither highbrows nor progressives and yet reached similar conclusions. Walter Duranty, of the *New York Times*, whose name has already been mentioned, expressed the views of many when he wrote: 'I don't care a whoop for socialism or totalitarianism, or any of their "isms".' But on Stalin he said:

I backed Stalin the way you back a horse until you think of it as 'your horse', though it may belong to Whitney or Widener or someone; you think of it as your horse, because you always backed it. That's how I felt about Russia, that's how I feel about Stalin.[5]

[4] Harold J. Laski, *Law and Justice in Soviet Russia*, London, 1935, p. 21.
[5] Walter Duranty, *The Kremlin and the people*, London, 1942, p. 15.

One such realist who did not care a whoop for socialism (because *inter alia* he was a multi-millionaire), and who yet regarded Stalin as his own horse, was Joseph E. Davies, American ambassador in Moscow in the late thirties. He was a lawyer, and sitting in at the trials he reached the 'reluctant conclusion that the state had established its case':

> On the face of the record in this case it would be difficult for me to conceive of any court, in any jurisdiction doing other than adjudging the defendants guilty of violations of the law as set forth in the indictment and as defined by the statutes.[6]

If at the time of the Radek-Pyatakov trial the situation still had Ambassador Davies guessing ('the simple fact is that ordinary psychology does not apply in this situation', p. 117), his doubts were dispelled by the Bukharin trial.

> All the fundamental weaknesses and vices of human nature, personal ambitions at their worst, are shown up in the proceedings. They disclose the outlines of a plot which came very near to being successful in bringing about the overthrow of the government. This testimony now makes clear what we could not understand and what happened last spring and summer ... But the government acted with great vigour and speed ... Then it came out that quite a few of those at the top were seriously infected with the virus of conspiracy to overthrow the government and were actually working with the Secret Service organizations of Germany and Japan ... Quite frankly we can't blame the powers that be much for reacting in this way if they believed what is now divulged at the trial (p. 177).

Thus Ambassador Davies to his daughter Emlen on 8 March 1938. Three years later he gave a talk to the University of Wisconsin Club:

> It was just three days after Hitler had invaded Russia. Someone in the audience asked, 'What about Fifth Columnists in Russia?' Off the anvil I said: 'There aren't any – they shot them' (p. 179).

Ambassador Davies' book was generally acclaimed as an authoritative work by most of the world's press at the time of its appearance.

Neither Feuchtwanger nor Laski nor Ambassador Davies had any background knowledge of Russia; they did not speak the language and had not spent any length of time in the country before. But

---

[6] Joseph E. Davies, *Mission to Moscow*, London, 1942, vol. 1, p. 39.

such background knowledge was absolutely essential, as Professor Pares once pointed out:

> One can always see at once whether anyone talking of Russia has really lived there; it is a kind of freemasonry independent both of class and views.[7]

Professor Pares certainly knew Russia from his frequent visits, beginning as a student at Moscow University in 1898; he was the author of many historical studies and towards the end of his life generally recognized as the leading British expert on Russia and the Soviet Union. This Russian expertise had only one major flaw; it did not care a whoop (as Mr Duranty would have put it) for socialism or Marxism or any other ism or ideology (though he hardly ever put it so bluntly); it was good old-fashioned empiricism, interested in action, not in words.

If we regard his actions rather than his words [one of Professor Pares' favourite sayings whenever dealing with Stalin] it appears that he [Stalin] has changed his course steadily and radically [away from Leninism].

Russia under Stalin appeared to Professor Pares

> as a nearer approach to true democracy than the liberal movement before the revolution; for then liberalism was a theory where the sense of its responsibilities was lacking, and now we are beginning to see that material of character and purpose out of which true democracy can be made.[8]

Of the trials and purges Pares took the conventional view:

> Zinoviev was now finally brought to book and died, still fawning, like the coward that he had always been . . . Nearly all the accused admitted having done so [conspiring] and on this point it is not necessary that we should doubt them, in whatever way their evidence was originally obtained. The bulky verbatim reports were in any case impressive.[9]

Of all the comments made at the time this one surely deserves to be repeated and remembered: 'The bulky verbatim reports were in any case impressive.' This was the outcome of fifty years of study of Russian history, of the Russian people, its country, its language.

[7] Bernard Pares, *Russia*, London, 1940, p. 256.

[8] Bernard Pares, *Russia and the Peace*, London, 1944, p. 33.

[9] Bernard Pares, *Russia*, p. 262. Pares was so impressed by Radek's 'confession' that he had it reproduced in *The Slavonic Review*, April 1937. Sir John Maynard also shed 'Light on the Trotskyist Trials', *Political Quarterly*, July 1937: 'the confessions have not been of the defiant kind. Rather they have been of the penitent kind, of a sinner making a clean breast of his sins and extenuating nothing.'

About the post-war world and Russia's role in it Professor Pares was very optimistic; did not the three major allies have certain principles in common? 'All three have alike had to grapple with the inescapable problem of reconciling a federal system with regional independence.'

One could have thought of a great many other similarities, such as the common need to build schools, to grow tomatoes, or to produce toilet paper. As for Stalin and his policy in the post-war world, Professor Pares thought

> that his deeds have been much more enlightening than his words. He has already travelled very far in very definite directions. To judge by his past my forecast of his future action would be: He has shown that his heart is in his own country, that he has set his reputation on a purely practical object of vast scope, its radical transformation for the benefit of all. Then he will need world peace . . . He can be credited with the good sense to see that he too must play his part in the building of world peace . . . It would not be sense to bring Poles or Czechs under Russian rule.[10]

The grand alliance of the second world war was followed by the Cold War and, over the last decade, by something of a *détente*. These comparatively recent events will not be discussed in detail in what is basically a comment on the writing of contemporary history, not on current affairs. In the post-Stalin period, too, there have been public utterances and publications that were stupid and uninformed. To get the facts straight and even the correct perspective does not *per se* constitute the truth; but it is difficult to imagine that any comment of relevance can now be made on Russia without a knowledge of the elementary facts of Soviet life. Whether the kind of social order established in the Soviet Union is the highest and most progressive way of life to be emulated by all mankind, or whether Soviet communism is evil incarnate, as some others argue – to take two extreme views – are ideological interpretations that will no doubt be inconclusively discussed for a long time. Such views can be neither rationally proven nor refuted because they include elements of belief and faith that evade rational discussion. What can be refuted is mis-statement of fact, whether it concerns standards of living or matters of government; it is unlikely that the story about the nationalization of women would be published by any leading newspaper now, or that a book like the one written by the Webbs would receive wide credence. All things considered, the general

[10] Bernard Pares, *Russia and the Peace*, p. 192.

17

level of knowledge and comment and the understanding of the Soviet Union have risen notably since the twenties and thirties. Partly, no doubt, because so much knowledge has been accumulated over the five decades. The specialists have collected a great amount of factual material ranging from the working of the Soviet railway system to the details of Soviet primary education. It is easy to scoff at these sometimes over-specialized studies, but taken together they constitute an impressive body of knowledge. Not all of this has filtered down to the general public or even to many students of world affairs, who should know better, but it makes a cumulative impact that should not be underrated. Many more people now read Russian, and the study of Soviet affairs has spread widely. Before the second world war the institutions, the economy, the culture of the USSR were nowhere studied in a systematic way. Today all this is different, and de-mythologization has reached a fairly advanced stage. If there still is a great deal of ignorance in the mass media and (let's face it) also sometimes in scholarly publications, the grosser acts of folly of the inter-war period are not likely to be repeated. If there are from time to time glaring mistakes or baseless interpretation and speculation in books, press, or radio on things Soviet – so there is on almost any other subject. The student of Soviet affairs has learned to take these things in his stride with philosophical equanimity. By and large the climate of opinion is far more sophisticated now than thirty or forty years ago and there may be cause for cautious self-congratulation.

Has this advancement in knowledge brought about a greater consensus of opinion on Soviet affairs or is it likely to have such a long-range effect? If there still are the widest possible differences of opinion about the French Revolution, its causes, character, and effects, it would be unwise to expect agreement about a far more recent event of even greater political and historical significance which has directly affected the lives of all contemporaries and provoked the most violent passions of our time. But there are important differences between the two revolutions: the French Revolution devoured its children within a period of five years. It had far-reaching repercussions, but it has remained to a large extent an unfulfilled promise; there is no saying what it would have achieved, or to what extent it would have failed, had it lasted longer. The Russian Revolution, on the other hand, established a régime that has been in power for five decades. It has devoured many of its children, but some of the grandchildren have devoured the revolution, the purgers of the purged have been purged several times over. Some of the revolutionary impetus has petered out and disappeared, some has been institutionalized in a new social system. The end of this process may not be in sight, but it is easier now than it was thirty or forty years ago to appraise the scope and impact of the Russian Revolution, its achievements and failures. We know so much less about the inner development of the Soviet Union than about France in the revolutionary period. But we know fairly accurately what the Soviet Union has achieved in the five decades of its existence.

This clearer vision will not necessarily make for agreement; some may think that hopes so far unfulfilled will be realized at some future stage. But if there is no consensus the middle ground of agreed opinion has surely grown; there is much less room now for illusory expectations, or for blind love or hate alike. The study of history may not be a guide to future action except in a negative sense, but it does offer on occasion a warning against the repetition of mistakes. Mistakes there have been in abundance, and the study of Soviet history, or, to be precise, the critical study of those who have written on Soviet history, may not be an altogether idle exercise. Provided, of course, it is done in the knowledge that 1967 is not the end of the line and that the last words of wisdom about our subject uttered now will most certainly be subjected to new criticism fifty years hence.

« 2 »

The Growth of Soviet Studies

Regular contacts between Russia and the West date back to the seventeenth century. Yet fifty years or so later, one of Peter the Great's envoys to a West European court reported that he found it exceedingly difficult to enlist specialists for work in Russia; not only was it generally believed that the country bordered on Red Indian territory; it was thought to be, quite literally, the end of the world. Most Russian notions of Europe at the time – and for many years to come – were even more fanciful.

Many foreigners went to Russia in the seventeenth century – British traders, French and Austrian diplomats, Italian churchmen – and some of them wrote useful and entertaining accounts of their stay there. But it was only after the Petrine reforms and the influx of more foreigners in the eighteenth century that Russia became an object of systematic study. Most of the foreigners who had settled in Petersburg and Moscow were Germans, and this, and its geographical nearness, made Germany the centre of early Russian studies. It is a sobering thought that almost two hundred years ago there was a German periodical which provided a critical bibliography of *all* books published in Russia; there was no such compilation in Russia itself at the time, nor for many years after, and there is none now in the West.

The early nineteenth century was the heyday of historical-philosophical theories and construction, formulated not only by travellers and historians, but also by men of such widely different background, outlook, and interest as Donoso Cortes, Moses Hess, Victor Hugo, and Nietzsche, who all commented at length on the present state and future destiny of Russia; most of them had never been near the country, but what they wrote was not necessarily more misleading than the accounts of the experts, for their knowledge too was slight. What Herzen knew about Russian agrarian institutions he had

20

learned from the account given by that well-known visitor the Baron from Westphalia.

Russian language and literature were taught in very few European universities. The first great expansion in political-historical studies, what would now be called 'area study' or *Zeitgeschichte*, came only around 1880. Mackenzie Wallace's *Russia*, subsequently translated into many languages, first appeared in 1877; the following year saw the publication of Rambaud's *Histoire de Russie* and Brueckner's *Kulturhistorische Studien*, and soon after the first volume of Anatole Leroy-Beaulieu's famous work was published. The first modern periodicals devoted to the study of Russia and Eastern Europe appeared only on the eve of the first world war. The Germans were first off the mark with Schiemann's *Zeitschrift für Osteuropäische Geschichte*, which did not, however, strictly speaking, deal with contemporary Russia; there had been such a journal, the *Russische Revue*, but it folded up in the early nineties. Bernard Pares' *Russian Review*, launched in Liverpool in 1912, was less academic, more lively, and far more concerned with contemporary affairs. It should therefore be regarded as the first of the modern journals devoted to the study of Russia – as distinct from the study of Russian history.

Great-power rivalries contributed much to the development of Russian studies; there is in the German archives a long memorandum dated 1912 or 1913, submitted by Professor Hoetzsch to the German Foreign Ministry, in which he urged the need to establish a German society for the study of Eastern Europe. One of his main arguments rested on the importance of Bernard Pares' activities in Liverpool, which he somewhat exaggerated. Obviously, Germany could not lag behind Britain.

It is instructive to compare the editorial statements in the first numbers of these journals. There was the brisk, optimistic, no-nonsense attitude of Bernard Pares, who announced in the first number of the *Russian Review* that

the Russian people does not as a whole share the idiosyncracies whether of extreme reactionaries or extreme revolutionaries, and seeks both the steady and normal progress of the Russian empire and the goodwill of our own country.

This was in 1912. When, ten years later, the *Russian Review* was reborn as the *Slavonic Review*, the same writer had lost most of his illusions, and had at least stopped projecting British mental attitudes on to the unsuspecting Russians. In his new preface he simply stated that it was important to know about Russia, because through the world war England had come into closer contact with that country. He also promised an impartial hearing to all schools; but this apparently did not extend to the communists themselves, for, as he put it elsewhere, 'it was never a question whether the vain experiment of Bolshevism could succeed in Russia'. He complained (as he had done in 1912) about the abysmal lack of knowledge in England of things Russian, as revealed in debates in Parliament, in the press, and elsewhere.

The *Monde Slave* was founded during the first world war, in 1917 to be precise; it is not surprising to find in its first editorial statement, fuller and more elegant than the British, many references to the German danger. *Osteuropa*, the German monthly devoted to Russian affairs, came into being at the time of the Soviet-German *rapprochement*, and soon became the leading periodical of its kind in any language. Its editor, Otto Hoetzsch, was a pro-Russian conservative, not unlike Bernard Pares in the scope of his interests, which were by no means limited to academic life. Usually a most prolific writer and speaker, he preferred on this occasion to be very brief; there is nothing quotable at all in his short introduction. Soviet-German relations were still a very fragile plant, and Hoetzsch probably thought, no doubt correctly, that whatever he said was likely to be misconstrued and give rise to suspicions.

Perhaps even more anti-climactic was the emergence of a journal of Russian studies in the United States – one day it simply existed. A project had been afoot in 1939 to establish an American review, but when preparations had been almost completed, a cable from Sir Bernard Pares from blitzed London induced the American editors to play host during the war to the *Slavonic and East European Review*. If America found itself without due preparation drawn in to playing a leading role in world affairs, its initiation into the field of Russian studies was similarly abrupt.

The study of Russian and other East European languages was, of course, the pre-condition for all other research. There was no lack of teachers in Germany or the United States; instruction in Russian was first given at Harvard in 1896, at the University of California in 1901. In England, on the other hand, there were very few men or women with the necessary qualifications; Forbes at Oxford and Goudy at Cambridge were well known, but the list of teachers and translators of Russian in the whole of Britain could still be printed on a single page of the *Russian Review*, and it included a reference to the Russian vice-consul in West Hartlepool. These linguists and students of literature were not as a rule deeply interested in contemporary Russia, being more attracted to philology than to politics. But there were a few who had chosen recent history, economics, or Russian institutions as their field of study, and who were themselves actively engaged in politics. Archibald Coolidge, Prince, Harper, Pares, all spent years in government service. Theodor Schiemann, the Nestor of Russian studies in Germany, was an adviser to Kaiser Wilhelm on East European affairs, and an editorial writer on the arch-conservative *Kreuzzeitung*. Of Baltic origin, he was violently anti-Russian, very much in contrast to his successor Otto Hoetzsch, who likewise played a prominent part in German politics. It is no exaggeration to say that all leading students of Russia at the time advised their governments in an official or unofficial capacity, though not all rose as high in rank as their erstwhile colleague Thomas Garrigue Masaryk.

Whether historians are superior to other observers in judging current political situations is open to doubt. The Russian experts, almost without exception, underrated the importance of the revolutionary movement. After the revolution their difficulties increased; they had now to deal with a country that in many essential respects had undergone radical change. Little had been known in the West about Russian socialism and communism; the comments on this subject published by German and British experts during the first world war must be read to be believed; one of them translated 'Trudoviki' as 'the weary ones' (this was not intended as a joke); another introduced Trotsky as a Ukrainian nationalist. In Germany, Staehlin, the leading historian of modern Russia, interpreted the Bolshevik revolution and subsequent events in terms of religious philosophy; Pares, after prolonged and bitter opposition to Lenin's Russia, came to display as much enthusiasm for Stalin's Russia as he had for Nikolai II's; in America, Samuel Harper, the only American scholar to deal with contemporary Russian affairs, began by declaring the Sisson papers, that crudest of anti-Bolshevik forgeries, authentic, and twenty years later described the big purge as a necessary stage on Russia's road to constitutional government.

Such *naïveté* was unfortunately very widespread; the judgment of intelligent journalists, from Mackenzie Wallace onward, has often been more reliable than that of the academics. The real merits of men like Pares or Hoetzsch lay in a different field altogether; they tried to explain to their governments and to the reading public that Russia was a very important country, that detailed information on things Russian was urgently needed. They fought an uphill struggle, and in doing so laid the foundations for the extensive and systematic study of Eastern Europe at a time when its need was scarcely recognized.

Today it is easy to underrate the difficulties faced by these men; financing Russian studies, for instance, was a major problem. Universities in the Western world were as a rule marked by an attitude of detachment from the life around them. Fashions might come and go, but why change the syllabus? Why study Russian, why not Assyrian? In Germany most of the money for Russian studies came from business men, particularly from exporters from the iron and steel concerns, who were interested in accurate economic and political information in connection with their trade. In America, after the second world war, the Foundations stepped in and made the rapid expansion of Russian studies possible. There were no such foundations in Britain, and big business showed little interest. As a result Russian studies in Britain were constantly faced with financial difficulties; it was a foreign government (Czechoslovakia) that paid for the building of the permanent home of the School of Slavonic Studies, and even rich American universities needed Polish and Czechoslovak subsidies until well after the second world war to maintain chairs for the study of the literatures of Eastern Europe.

The institutions that had been founded before the first world war continued to exist, but did not really grow. In America the academic experts were enlisted into government service for long stretches of time, while those who continued to teach, such as Patrick, Noyes, and Karpovich, had few students. Russian studies were, moreover, impeded by an unfavourable political climate which reinforced the prejudice and resistance in the academic world to area studies. Nor were there enough qualified men at the time in the United States; despite the presence of so many millions of immigrants from Eastern Europe and their descendants, interest in Russian and East European affairs was selective and strictly limited.

In Britain there was similar stagnation, though a School of Slavonic Studies had been founded in the nineteen-twenties. There were close relations with many East European countries (owing to the contacts of such men as R. W. Seton-Watson), but there was much less activity in the Soviet field. There were individual historians, economists, philosophers, theologians, and linguists studying specific aspects of Russian history, philosophy, etc., but their work was unco-ordinated and taken all together did not add up to 'Russian studies'. In his efforts to introduce Russian studies in Britain before the first world war, Pares had had the active support of leading personalities and friends of Russia outside the academic world like Mackenzie Wallace, Aylmer Maude, Constance Garnett, Maurice Baring. After the war, these old friends dropped out; the new friends of Russia were not interested in making the country they admired a subject of detached enquiry. As a result Russian studies were pursued on strictly academic lines, that is, with hardly any reference to contemporary affairs.

The *Slavonic Review* went through a similar development; originally founded to study contemporary Russia and its institutions, it became less and less interested in topical questions and was gradually transformed into an eminently respectable academic journal. Much of the stagnation in Russian studies in the West was due to the difficulties of communication with Russia, of obtaining Russian books and newspapers, not to mention the obstacles to visiting the Soviet Union for many years after 1917. Not that this prevented the Germans from forging ahead; the years 1920–33 were the heyday of Russian studies in Germany. An association of sponsors similar to the English in scope had already been founded before the first world war; subsequently a number of Russian and East European research institutions came into being in the universities at Breslau (1918), Koenigsberg (1922), and Leipzig (1928). Hoetzsch pursued very actively his policy of cultural exchange; *Osteuropa* frequently published contributions by Soviet experts, German students of East European affairs often went to Russia. There were more 'Russian experts' in Germany than in any other country, and more publications – and these by and large on a fairly high level. The Germans before 1933 were on the whole the best informed people on Russia, meaning that those few thousands who had an interest in foreign affairs had a fuller and more realistic picture of the state of affairs in the Soviet Union than their counterparts in other countries.

After 1933 this changed very rapidly. Some leading students of Russian affairs were forced to emigrate; others (including Hoetzsch) had to resign their academic posts. With the progress of nazification, the conditions for objective scholarly study disappeared. Some valuable research was still done in more specialized fields such as economics, but even those who did not believe in official Nazi doctrine on Russia and the Slavs had to pay lip service to the new dogma. Many German students of Russian affairs became involved in activities of a non-academic kind that they were later to regret. Even so, the orthodox Nazis were never quite satisfied with the state of affairs in the field of *Ostforschung*. They criticized their colleagues for not paying sufficient attention to racial factors in Eastern Europe, for regarding Russia as a national entity, neglecting the minorities, and, generally speaking, for being too well disposed toward Russia. Even Schiemann was posthumously hauled over the coals.

By the end of the thirties, with the growing involvement of the Soviet Union in world affairs, the demand in the West for information on Russian affairs expanded rapidly, but the universities and other academic research institutes were quite unable to meet it. In consequence what information was available came largely from communists, or ex-communists, or from journalists who had been stationed in Moscow. Some of these men and women wrote excellent books, but their work could not replace systematic study, especially on the more technical aspects of Soviet development. Only the second world war brought a decisive change in this respect; it had been said that war gives (or used to give) a powerful impulse to discovery and technical advance. It certainly did so in the field of Soviet and East European studies, for hundreds of experts were now needed, and since only a few existed, they had to be produced as quickly and expediently as possible.

It is not the intention here to provide a catalogue of Russian research or even a review of the main stages of its development; those interested can refer to the detailed studies published in recent years.[1] The study of Russian, East European, and communist affairs has made great progress since the second world war, large research centres have come into being, libraries and other facilities have been developed, and the lists of members of the various professional

---

[1] E.g. Harold Fisher on *American Research on Russia*; Manning's *History of Slavic Studies in the United States*; Seton-Watson's and Bolsover's essay on Russian studies in Britain; Jens Hacker's surveys of East European and Russian studies in West Germany and Austria; Berton-Langer-Swearingen on Japanese research in the Russian field; and the briefer notes on work in Italy (Hartmann), Spain (Ronay), and France (Kerblay and others).

organizations have become longer and longer.[2] This growth has levelled off in recent years; the Soviet Union, however important, is not the only field of interest in today's world; Africa, Latin America, and the Far East have also figured prominently in area studies. Even so, the growth of Russian and East European studies especially in the United States, has been astounding, considering how ill-prepared academic institutions were for such an expansion. Unfortunately, this quantitative growth has not always been matched by a parallel advance in quality. There are some basic shortcomings in contemporary Russian and East European studies, and in some respects developments over the last decade or so seem to have gone in the wrong direction. This has been due largely to prevailing customs and intellectual fashions in the academic world. Universities try to inculcate a spirit of objectivity and detachment, and put a high value on thoroughness; these are admirable qualities, but they are accompanied by drawbacks which sometimes provoke the question whether or not the universities are the best place in which to pursue Russian studies.

One of the most striking developments since the second world war, particularly in the United States and in Germany, but to a lesser extent also in other countries, is the gradual disappearance of the senior professor as an active participant in these studies. (It is hardly necessary to add that there have been, and are, some notable exceptions.) Most of the articles and books published these days are dissertations or parts of dissertations, or 'papers' written by young lecturers aspiring to higher positions in the academic world. Since a brilliant writer is not necessarily a good teacher, and vice versa, and since both teachers and writers are needed, the system which, as in America, insists that everyone shall publish seems both mistaken and wasteful. In the past the most important contributions to learning came from men at the height of their mental powers and experience; today the publication of a book or even an essay by a leading member of the profession is an event, and unfortunately not always a joyful event. Administrative responsibilities of various kinds have grown to such an extent that substantive work is often impossible. Trapped in countless board meetings, committees, and other extraneous activities, those who could and should be leaders in

---

[2] Between 1850 and 1950 some 250 doctoral dissertations on Russia and the Soviet Union were approved in American universities. The number accepted since 1950 is estimated at 1,000 and has probably already exceeded this figure.

their field do not always find the time even to keep abreast with current developments. Hoetzsch was a scholar, a public lecturer who drew large audiences, a member of the German parliament, a well-known editorial writer; he not merely found the time to follow current events but wrote for many years a monthly political survey in *Osteuropa*. Sir Bernard Pares' many public activities hardly affected his output as an historian and a student of current affairs. Today it is exceedingly difficult to imagine a professor anywhere in the world with enough time (and the urge) to achieve half as much as his predecessors; and since there is no reason to assume that academicians today are inferior to those of the twenties, it can only be concluded that something is very wrong with the whole system.

It has been suggested that in part this is the inevitable result of specialization and fragmentation in the study of international affairs. It is certainly true that it has become much more difficult to master all the important material than it was forty years ago, what with the multiplication of countries and their spokesmen, not to mention books, journals, and microfilms. Yet for all that, the need not to lose sight of the broad lines of development in each field is no less pressing than it was. Unfortunately, the prevailing fashion at universities has aggravated the situation. There is still the belief that the study of contemporary problems is not a suitable subject for academic research. This is supposed to be the traditional approach, yet leading philosophers and historians of the eighteenth and nineteenth centuries would certainly not have assented to this doctrine. Nowadays a scholar who publishes a book on some present-day topic will frequently retreat in his next work to safer ground in order to re-establish his academic respectability. The trend towards specialization is not combated but encouraged; it is much easier to obtain support for a highly specialized project of uncertain value than for a work of more general character. Obviously, there is no such thing as an 'all-round, all-purpose Soviet expert'; there is no earthly reason why a student of Soviet poetry should be well informed about current developments in Soviet agriculture. But it is disconcerting if the student of poetry is totally unaware of developments in the other arts, or if the student of agriculture approaches his subject in isolation from other socio-economic developments. This lack of broad perspective is frequently coupled with a false image of scholarship. The 'sound scholarship' praised in a book review often simply refers to the number of footnotes; no wonder that students want to conform and think it necessary to quote an authority for the bold statement that the first world war broke out in 1914. This concept of the scholar puts a premium not on fresh insights, on independent thought, on a contribution to knowledge, let alone on a clear intelligible style; its ideal figure is more likely to be the author of a monograph on an obscure subject, written in a professional jargon that will be intelligible at most to a small group of like-minded people, and of course plentifully supplied with footnotes. As a result, scholarship and academic standards have sometimes become synonyms for sterility and irrelevance.

Often there is a breakdown in communication between the expert and the wider public; academics these days seem too often to be capable of producing books that are read only by fellow professors and occasionally by their students. But there is perhaps no more urgent job to be done; intelligent popularization and generalization is needed not only to combat the dangerous trends towards over-specialization; it would in many cases be a most useful intellectual exercise. Unsheltered by professional jargon and accepted methodology, those trying to expose their findings in intelligible terms may find themselves rethinking some of their basic assumptions.

Innovators have been at work during the last decade and one feels reluctant to criticize attempts to experiment with new methods and concepts. Yet the sad truth is that the contribution to the field of Soviet studies of the *avant-garde* trends in sociology and political science has been on the whole negligible. Some of the early straight historical accounts, such as Louis Fischer's book on Soviet foreign policy or W.H. Chamberlin's *History of the Civil War*, have retained their value for fifty years or more. It is difficult to think of books published in the fifties by a political scientist of the behaviourist school whose prospects are equally bright. Some sociological studies have broken fresh ground by marshalling and analysing new material on various aspects of Soviet life, but the contribution they have made to our knowledge comes from their broad factual content, not from their revolutionary methodological approach, their model-building, theory of communication, or quantification. One recalls even among the best samples of the species those great projects with their weighty emphasis on methodology and their even weightier discovery of the obvious. One recalls, on a different level, the futile endeavours to find sundry operational codes and unravel rituals, or, in different fields, ill-written page upon page of un-mitigated trivialities, of pseudo-academicism and bogus scholarship, of a pomposity that passes for profundity. It has been a very sheltered world in which a professor's word carried great weight and an out-side critic's very little, for he had neither academic standing nor academic patronage. This lack of a critical approach was often reflected in book reviews.

Seen in a broader context the picture is admittedly far less bleak; most of the shortcomings noted are common to many other fields of study, which suffer in addition from a number of disorders from which Soviet studies are free. And no one will deny that in compar-ison with the immediate post-war period tremendous progress has been made, particularly in the United States but also in England.

That Eastern Europe has attracted less interest than Russia as a field of study is not surprising; Bulgarian foreign policy is intellect-ually not a very important topic and Albanian cultural life not a very stimulating one. Yet it is not only a neglected field of study; the lacunae are more glaring than in Soviet studies, standards seem to be lower, and, to put it bluntly, the likelihood that outrageous nonsense may be produced is considerably greater. The field of East European studies is to a considerable extent manned by friends and enemies of a certain country rather than by students who approach it with an open mind; personal considerations seem to play an important part. Nationalist passions in Eastern Europe have always run high and their impact on academic life has usually been disastrous; to see some of the old battles fought out over again on a new continent is a strain to which the uninvolved public should not be, but often is, subjected.

Soviet and East European studies in the United States require a fairly extensive appraisal, for since the second world war America has unquestionably taken first place in this field. In Britain, by contrast, new academic fashions have had much less effect. Individual writers have fortunately not hesitated to tackle large subjects; over-specialization certainly has not been a major danger in this country. At one time in the fifties it appeared as if uncritical attitudes were to prevail, but subsequent events have not borne out these fears; prolonged exposure to the facts of life has a corrosive impact on all but the most tightly closed minds. Some of the old habits may linger on in certain quarters but this has to do with the general political and intellectual climate in Britain; it is certainly not peculiar to students of Soviet and East European affairs alone. More disconcerting perhaps is the narrow basis of Soviet and East European studies in Britain. The fact that some leading members of the profession are very much in demand as lecturers and writers abroad tends to make one forget that the number of students is very small indeed, and does not appear to be growing.

West Germany faces the opposite problem. A great proliferation of Soviet and East European studies has not so far produced many outstanding individual works. There has been some encouraging specialized writing – for instance on Soviet medicine, and in legal studies – but at the same time the once so prolific German professors have on the whole all but stopped publishing. The burden of organizational and administrative duties weighs heavily there as it does in other parts of the world.

But there may be other reasons as well; a certain reluctance to express opinions on current affairs; the recent past has taught them the great advantages of caution. Apart from some general textbooks and some compilations of documents it is difficult to think of any outstanding work done by Germans in a field in which they were once the undisputed masters.

Many French intellectuals have shown interest in communism and some have studied Marxist and Marxist-Leninist philosophy. Yet this interest has not extended far into Soviet and East European affairs; Frenchmen have traditionally been less interested than other people in foreign countries; what interest there was has been restricted to immediate French preoccupations. Individual Frenchmen have made valuable contributions to our knowledge, but a French school of Soviet studies has come into being only of late.

In Italy publishers and newspapermen have shown more awareness and initiative than the academics. While the Italian press has had for some years now the best news coverage from Moscow, and while Milan and Rome publishing houses have brought out Italian translations of Soviet writers whose names were not even known to all the specialists in England and America, no comparable contribution has been made by Italian universities. Italy may be an extreme example, but its case raises one most important question, namely the impact of Soviet studies on public opinion. We shall have ample opportunity to return to this central issue.

31

« 3 »

1917

Revolutions seldom, if ever, come as a bolt from the blue; like a thunderstorm, they are usually preceded by unmistakable warning signs: the *grand peur* in 1789, the universal expectation of a revolution years before 1848. There had been black clouds on the Russian political horizon for almost one hundred years; Herzen wrote in 1853 that any day Russia could be drawn into the maelstrom of a terrible revolution. The writings of other Russian radicals in the nineteenth century are full of similar predictions. Few doubted that ultimately there would be a more violent and radical revolution than anywhere else in Europe.

After a great upsurge the revolutionary movement suffered temporary defeat in 1905, but the Tsarist régime had been revealed in all its weakness; it was neither willing nor able to reform itself. How much longer could it last? Turgenev once compared the whole régime to a rotten fence; no one was likely to mistake it for a solid wall that could serve as a foundation on which one could build. The middle classes, and in particular the intelligentsia, were disaffected, the workers hostile, and even the peasants were awakening from their age-old apathy. Liberal demands had made inroads even among the aristocracy, and (as Peter Struve wrote in 1906) who could guarantee that in an extreme situation a part of the army would not join the revolutionary movement?

The German ambassador in Petersburg predicted in 1914 that a Russian declaration of war would start a revolution; he was wrong, as his French and British colleagues noted: on the contrary, there was a great outburst of patriotic feeling. Everyone, or almost everyone, promised not to rest until the enemies of Russia and Slavdom were defeated. All political differences were forgotten, strikes were called off. But the enthusiasm did not last. Even in court circles there were no illusions about Russia's ability to fight a long war. Durnovo, Minister of the Interior and an extreme reactionary, had written in a confidential memorandum for the Tsar that the suppression of the socialist movement would not be too difficult in time of war, but in the event of a defeat a social revolution with extreme consequences was inevitable. 'Workers and peasants,' he wrote, 'do not look for political rights, but the peasants want land, and the workers a redistribution of property.' The reasons for Russia's grave setbacks in the war are well known. Militarily and economically the country was unprepared; the war disrupted both industry and agriculture, the cost of living rose, there was a fuel crisis, and, even more damaging for the war effort, an ammunition shortage and a food crisis. The military leadership was lamentable. The Tsar left for headquarters; the management of affairs of state was partly in the hands of his wife, who was dominated by Rasputin. This in itself was enough to spread despondency even among the staunchest pillars of autocracy. By 1915 there was deep pessimism; Paléologue, the French ambassador, tells of a meeting with Putilov, a leading industrialist, who was absolutely certain about the coming catastrophe.

The March revolution was spontaneous. Proudhon's observation about Paris in 1848 applies also to events in St Petersburg: *'Le 24 février a été fait sans idée'*. There had been bread riots, some strikes – 'nothing serious' as Sir George Buchanan cabled Balfour. There was also an acute conflict between the Tsar and the Duma. But the troops that were sent to quell the disorders refused to obey and this, as Struve had predicted twelve years earlier, was the end of the Tsarist autocracy. The revolution had been without a plan or a central leadership. Almost everyone had talked about the coming revolution in a general way; but when it actually happened it took everyone by surprise. The extreme left was no exception. Sukhanov, the Boswell of the Russian revolution, noted in his diary that not one party was prepared for the great overturn. Lenin in his Swiss exile had been lecturing about the lessons of 1905: the coming years would lead to popular uprisings under the leadership of the proletariat and they could not end otherwise than with the expropriation of the bourgeoisie and the victory of socialism. But he ended his lecture on a somewhat resigned note: 'We of the older generation may not see the decisive battle of the coming revolution' – exactly two months before the revolution broke out.

Trotsky was in two minds about the revolution: 'It was led by conscious workers educated for the most part by the party of Lenin', he wrote on one occasion. On another he said that it was a spontaneous uprising spurred by universal indignation; the Bolsheviks were a headless organization with a scattered staff and weak illegal groups.

How Russia would have developed but for the outbreak of the first world war has been a topic of debate for a long time: would the rapid industrial development and the agrarian reforms have initiated a period of greater stability and, eventually, constitutional government? Some historians and economists have since argued that, grave as the tensions were, a peaceful solution of Russia's problems was not impossible but for the outbreak of the world war. The political struggle would have continued and eventually led the workers' movement to reformism. Russia on the eve of war was on the way towards Westernization, or, as Professor Gerschenkron has written, 'perhaps more precisely, towards a Germanization of its industrial growth'. Others maintain that a revolution might well have happened in 1917 even without war. The prospects for non-revolutionary trade unionism were dim; the trade unions continued to be harassed by the police and were legal only on the local level. It is doubtful whether the workers would have benefited substantially from economic prosperity. The Stolypin reforms might have brought a change in the long run in the situation of the peasants, but it was thought that the reforms would need fifty or perhaps even a hundred years to take full effect. Many observers thought, moreover, that trouble in the countryside was inevitable as long as the estates of the nobility were excluded from the reform.[1]

The March Revolution

The conviction that Tsarism could not survive a protracted war and that more than a change of government was necessary is now shared by most historians. With the emergence of the Provisional Government views begin to differ; there is not even unanimity as to how to define the events that occurred in 1917. According to the Bolshevik interpretation there were two revolutions in 1917 – first a bourgeois one

[1] Michael Karpovich, *Imperial Russia 1801–1917*, New York, 1932, pp. 93–4; Alexander Gerschenkron, 'Problems and Patterns of Russian Economic Development', in C. E. Black, ed., *The Transformation of Russian Society*, Cambridge, Mass., 1960; Leopold Haimson, 'The Problem of Social Stability in Urban Russia 1905–1917', *Slavic Review*, December 1964 and March 1965; Hans Rogger, 'Russia in 1914', in *Journal of Contemporary History*, October 1966.

in March and then a proletarian one in November. That there were in 1917 two uprisings against the existing political order no one denies, but strong exception has been taken to the use of 'bourgeois' and 'proletarian' in this connection. According to Marxist theory a revolution is not a *coup d'état* but a radical change in the social order. Did capitalism triumph over feudalism in March, and socialism over capitalism eight months later? If not, what was the real political character of the two uprisings? The Bolsheviks had for a long time debated whether the transition from Tsarist autocracy to proletarian dictatorship would proceed in one bound or in a series of stages and how long these stages would last. But when the hour of decision came Lenin and Trotsky were scarcely influenced by their past theories; they acted in accordance with the balance of power and tactical considerations. The Bolsheviks had an elaborate and much discussed agrarian programme, but, again, in 1917 they adopted the agrarian programme of the Social Revolutionaries in preference to their own blueprint.

The overthrow of Tsarism is not really a bone of contention between historians, nor are there wide divergencies about the importance of the pre-1917 doctrinal discussions. The policies of the Provisional Government, on the other hand, continue to be the subject of polemics even today. Were they bound to fail because they were wrong or half-hearted? Or was it simply the absence of strong leadership that caused its downfall? Could the Western allies have affected the outcome decisively by releasing Russia from its military obligations? To what extent was it Kerensky's personal failure – or was Kerensky sabotaged by enemies and rivals from both the right and the left? What explains the growing influence of the Bolsheviks from near-insignificance in March to decisive importance in November? There is no lack of personal accounts and apologies; almost everyone involved in Russian politics in 1917 subsequently commented on his own part in the revolution, usually with additional reflections on the general course of events: Shulgin and Nabokov, Rodzyanko and Milyukov, Kerensky and many of the generals, Chernov and Tseretelli, Dan and Abramovich, Trotsky and many others have published their own versions. Most of the writers, excepting only the Bolsheviks, maintain that the odds against them had been too heavy; most of their anger and bitterness is directed not against the enemy on the other side of the barricade but against leaders and parties much nearer to the writer's own position in the political spectrum. For the Monarchists Milyukov and Guchkov were the main enemies; for Milyukov, Kerensky (and vice versa); Lenin's main attack was directed against the Mensheviks and the Social Revolutionaries.

About the weakness of the Provisional Government there is but one opinion. It did not have a clear line of policy but muddled along; what little real power it had, it was obliged to share with the Soviets. The army was demoralized, some units already in a state of disintegration. There was the sharpening economic crisis on the home front and the growing demand for peace. 'Peace' and 'Bread' rapidly became the slogans of the demonstrators in the street, but the Provisional Government ignored these demands or was powerless to do anything about them. Milyukov, Chernov wrote, staked everything on Russia's patriotic enthusiasm. But Milyukov misread the signs of the times; nothing was left of the enthusiasm of 1914. Popular opinion still opposed a separate peace, which had been associated with the most reactionary clique at court, but popular opinion was changing fast. Milyukov regarded the alliance with Britain and France as the cornerstone of his policy. This involved the full acceptance of the open and secret treaties Tsarist Russia had entered into with its allies – the annexation of Constantinople and the Dardanelles, the unification of Poland under Russian rule. Such an ambitious programme was far beyond Russia's power and there was growing pressure for a restatement of war aims. The left-wing parties, refusing to be bound by the Tsarist secret treaties, demanded a peace without annexations. This was sharply opposed by Milyukov, the Foreign Minister, who thought that all approaches for peace were futile. He had to go after the demonstrations against him in early May. Milyukov regarded this as a turning point; the capitulation of the Provisional Government to the socialists was a disaster – the first step towards the victory of the Soviets.[2]

Kerensky now became the leading figure in the Provisional Government. For fifty years his supporters and those of Milyukov have continued to quarrel about the rights and wrongs of their policies in 1917. Time has done little to make these polemics less acrimonious. After Milyukov's death his friends continued to defend him: Milyukov, they said, was both a statesman and a great historian and linguist who by training had a far better grasp of foreign affairs than Kerensky, a provincial lawyer. Kerensky and his

[2] P. N. Milyukov, *Istoriya Vtoroi Russkoi Revoliutsii*, Sofia, 1921, vol. 1, p. 117.

political friends had argued that while Milyukov may have been a great historian, he changed his political views too often – moving from the extreme right to the left and back. He kept fighting for ideas he thought correct.

though they had not a ghost of a chance to be implemented . . . today it is perfectly obvious that his political concepts (gaining possession of Constantinople and the Straits) could never have been translated into reality under conditions of a revolutionary upheaval.[3]

Kerensky had been upbraided by many critics for shilly-shallying inactivity, mere rhetoric and, generally speaking, for not being up to what was required of him. Kerensky countered by claiming that he tried his best but that he was betrayed by most of those around him and that single-handed he could not save Russia at a time of disaster. Had it not been for the Kornilov mutiny, Kerensky argued, his government would have been able to weather the storm and there would have been no Bolshevik *coup* in November. Kerensky's accusers on the right maintain that there was no Kornilov mutiny, that, on the contrary, Kerensky betrayed Kornilov and thus delivered Russia into the hands of the Bolsheviks.

The facts behind this dispute are very briefly these: Kornilov had been made supreme military commander in July 1917. He had Kerensky's support in his efforts to check the disintegration of the army, but his demand for corrective measures to curb the soldiers' councils was resisted by Kerensky who feared the reaction of the Soviets. Behind this tug of war was the rift between most of the officers who wanted a more stable government and sympathized with the right, and Kerensky, who stood for a coalition with the left. There were inconclusive negotiations through intermediaries and probably some misunderstandings. Eventually Kornilov dispatched a military unit to Petrograd; Kerensky, sensing a *coup*, deposed Kornilov on 26 August. Kornilov surrendered peacefully after the advance of his cavalry corps had been held up by railway workers.

Kerensky was convinced that there was a plot – and that it was suicidal. It helped the Bolsheviks to make a political comeback, undermined the prestige of the government and fatally weakened the army. Lenin's fortunes were at their lowest ebb in July 1917; his

[3] See Boris Elkin, 'The Kerensky government and its Fate', in *Slavic Review*, December 1964, and the rejoinder by Marc Vishniak 'A pamphlet in the guise of a Review' in *Slavic Review*, March 1966, summarizing a dispute that has been going on since 1918.

party had been suppressed following earlier attempts to engage in small-scale armed insurrections. The food position in the country was improving, transport had been partly restored, the Constituent Assembly was to meet in November. Kerensky believed that with the convening of this first parliament the power of the Soviets, which had outlived their function, would have been curtailed. But the right-wing mutiny gave a decisive impetus to the Bolsheviks, who took a prominent part in organizing the workers' resistance to it and thus gained much popular support. A historian of the revolution notes that the two most important Soviets in the country went Bolshevik immediately after the Kornilov affair; Petrograd on 13 September and Moscow on 18 September.[4] The Kornilov *putsch*, Kerensky maintained, was a stab in the back at the 'mortal hour of Russia's existence'.

No one now denies that it was a calamity. But Kerensky's critics assert that there was in fact no Kornilov *putsch*. According to their version the Commander of the army tried very hard to collaborate with the head of the Provisional Government but Kerensky, as usual, procrastinated. He pretended to agree with Kornilov but broke his promise, and Kornilov defied Kerensky's order of dismissal in the end only because he thought that Kerensky had betrayed him and become a tool of the Petrograd Soviet. This, in Milyukov's eyes, was Kerensky's crime against Russia – his taste for power took precedence over actions which were imperatively dictated by the country's interests. Or, as Zinaida Gippius somewhat melodramatically wrote in her diary at the time, '. . . a cowardly and irresponsible person . . . he alone is guilty of Russia's fall to the bottom of a bloody pit'.[5] Kerensky, in brief, came under fire from both right and left. He was accused by the right and centre parties of betraying the country by intensifying the revolution and weakening authority. At the same time the left attacked him for pursuing the old reactionary policies. Kerensky had initially enjoyed great personal popularity, but he failed to achieve incompatible aims; revolutionary appeals to the soldiers did not go down well with commands to pursue a war that was definitely not revolutionary in character. Disillusionment with him and his policies was quick and almost total.

[4] W. H. Chamberlin, *The Russian Revolution 1917–21*, London, 1935, vol. 1, p. 221.

[5] A. F. Kerensky, *Delo Kornilova*, Moscow, 1918, and many subsequent accounts; P. N. Milyukov, loc. cit., pp. 216–17; Leonid I. Strakhovsky 'Was there a Kornilov Rebellion?', in the *Slavonic and East European Review*, June 1955; Abraham Ascher, 'The Kornilov Affair', *The Russian Review*, vol. 12, no. 4, 1953.

Kerensky's personal shortcomings are regarded by some as the main cause of the downfall of the Provisional Government; others have seen the source of all evil in the activities of sinister forces, mostly behind the scenes, throughout that fateful year.

Conspirators

This refers, above all, to the role of German money in the Russian revolution, and the part played by Freemasons and by Jews. It was known already in 1917 that there had been connections between some Bolsheviks and certain political agents of the German army and the German foreign ministry. There were accusations of treason and they redoubled after Lenin's return via Germany in the famous sealed compartment. There was a revival of interest in this question in the nineteen-fifties when the German archives were opened and documentary evidence was found for some of these transactions. Some writers chose to ignore or belittle these contacts, others maintained that the Germans played an important if not a decisive role in bringing Lenin and the Bolsheviks to power (Possony's Lenin biography, Alan Moorehead's *The Russian Revolution*). We shall have to return to this controversy.

The role of the Freemasons in 1917 has also attracted much interest and, on occasion, caused great commotion – though more on the popular than on the scholarly level of discussion. There were in the Provisional Government, and especially in the Liberal party, strong masonic influences. Tereshenko (who succeeded Milyukov as Foreign Minister in May 1917) was a prominent Freemason, and so was his colleague Nekrasov; both took a strongly pacifist line. These Freemasons were accused, mostly by the right wing, of having had a baneful influence in 1917 from the very beginning. Obscure ties between Brothers and army generals, between liberal political figures and left-wing revolutionaries, were said to have existed. There was in the early twenties a considerable literature on masonry and the Russian revolution. The belief that the Freemasons (together with the Jews) had played a leading, if not *the* leading role in the Russian revolution became part and parcel of the right-wing *émigré* ideology in the nineteen-twenties. This version gradually lost ground but there was a revival of interest in their role in the nineteen-fifties – this time not on the part of the extreme right (G. Aronson, G. Katkov). The assumption that masons had collectively played an important part in the revolution has not been accepted by the majority of students of Soviet affairs. If Tereshenko and Nekrasov were masons, so were others, who stood for the continuation of the war and for annexations. Since it has not been shown that there was political solidarity and concerted action, the masonic background of certain individuals is not of great significance.

The role of the Jews in the Russian revolution also featured prominently in the debates of the nineteen-twenties, and National-Socialism did what it could to dramatize this issue. Since the second world war discussions on the Jewish question in the USSR have been of a different character altogether. There are very few Jews occupying high positions in party, government, the foreign ministry, the army, or other key institutions. In 1917, however, there were many Jews among the Bolshevik leaders, such as Trotsky, Sverdlov, Zinoviev, Kamenev, Sokolnikov, Radek, Uritsky and others. Antisemites exaggerated their number and influence by alleging that Lenin and other communist leaders were also Jews. The reasons for this Jewish prominence and, incidentally, for the high representation of some other minority groups in the party of the revolution are obvious; reacting against Tsarist oppression, many young Jewish intellectuals were attracted by the radical left. With the revolution many opportunities opened that had been closed to them before. At the same time there was a real need for their talents, since many members of the old intelligentsia refused to co-operate with the new régime. There certainly was social significance in these developments; but what was their political meaning?

If there were comparatively many Jews among the Bolsheviks, there were more among the Mensheviks. But the decisive argument against attributing undue importance to the Jewish issue in 1917 is that there really was no Jewish cohesion and concerted policy. Jews who joined the Bolsheviks in 1917 did so as individuals; they cut themselves off from their community, they were Jews by origin but not by religious or national conviction. They were bitterly opposed to any manifestation of Jewish national, social, or religious autonomy. They regarded themselves as loyal members of the Russian revolutionary movement – and nothing else. The idea shared by most right-wing authors in Russia and abroad that, together with Jewish high finance and the Zionist movement, they represented a hidden Jewish world government was sheer fantasy. Subsequently, most Bolsheviks of Jewish origin joined the opposition; some became loyal Stalinists.

By the late nineteen-thirties most of them had disappeared from the political scene; many had perished in the purges.

The Bolsheviks

All eye witnesses agree that the revolution in March was spontaneous and that no political party was prepared for the rising. The Bolshevik leaders were, as were the leaders of the other left-wing parties, either in Siberian exile or in the West European emigration. Individual Bolsheviks took a leading part in the demonstrations but no clear lead was given by this or any other party; Antonov-Ovseenko, one of the leaders of the November rising, wrote subsequently that no one knew what slogans had been given out by the Bolsheviks. In later years, however, beginning with the nineteen-thirties, a more active role was ascribed to the Bolsheviks in the Soviet Union. According to this version the big political strike in Petersburg had been called by the Bolsheviks who subsequently decided to turn it into a general strike and then into an insurrection:

The Bolsheviks were the only party to offer the people a revolutionary programme, and to call on the masses to overthrow Tsarism ... The Romanov monarchy collapsed under the shattering blows of the people inspired by the Bolshevik party.[6]

Whatever the role of the party at the time of the deposition of the Tsar, Bolsheviks and their critics agree that the real turning point in the activities of the party came only with Lenin's return in April. Up to that date the leaders of the party in Petrograd (Kamenev, Stalin) had given limited support to the Provisional Government; they had envisaged a union with the left wing of the Mensheviks and expressed the belief that 'Down with the War' was not a practical policy. Lenin immediately began to fight for a reversal of this policy (the 'April Theses') and within a comparatively short time succeeded in winning over the party majority. The differences between Lenin and the other party leaders (and the party organ *Pravda*) were played down in the Stalin era, because Stalin had been one of the 'conciliators'. Since Stalin's death the mistakes of the 'conciliators' are freely admitted. It is now said in explanation (and mitigation) that the Bolshevik party faced in March 1917 a situation rarely met in history – dual power shared by the Soviets and the Provisional Government. Before Lenin's arrival, the party leaders

[6] *History of the Communist Party of the Soviet Union*, Moscow, 1960, pp. 206–7.

did not understand the magnitude of the tasks ahead and chose an incorrect tactic towards the Provisional Government.

Lenin was convinced that the most immediate assignment of a revolutionary party was to end the war, and that this could be achieved only by a second revolution. The opposition to the war grew with each day but no party, with the exception of the Bolsheviks, dared to call openly for immediate peace. Lenin put himself into deliberate opposition to the Provisional Government. He was of course aware that his call 'All power to the Soviets' would have meant the transfer of power to the Social Revolutionaries and the Mensheviks, who at the time dominated the Soviets. But he was confident that the Bolsheviks would gain the ascendancy in the Soviets because their rivals had no clear policy on ending the war, and this assumption was borne out by subsequent events: the influence of the Bolsheviks increased steadily. The party faced a crisis in May, and again in July, but these were not lasting setbacks. In May, during the demonstrations against Milyukov, the then foreign minister who supported the imperialist war aims of the Tsarist government, Bolshevik armed units had clashed with army officers and attacked groups of other political parties. According to the official party history a small group of members of the St Petersburg committee had adopted an 'adventurist line' and wrong slogans ('Down with the Provisional Government'). They were disavowed almost immediately by Lenin. Other historians, quoting Trotsky as witness, believe that the May insurrection was regarded by Lenin as a trial balloon. What really happened is now almost impossible to establish. It is unlikely that Lenin thought that the time was already ripe for an armed uprising. Though the Bolshevik party was more disciplined than its rivals, its discipline was far from complete; there seem to have been conflicting orders to party units in a rapidly changing situation.

The July Crisis

The July crisis was an event of much greater importance than the May incidents. Kerensky's military offensive, which had been planned in collaboration with the allies, had failed. On 16 July part of the capital's garrison and the Kronstadt sailors rebelled and demonstrated in the streets. The Bolshevik party was not averse to taking action against Kerensky's government, but it thought the rising premature. The insurrection of the soldiers and sailors forced Lenin's hand, and the Bolsheviks decided to support the rising after all. The Provisional Government succeeded, however, in suppressing the rebellion within two days, and it also took action against the Bolsheviks. According to the party history, the Bolshevik leaders were in a real dilemma; they did not want to disavow 'the masses' though they were quite certain that their party was not yet ready to hold power, even if it succeeded in overthrowing Kerensky. A decision was taken not to join the revolt, but since it was no longer possible to restrain the masses the party annulled its decision. The revolt was suppressed, but the Bolsheviks were able to retreat in good time and withdraw their main forces. According to the party history the July crisis constituted a radical change in the political situation: the Mensheviks and the Social Revolutionaries had now finally deserted to the camp of counter-revolution. With power in the hands of the bourgeoisie, the stage of peaceful development had ended; the working class could take power only by an armed insurrection.

So much for the Bolshevik version of the July events.

Non-communist historians do not on the whole accept it. In their view it was entirely by their own choice that the Bolsheviks decided against their better judgment to support a military rebellion against the Provisional Government. The Bolsheviks seemed to have subsequently regretted their party's involvement in the abortive coup; it is difficult therefore to understand their anger about the Mensheviks and Social Revolutionaries who opposed it. Not they, but the Bolsheviks, had brought about the 'end of the peaceful development of the revolution'. The Mensheviks and the Social Revolutionaries did not change their policy in July – the Bolsheviks did. Perhaps Lenin needed this argument (that his rivals had gone over to the camp of counter-revolution) as a justification for preparing an armed insurrection. But he had not been exactly a believer in non-violence even before July.

The situation in July was certainly confusing and later the party felt more confident about it than it did at the time. Lenin subsequently wrote that his party had committed many blunders in July but he did not specify them. The party was isolated; even the left-wing Mensheviks thought that the policy of the Bolsheviks had been disastrous; Sukhanov wrote that the 'vast energies of the revolution had been squandered in vain'. He also says that he was told by leading Bolsheviks at the time that their party intended to carry out a *coup* in July; subsequently (in 1920) this was denied by Trotsky and Lunacharsky. Soviet historians now maintain that the party line was correct all along. If there were some precipitate actions, it was all the fault of the reactionaries; street fighting developed only after reactionary units had opened fire on the demonstrators, killing and wounding many of them.

Certainly Bolshevik policy during July did not do much good to their own party, but it harmed their left-wing rivals even more. To suppress the Bolshevik insurrection, Kerensky had to call in right-wing Cossack units. The democratic forces in the centre were thus crushed in the struggle between the extreme left and the forces of restoration, and a civil war became more and more likely: Lenin had achieved what has been the ideal of the communists everywhere since, Franz Borkenau wrote, a 'political constellation in which there is less and less freedom for manœuvre between a dictatorship from left and from right'. Whether this was deliberate policy or whether the situation developed by the logic of events is, however, by no means clear. The general situation was steadily deteriorating, the government and the parties did not know how to get out of the crisis. The country was unable to prosecute the war; 'revolutionary defencists' like Dan subsequently admitted that theirs was a mistaken policy. When Lenin said that the Bolshevik party was to the left of the central committee, and that the masses were more radical than the party, this was not wishful thinking but reflected the general radicalization of the masses throughout 1917.

To some these masses were an unbridled drunken mob, purely destructive, evil incarnate. For others these were the heroic fighters for a glorious revolution; the crowd already embodied a new world, free of oppression and exploitation. The story of the crowd in the Russian revolution remains to be written. All we have now are some striking word pictures of the people of the slums, of the attics and basements, in threadbare coat or grey uniform, with caps or heavy shawls still on their heads, the mud of the streets soaking through their shoes, an autumn cough catching at their throats, listening tire-lessly, hungrily, passionately, demandingly to Bolshevik speakers (Trotsky). Dan wrote that the mainstay of the Bolshevik revolution were the soldiers who threw away their rifles and returned home in casual groups, plundering and committing acts of violence because there was no other way of getting provisions and transport. Anti-communists saw in the crowds in the streets, that grew more and

44

more lawless and insolent, the coming triumph of anarchy. Where the Bolsheviks saw only class-conscious workers acting in the best tradition of the Russian working class and hungry and tired Red Guards hurrying to do their duty, the anti-Bolsheviks saw only murder, assault, looting of private houses and wine shops.

After the Bolsheviks had obtained a majority in the Petrograd and Moscow Soviets, Lenin pressed for an armed take-over. He thought that victory was certain and that, most probably, it could be accomplished without bloodshed. To wait would be a crime against the revolution. That the Bolsheviks were preparing for armed insurrection was fairly widely known; there were editorials about it in the newspapers but there was no determined opposition. Some thought that, given the chaotic state of affairs, no party could stay in power for long; the more sensible Bolsheviks would be ready for a coalition government. The Provisional Government was in a state of disintegration; there was a paradoxical situation in which no one wanted power because it seemed so intractable. Milyukov observed an angry worker shaking his fist at the reluctant Chernov, the leader of the Social Revolutionaries, shouting, 'Take power, you son of a bitch, when it's given to you'. This contrasted starkly with Lenin's supreme self-confidence when he shouted, '*Est takaya partiya*' – 'there is such a party' – in reply to a speaker at a meeting who had rhetorically declared that in the present situation no one party wanted to be solely responsible for the management of affairs. The Mensheviks waited for an initiative by the Social Revolutionaries, who were split: their right wing did not really want to act without the Cadets. Kerensky was a great orator but the effect of his speeches was of limited duration. Bruce Lockhart, English Consul in Petrograd, wrote years later, commenting on one such speech: 'It was an epic performance, the soldiers were in a frenzy of hysteria, the generals wept. It was more impressive than any speech of Hitler or any other orator I ever heard. The speech lasted for two hours. Its effect on Moscow and the rest of Russia lasted exactly two days.'

The facts about the preparation of the November uprising and the actual course of events are not in dispute, but there is controversy about their interpretation. Was it a Blanquist *putsch* or a real, popular revolution? Who did in fact prepare and lead the uprising? The former question is largely semantic in character, and the answer to the latter is fairly obvious. Revolutions are always carried out by a small militant minority, convinced of acting on behalf and in the best interest of the great majority. Whether they actually have the support of the majority will usually be a matter of conjecture, for no votes are taken in a revolutionary crisis. Lenin and Trotsky were certain that in October (in contrast to July) they had the support of the majority of the working class, the vanguard of the revolution. The Russian people were near despair, and the international situation made the seizure of power imperative. Trotsky wrote that insurrection and conspiracy were not mutually exclusive: the overturn had to be prepared consciously: 'Just as a blacksmith cannot seize the red hot iron in his naked hand, so the proletariat cannot directly seize power.' The ruling classes had shown their inability to lead the country out of the deepening crisis; they had lost faith in themselves. The old parties were in a state of disintegration, there were bitter struggles between the various groups and cliques. From the Bolshevik point of view there was a 'favourable combination of historic conditions, both domestic and international, the Russian proletariat was headed by a party of extraordinary political clarity and un-exampled revolutionary temper'.[7] Was there a conspiracy? Yes, but it was a preparation by the minority who had mass support of a majority insurrection. Was it, as the Mensheviks and the Social Revolutionaries argued, a soldiers' rather than a workers' revolution? The Bolsheviks explained that an insurrection had by necessity to be military in character; revolutions are seldom carried out by unarmed people. The old and discredited régime would not capitulate voluntarily. They also argued that the support for Bolshevism came mainly from the working class, and that only under the impact of the workers did the Petrograd garrison and other military units join the Bolsheviks on the eve of the insurrection. These soldiers were not necessarily class-conscious workers, imbued with the spirit of Marxism; most of them were peasants, 'united by a single sentiment: overthrow Kerensky as soon as possible, disperse and go home and institute a new land system'.[8]

The argument of the critics of Bolshevism that the insurrection was the action of a relatively small minority does not therefore greatly affect the Bolsheviks. Had not all other parties virtually abdicated? The Bolsheviks had never been believers in 'formal' bourgeois democracy: the fact that history was on their side weighed more heavily than the votes of a few million illiterate peasants befuddled by the propaganda of the reactionary parties. Hence, they

[7] Leon Trotsky, *The History of the Russian Revolution*, p. 1024.   [8] Ibid., p. 1033.

were not greatly perturbed that their party had no majority in the Second Congress of Soviets, which was to convene on 7 November, and that they would be outnumbered in the Constituent Assembly which was to meet a few weeks later. The Constituent Assembly was in their eyes a 'liberal pleasantry'; when it appeared that there was a big anti-Bolshevik majority it was dispersed without further ado.

The Bolsheviks then (to summarize their argument) merged into a single revolutionary torrent the movement for peace and the peasants' fight for land, the struggle of the proletariat for socialism, and the resistance of Russia's subjugated minorities to national oppression. The masses entrusted their fate to the only revolutionary and wholly consistent defender of their interests. The dictatorship of the proletariat was established, the proletariat became the ruling class. The proletariat was not the majority, but it constituted the vanguard, and it had also the backing of the poor peasants.

Non-communist historians agree about the growth of Bolshevik influence after July; quite a few Mensheviks had joined them and the left-wing Social Revolutionaries were willing to collaborate with them. They were still a comparatively small minority group, but the majority was either disorganized or apathetic, and there was not much organized resistance to them. The Bolsheviks, after all, seized power not only in Petrograd and Moscow but also, without undue difficulty, in most other centres. What they lacked in numbers they made good by their confidence, their intense belief in their mission on behalf of their party, the working class, and world revolution. They were conscious of being a small minority, especially immediately after the seizure of power. John Reed said that if ever men were alone it was that handful of Bolsheviks on that cold morning in November in the storms that raged over them from all sides. Within the Bolshevik party leadership a sizeable minority stood for a coalition with the other left-wing parties, a demand that was firmly resisted by Lenin. Lenin warned them in the strongest terms against 'parliamentary illusions' and threatened to 'go to the sailors'. He knew that only if unhampered by a coalition with the 'compromisers' could there be a revolutionary transformation. Lenin's view prevailed; Russia was to be ruled by one party. Whether this was the point of no return, or whether, as Professor Schapiro contends, there was a second chance in 1921 of burying past enmities and carrying the vast majority of the country with him in an attempt to rebuild the country, may still be debated; but victorious revolutionaries are seldom willing to share power and Lenin was the leader least likely to do so. It was a momentous decision and it has shaped Soviet history ever since.

The identity of the leadership of the November revolution has been something of a problem, but mainly for Soviet historians. There is no doubt that the decision for an armed uprising was taken by Lenin, who was in this, as in all other decisive questions, the supreme authority. But Lenin was in hiding, and contact between him and the other party leaders was by necessity infrequent. During the early years after the revolution it was generally agreed that (as Stalin put it in an anniversary article in 1918)

all the work of practical organization of the revolution was conducted under the direct leadership of the president of the Petrograd Soviet, Comrade Trotsky. It may be said with certainty that the swift passing of the garrison to the side of the Soviet, and the bold execution of the work of the Military Revolutionary Committee, the party owes principally and above all to Comrade Trotsky. Comrades Antonov and Podvoisky were Comrade Trotsky's chief assistants.

The first edition of Lenin's works also stated that Trotsky organized and led the insurrection of 25 October. Many other Bolshevik leaders were involved in one way or another in the preparation or the execution, but on the overall leadership there was no doubt until 1924–5. When Trotsky had gone into opposition, it was found that in addition to the Military Revolutionary Committee another committee had been established by the party in mid-October, consisting of five Central Committee members (including Stalin, but not Trotsky) which (it was now argued), also played an important role in the uprising. Trotsky asserts that such a resolution was indeed passed but never carried out; the new committee never met. Its members collaborated individually with Trotsky's Military Revolutionary Committee. Contemporary documents bear out this version. But when Trotsky's policies became more and more opposed to Stalin's his historical role, too, was affected. From being the leader of the uprising he had become by 1925 merely one of the leaders; after 1930 his standing further declined, until in the *Short Course* of 1938 he appears as the main enemy of the revolution. The names of Podvoisky and Antonov-Ovseenko disappeared from the history books and with them the names of many other old Bolsheviks. Stalin – it was now said – had been the chief architect of the revolution, together with Lenin; among Stalin's assistants there had been

Molotov, Kaganovich, Zhdanov, and others. Since Stalin's death
the merits of Podvoisky, Antonov-Ovseenko and others have again
been recognized. But while Stalin has been demoted Trotsky has not
yet been reinstated; it is still alleged that he boastfully blurted out
to the enemy the date fixed for the revolution, and that he wanted
to postpone it. In present-day Soviet historiography Lenin takes the
first and only place in the preparation of the uprising; he not merely
decided on it but also organized and supervised it.

The Mensheviks and the Social Revolutionaries

On the reasons for the victory of Bolshevism all that can possibly be
said by friends, enemies, and neutrals has by now been said. Far less
attention has been devoted to the policies of the losers in 1917. The
anarchists, for instance, played a certain role in the year of the
revolution and they were among the first against whom methods of
suppression were applied. Disillusioned anarchists who left Russia
after 1917 have published their reminiscences, but there has not really
been a postmortem on anarchist policy. The anarchists were not a
party, nor even a political movement. There were Tolstoyans and
terrorists among them, and local peasant groups such as the Makhno
movement in the Ukraine. These constituted a movement of congenital protest; they did not aspire to lead the masses and to provide
an alternative government. They complained that in no capitalist
country were the anarchists so repressed as in the Soviet Union.
Communist historians have, with one or two exceptions, ignored
anarchism in their writings; apparently it was not deemed to be a
subject of sufficient importance.

Menshevism was a different proposition. With all its splits it had
more cohesion and, above all, a distinct ideology. The Mensheviks
had been divided throughout the summer and autumn of 1917 into a
left internationalist wing headed by Martov, and a 'centrist group'
led by Dan and Lieber, which took a more hostile position towards
Bolshevism than the Martov faction. After November Martov and
Dan joined forces; their policy was one of qualified support for the
Soviet government. They were in favour of defending the revolution
against both its internal enemies (Kolchak, Denikin) and foreign
intervention. An armed struggle against Bolshevism, they said,
could only lead to the victory of extreme right-wing reactionary
forces. A minority Menshevik group led by Lieber thought that any

compromise with the Bolsheviks was tantamount to betraying the working class; the main task was to establish a united front of all democratic forces to overthrow Bolshevism. All factions agreed, however, that Bolshevism should be opposed only by constitutional means. Menshevism continued to exist, severely hampered in its activities, for about four years after the revolution until, with the end of the civil war, it was finally suppressed, its leaders deported or imprisoned. To quote Leonard Schapiro:

The Mensheviks perished without firing a shot. By the irony of history, their faith in democratic freedom had contributed not a little to their undoing. By refusing to take power themselves and by failing to support the coalition of anti-bolshevik parties between March and November they helped Lenin to power. After the October revolution, with large numbers of the working class behind them, an advantage which no other opposition party ever enjoyed, they refused to resort to anything but strictly constitutional means to overthrow him.[9]

Leading Mensheviks have often commented on their policies in 1917–20, adducing many mitigating circumstances for their defeat. Was not their party doomed to fail? As social-democrats their freedom of action was narrowly circumscribed. Being orthodox Marxists they believed that Russia in 1917 was not ripe for socialism; they could argue that subsequent developments have borne out their predictions. It was impossible for them to join forces with the centre and right-wing opponents of the Bolsheviks; equally they could not enter a coalition with Lenin: such tactics would have been a betrayal of their basic principles. Their line appears quixotic in retrospect and it certainly reduced them to political impotence, but it is far easier even with the benefit of hindsight to criticize them than to propound alternative solutions. Menshevism was congenitally unable to cope with a severe revolutionary crisis. Social-democratic parties were crushed subsequently in many European countries in the struggle between the radical right and the extreme left; they had very little chance in a country in which tensions were even more acute than in Central Europe and which had no democratic tradition. Menshevism, in brief, could not jump over its own democratic shadow. Or could it? There have been a few social-democratic leaders and parties unafraid of seizing power and clinging to it in a crisis. The Mensheviks individually and as a party had many sterling qualities, but toughness was not one of them. Whether toughness alone would have

[9] L. Schapiro, *The Origin of the Communist Autocracy*, London, 1955, p. 209.

been sufficient to ride the revolutionary wave in 1917 is a question that could be discussed inconclusively for a long time.

Among the Social Revolutionaries dissension was even more widespread and deeper than among the Mensheviks. Unlike them, they were not Marxists; they did not necessarily believe in gradualism and therefore had, in a way, greater freedom of manœuvre. They also had more influence, especially in the countryside; on paper they were a much bigger party than the Bolsheviks until well after the revolution. But by November 1917 the left wing of the party was hardly on speaking terms with its right; it co-operated closely with the Bolsheviks in the preparation of the insurrection. Several of its members entered the first Bolshevik government. The right wing, on the other hand, did not hesitate to support the offensive of the Czech troops against Bolshevism, and it established its own counter government at Samara. It would be too tortuous to describe in detail the activities of a centre group headed by Chernov which attempted the impossible – to reconcile the views of the two extremes.

The Social Revolutionary party has, in contrast to the Mensheviks, found a historian who in great detail describes and analyses the fortunes of the party in 1917–18.[10] Professor Radkey complains that previous writers had erected a screen of virtue around the right wing of the party, who have been generally considered exponents of democracy because of their support for the Provisional Government and the allied war effort. Radkey, on the other hand, does not think highly of the right wing of the party – a clique which had long before become a satellite of the bourgeois *Kadets* without whom they were not willing to move. ('They had become Kadets without admitting it.') The Social Revolutionary right wing had ceased to be revolutionary at a time when the country was becoming so in the broadest and deepest sense of the term,[11] while the 'left centre' under Chernov was a group of decent but weak men; in the name of party unity they supported a war which they abhorred in their hearts. The right wing failed because it subordinated peasant interests to the preservation of the Tsarist empire and its needs. The left Social Revolutionaries

---

[10] Oliver Henry Radkey, *Russian Socialist Revolutionaries February to October 1917*, New York, 1958. Professor Radkey has been criticized for an account that is too detailed – one page for each eight hours of the history of this party in 1917–18 (Richard Pipes). I am not sure whether this criticism is quite fair; not only does Professor Radkey compare favourably with John Reed – let alone James Joyce; was it not Machiavelli who said that God was in the details?

[11] O. H. Radkey, *The Sickle under the Hammer*, New York, 1963, p. 468.

helped Bolshevism to gain power, but is their historical responsibility greater than that of the majority of the party which failed in its duty to defend the interests of the rural toilers? Radkey believes that a brave and earnest effort should have been made, even if it ended in defeat, 'for the rule seems to be that no matter what happens in Eastern Europe the rural toilers always lose'.[12]

Radkey's conclusions have been criticized by some surviving Social Revolutionary leaders (in greatest detail by Vishniak) and by other historians. His account has been contested both on questions of fact and on interpretation, above all for over-rating the freedom of action of a movement that was essentially democratic in inspiration and structure. The debate is unfinished. Was their basic dilemma the same that faced the Mensheviks, of democratic convictions that seemed to be incompatible with toughness and the will to power, or would they have fared better had the right-wing majority not betrayed its principles, as Radkey argues?

The Civil War

The Bolsheviks had prevailed in most important centres but their position continued to be precarious. Soviet rule was seriously threatened both by internal enemies, the armies of Yudenich and Denikin, and by the revolt of the Kronstadt sailors. It would have been even more seriously menaced by large-scale allied intervention, but the internal enemies never made common cause and allied intervention was never more than a gesture. A recent historian of allied intervention has little doubt that the Allies could have forced their way to Moscow and overthrown the Bolshevik régime had they sent two or three divisions to Arkhangelsk rather than 1,200 men.[13] Such a force could not have ruled Russia, but it might have served as a rallying point for 'loyal' (i.e. anti-Bolshevik) Russians.

The decision to intervene and the course of allied intervention has been the focus of much bitter controversy in West and East. In the Soviet view it was a case of naked imperialistic aggression; the foreign bankers did not want to lose their investments in Russia. They were also afraid that the Soviet government would set an example to the working people of other countries. Occasionally this view has received the support of Russian right-wing authors who

[12] O. H. Radkey, *The Sickle under the Hammer*, p. 496.
[13] Richard H. Ullmann, *Intervention and the War*, Princeton, 1961, p. 333.

were convinced that some of the allied decisions (the British move into the Transcaucasus) were motivated by old-fashioned predatory imperialism rather than the wish to support the Russian 'loyalists'. But more often the Allies have been criticized for not giving sufficient help to Denikin, Kolchak, and Wrangel when it was most needed; they have been accused of betraying them after initially encouraging them. But the position of the Allies in 1917–19 allowed them little freedom of action. While the war was going on troops could not be spared: after the war had ended no one wanted to go on fighting. Public opinion in Britain and France, let alone the United States, would not have stood for dispatching 100,000 men to Russia. Two or three divisions might have been sufficient for a landing in Arkhangelsk, but in addition military intervention in South Russia and elsewhere would have been needed.

The conservative press in London and Paris was clamouring for intervention and protested against the desertion of friends and allies. They had the powerful support of Churchill who, in countless speeches and articles, demanded the dispatch of troops to Russia. But those in power thought (as Balfour wrote to Bruce Lockhart in February 1918) that the 'internal affairs of Russia are no concern of ours, we consider them in so far as they affect the war'. Lloyd George's stand was similar. There was an attempt to bring America in, but the Americans, as Lord Robert Cecil wrote to Clemenceau, had a special tenderness towards the Russian Revolution. When Wilson at last came around it was to be intervention only on a minute scale. It took place mainly by proxy – the Czech legionnaires in Siberia and the Urals, the Japanese troops in the Far East. France officially recognized General Wrangel in the Crimea, but when Poland made peace with Russia, this meant the end of Wrangel too, and the idea of intervention had to be given up altogether. The conservative press in Paris and London wrote mournfully that the Russian people could from now on count only on themselves in their effort to overthrow Bolshevism.

The reasons for the outcome of the civil war have been debated for a long time in the centres of the Russian emigration. To some it all seemed inexplicable, for the position of the Bolsheviks had initially been so weak. They had won the struggle in Petrograd and Moscow under the slogan of 'peace and bread'. But the situation of workers and peasants continued to deteriorate after the revolution – nor was there an end to the fighting. William Henry Chamberlin in his history of the Russian Revolution writes that if all the hatreds which the activities of the Soviet government generated in the various classes of the people had ever found concentrated expression at one time under a single leadership, the Bolsheviks would have been swept out of existence.[14]

Instead, the Bolsheviks gathered strength. The leaders of the White movement were pre-war generals and admirals, without a positive programme, accustomed to commanding, not to persuading and agitating, 'quite incapable of appealing to the masses as Lenin and Trotsky could appeal to them'. About the profoundly reactionary character of the White movement there was unanimity: Alfred Rosenberg, the Nazi leader, commenting on the memoirs of a White general (Zakharov) wrote a few years later that the Whites lacked a central idea; they were mere reactionaries and their cause was therefore doomed. Chamberlin asserts, and almost all observers concur, that the White generals' government was separated by an impassable gulf from the peasant majority of the country on whom in the last resort the outcome of the struggle depended: 'One year of Kolchak's rule was sufficient to turn Siberia into a hornet's nest of rebellious peasant partisans who did half the Red Army's work for it.'[15] Among many who wavered in the struggle the conviction grew, as the official Communist party history puts it, crudely but probably correctly, that the Red Army was fighting for the interests of the people, whereas the Whites and the interventionists were fighting against the people – for the restoration of the old order and the old privileges. Intervention antagonized many Russian patriots who opted for supporting a Russian government, however disagreeable, against foreign attack. The Bolsheviks were a minority; their plans for the transformation of the country were supported by only a small part of the people. But there was the growing belief that they fought for Russia, whereas the White movement merely defended the old régime.

Views of the Revolution

On the origins and causes of the November revolution every possible viewpoint has by now been expressed; there is, of course, no agreement and interpretations still continue to change. These new inter-

---

[14] W. H. Chamberlin, *The Russian Revolution*, London, 1935, vol. II, p. 454.
[15] Ibid., p. 455.

pretations are not based on new facts that have come to light; they are shaped by the general course of Soviet history since 1917 and by developments in the West. Reinterpretations of the French Revolution too may be ideologically inspired, but to carry conviction they have to be based on detailed research into the living conditions of, for instance, the peasants in the North of France or the *sans culottes* in some Paris suburb. The facts that have come to light in recent decades about 1917 are neither detailed nor reliable enough to provide a basis for a re-examination of the revolution. The debates about its significance are therefore mainly moral, ideological, even theological in character; if new aspects and facts come to light from time to time, they do not decisively affect the arguments. Most historians now agree that Tsarism as it existed in 1914 could not survive for long; whether peaceful change was still possible is doubtful. The war and military defeat accelerated its downfall. They also agree that great tensions, bitter class hatred, general resentment accumulated as the result of the inequities of the old régime. The prerequisites for a major eruption all existed. But there is the widest disagreement as to whether the actual form it took was accidental or inevitable. Russian *émigrés* and probably the majority of Anglo-American scholars have traditionally emphasized the accidental elements. Their sceptical empiricism, as Professor Billington notes, 'inclines them to reject deeper patterns of explanation, their native political traditions subtly incline them to regard sudden and convulsive change as a distasteful aberration from the norm in human events'. 1917 was, as many Russians said at the time, a 'crazy year' – anything could happen. It became quite fashionable to compare it with the *Smutnoe Vremia*, the time of troubles and anarchy at the end of the sixteenth century. The ineptitude of Milyukov, the lack of firmness displayed by Kerensky, are mentioned in this context, the short-sightedness of the Allies in their attitude towards the Provisional Government, the stupidity of the German General Staff in bringing Lenin to Petrograd, the political failure of the Mensheviks and the Social Revolutionaries, and, last but not least, the excellent organization of the Bolsheviks and their luck in having a political leader of genius. The revolution was caused, in other words, by a mixture of adverse circumstances and human frailty and stupidity. It was a natural disaster, a catastrophe (a 'powerful geological upheaval', in Milyukov's words). Some regarded it as a completely senseless disaster against which nothing could have been done, others compare it with a spring flood that could have been stemmed, had dykes been erected in time.

According to the Soviet interpretation, the November revolution was inevitable. The Tsarist régime, its reactionary character quite apart, was an obstacle to Russia's further social and economic development. The Liberals, the Social Revolutionaries and the Mensheviks were bankrupt; they had doomed Russia to backwardness and stagnation. Only the Bolsheviks, a party of a new type, could lead the country out of the immediate crisis and build a higher social order. Orthodox Marxism is invoked in this context – the inevitable progress of mankind from feudalism to capitalism to socialism. But was not the revolution to prevail first in the highly industrialized countries? At this point Lenin's genius comes in. He realized that precisely because the capitalist elements were as yet weak in Russia, it would be easier for the revolution to win – the theory of the weakest link in the chain. Victory was not therefore entirely automatic; there is room in the Soviet interpretation for the human factor – the heroic working class with its party steeled in the fight and its gifted and resolute leaders. Some Bolshevik historians (Pokrovsky) have put greater stress on inevitability, others on voluntaristic elements (Lenin's greatness, the heroic stand of the Petrograd workers and soldiers). All agree that the Bolshevik victory was not accidental.

The longer a régime lasts, the more rooted it becomes and increases its power, the more people are convinced that what happened could not have happened in any other way. Given the chaotic situation in 1917, an extreme uncompromising left-wing party that offered radical solutions, was not afraid of power, and did not bother unduly about democratic processes, seemed in retrospect greatly favoured to prevail over its opponents, even if its victory was not preordained. Accidental or inevitable, there is a wide range of possible judgments on the revolution; a disaster, too, may be inevitable. A religious thinker may view it (as some indeed did) as a scourge of God to punish those who had sinned. An accidental event, on the other hand, may come to others as a great blessing. The number of variations is almost unlimited, even if we disregard the more fanciful explanations invoking cosmic or conspiratorial forces, or that version which interpreted the Russian revolution as a revolt of the racial (non-Aryan) underworld against the Nordic elements in Russian society.

The question of the achievements of the Russian revolution will feature prominently in subsequent sections of this book. It is not at all identical with the quest for its causes and origins. But it is in practice difficult, often impossible, to maintain a clear-cut division between the two. The performance of the Soviet state has influenced the judgment of the historian at every step.

Of those who had viewed the revolution as an unmitigated disaster quite a few came to see subsequently its tragic grandeur. Some went further and wholeheartedly accepted it. Of the most enthusiastic supporters of the revolution who had praised the selflessness and the heroism of the Bolsheviks, many came to oppose it, for it did not fulfil its promise – as Mephistopheles said at Faust's burial – 'such a great outlay squandered! Oh, the shame'. James Billington, following Niebuhr's concept of 'irony', has defined the ironic view of the Russian revolution as one dealing with its perplexing incongruities without belittling or rejecting the hopes of the revolution.

Was there not irony in the fact that the revolution triumphed in a country in which Marxists had least expected it, and that its victory depended so much on the leadership of one man? Was it not ironic that the attempt to establish the freest régime in the world resulted in a giant bureaucracy, and that, in contrast to ideological expectations, political power came to control economics? Was it the historical function of the November revolution to industrialize and modernize a backward country, or has it not yet spent its force and dynamism? Only the course of Soviet history in coming decades will show. The revolution may be finished, but it has resulted in the creation of a new society; the achievements of the revolution are therefore inseparably connected with the performance of this society. This society is still changing and our appraisal cannot be final in character. Should judgment therefore be suspended? The question is rhetorical, for no one does suspend judgment.

There remains the question of the significance for the rest of the world of the Russian revolution, which was not an event of purely Russian interest, though at first many thought so. Gradually, its enormous historical import dawned on observers and increasingly influenced the writing of European and world history. Up to the nineteen-twenties the study of Russian history figured somewhere on the sidelines; a few specialists devoted their energies to research into a subject that was generally believed to be outside the mainstream of Western civilization. All this has changed since the second world war; the changes in the balance of world power have had a great impact on the writing of history. After the first world war America had come into its own, after the second Russia, and since the nineteen-fifties more and more attention has been devoted to the history of the newly independent states of Africa and Asia.

Historians have always been influenced by the *Zeitgeist*; in so far as the history of these countries had been neglected in the past, the impetus given to their study is of course to be welcomed. Occasionally, the enthusiasm has been excessive, especially among new converts who previously had neither known nor greatly cared about the subject which suddenly seemed all-important. Among them there arose the demand for a revolution in the writing of world history, at the expense of the decadent West, which was a spent force, and in favour of the 'wave of the future'. Not only had the balance of world power changed, the future of civilization, too, was no longer connected with Europe but with the new forces. About one of the prominent spokesmen of this school Pieter Geyl wrote that when Stalingrad was relieved by the Russians in 1943 he suddenly awoke to the fact that he had misspent his life – he knew all about the machinery of papal diplomacy in the thirteenth and fourteenth centuries, but very little about the Ruriks, the Przemyslids, and the Piasts.[16] That the idea of universal history is now generally accepted and that Europe's place in the world has changed, need hardly be restated at this stage. Some historians were slower than others to sense these changes. But is exchanging one form of provincialism for another the right way to adjust oneself? The world significance of the Russian revolution as a social movement is now undisputed. But future ages may perhaps attribute equal or perhaps even greater importance to the fact that it triggered off national revolutions and independence movements in many parts of the globe. The effects of all this on the Soviet Union and the world at large are only beginning to be felt. But the wider the repercussions of this revolution, the less of its original inspiration remains; the connection between Marx and present-day events in China, or between Lenin and the guerrilla war in the Congo, is not readily obvious. And the course of world revolution has led from the Finland Station to Peking airport.

[16] Pieter Geyl, *Encounters in History*, London, 1963, p. 260.

« 4 »

Lenin: For and Against

When Lenin came to power at the head of the Bolshevik party in 1917 little was known about him in Russia and nothing at all abroad. At the time of his death seven years later there were tributes from all over the globe and grudging respect even on the part of those who had once thought him wholly insignificant or who had only very recently attacked him as evil incarnate, the scourge of God. Seldom in recorded history has one man emerged so rapidly from obscurity to the foremost place on the historical stage: seldom has contemporary judgment changed so rapidly and so radically.

Before 1917 Lenin's name was familiar only to Russian socialists. A few social-democrats in Europe had heard of him or had actually met him but he certainly had no friends among them: he had the reputation of being a quarrelsome and an obstinate sectarian. His disputes with the other Russian factions took up an inordinate amount of valuable time at the sessions of the Socialist International. After the March revolution Lenin's name was occasionally mentioned in the world's press; a correspondent in Stockholm informed the liberal *Berliner Tageblatt* in early May 1917 that the main danger to the Provisional Government came from the revolutionary social-democrats led by Lenin, a 'strong personality of great culture and ruthless consistency'.[1] This, however, was an exception, most foreign commentators were certain neither of the spelling of his name nor of his political orientation. Was he head of the pro-German party in Russia, an anarchist, or perhaps a 'Maximalist' (whatever that meant)? Few had read his books and brochures, which had not exactly been best-sellers, he had not even been a deputy in the *Duma*. If Lenin received publicity in the summer and autumn of 1917 it was largely in connection with the 'sealed train' affair

[1] Hans Vorst, *Das bolschewistische Russland*, Leipzig, 1919. Vorst first coined the expression 'Iron Curtain', ibid., p. 229.

and 'German money'. This helped to make his name a household word in the then Russian capital, but these reports did not provide a well-rounded picture nor were they a key to what was to follow.

After the revolution Lenin's name became a symbol – a ray of hope to communists all over the world. He did not fare equally well in British, French, or American public opinion. Nor was there much factual knowledge: 'A German spy whose real name is Goldberg', announced *Le Matin*; the right-wing German press called him for years 'Lenin-Zederbaum'. 'The head of a gang of apostate Jews,' announced the British and French press, 'traitors to their own community and their country, traitors to their allies and mankind in general.'[2] The fact that Lenin was considered a traitor in Paris and London did not cause sleepless nights to those in authority in Berlin, but about his politics the Germans knew little more than their enemies.

Mirbach, the ambassador, reported from Moscow that the new régime was doomed; he expected its downfall any day, and he was not alone in this assumption. After all, Lenin himself, after a few months, was surprised that he was still in power. In 1918, the first visitors from abroad began to arrive. For the communists and their sympathisers his greatness was now beyond doubt; Zinoviev said that a man like Lenin was born only once every five hundred years. George Lansbury, the British Labour Party leader, talked about him as 'the gentle Lenin', a man of such devotion to the cause of humanity as to compare with no other whom he had ever encountered. But for Lansbury's party comrade, Mrs Philip Snowden, he was the 'Prince of Slaves and the Slave of Dogmas'. In Winston Churchill's judgment Lenin was the Grand Repudiator:

---

[2] Boris Souvarine wrote in 1924 in an essay about Lenin that out of one hundred news items published in the French and British press since the revolution, ninety-nine were mendacious and all hundred tendentious even if they accidentally revealed a fact that was correct. This statement refers to 1917–19, and it is an exaggeration. While leading conservative papers (*The Times*, *Morning Post*, *Daily Telegraph*) took an uncompromising anti-Bolshevik line, the *Daily Herald* usually defended the Soviet point of view, and the *Manchester Guardian*, the *Daily News* and others often gave the Bolsheviks the benefit of the doubt – for instance, by calling Litvinov 'above all a Tolstoyan and only incidentally a Bolshevik'. Of the many books and pamphlets which also had a great effect on public opinion, a substantial part was written from a point of view sympathetic to the new Russian régime. This refers to accounts by newspapermen (Phillips Price, Arthur Ransome, W. T. Goode, B. Beatty, L. Bryant, A. R. Williams, R. Marchand and others); there were also the books by G. Lansbury, H. N. Brailsford, Colonel Malone, Sylvia Pankhurst – not to mention official Soviet literature in English. Such support came not only from the left wing; Sorel's *In Defence of Lenin* ought to be mentioned at least in passing.

Lenin repudiated everything. He repudiated God, King, Country, morals, treaties, debts, rents, the laws and customs of centuries, all contracts written or implied, the whole structure - such as it is - of human society.

When 'revolutionary terror' was introduced, Lenin became the arch-murderer, the Great Destroyer, the Antichrist, a man motivated solely by hatred – hatred of the old order, of capitalism, of every tradition. Historical comparisons were made – mainly with Attila and Tamerlane.[3] But it was also thought that this was giving Lenin undue honour; he was not really that important; Lord Birkenhead denounced the myth of Lenin's greatness, which was a typical example of 'this modern cult of success'.

The years passed, the civil war came to an end, the Bolshevists stayed in power. More visitors came from abroad, but they too did not quite know what to make of Lenin. H. G. Wells, who came to see him in 1920, was somewhat patronizing. No giant himself, he wrote of Lenin as that little man whose feet hardly touched the ground even when he sat on the edge of his chair; and of Lenin's works – 'short, uncouth pamphlets'. But Gorky, who had so bitterly denounced Lenin in 1917–18, had now come round to admire him. He, too, subscribed to the analogy with Peter the Great; but in some ways Lenin's significance was much greater, for he wanted to change not merely Russia but the whole world. One of Gorky's most famous poems was a tribute to the 'holy madness of the brave' – and he was now singing his song to the first and foremost of these raving heroes – an irreverent comparison, but one in the style of the Russian revolutionary movement, which could still pass in the early twenties. Tributes to his greatness and historical significance came after his death from unexpected quarters. French statesmen like Painlevé and Herriot wrote about his great energy and force, his gifts as a statesman and his wide education. Thomas Mann wrote about the 'human organism of new democratically titanic dimensions, the powerful combination of the *Wille zur Macht* and asceticism, the great pope of the idea . . .' Romain Rolland, not yet fully converted to the cause, called him the greatest man of action in our century and, at the same time, the most selfless. Bertrand Russell and Shaw compared him with Einstein ('our century will go down in history as theirs'); what made Lenin's greatness was not his destructive activity, but his harmoniously creative mind; he was a philosopher, a practical

---

[3] Some early comparisons were more laudatory. Aldanov-Landau, in what is probably the first biography on record, drew a parallel with Peter I.

systematizer. Shaw, moreover, predicted that a Lenin statue would be erected in London alongside that of George Washington; for had not Washington like Lenin been vilified by the British press of the day?[4] This was only a few years after Lenin had been the chief of a group of bandits in German pay, the head of the Elders of Zion.

With his death began the process of deification. According to a peasant legend, Lenin in 1922 had sent for a doctor and asked him whether he could arrange for him, Lenin, to seem to be dead. For, he explained: 'I want to see what becomes of Russia if they think me dead; at present they put everything on my shoulders and make me responsible.' The doctor suggested a glass case from behind which Lenin could watch. Lenin agreed, and nobody was let into the secret apart from the doctor and Krupskaya, Lenin's wife. Lenin's death was announced, everyone mourned him and he was put into the mausoleum. But on the third week (or was it the third day?) after his death, he rose quietly one night and went out of the mausoleum by the back door – straight into the Kremlin; the sentries let him by for he carried a pass and no one recognized him, for he had pulled his hat down over his face. In the Kremlin he listened contentedly to a session of the Council of People's Commissars and then went to his glass case again. But on another night he went to a factory and on a third he went among the peasants. No one knows how long Lenin will lie in his glass case pretending to be dead.[5]

Forty years after Lenin's death huge placards throughout the Soviet Union proclaimed that 'Lenin is more alive than all those living now'. It is an interesting slogan, somewhat mystical for a party that has inscribed atheism and scientific materialism in capital letters on its banner. But it is a typical illustration of the central importance that Lenin and everything concerning him still retains in the Soviet Union. His birthday and the day of his death became the most important anniversaries. Lenin collections (*Leninskie Sborniki*) were put out, including even the most insignificant marginal notes; never in human history have anyone's papers been published so systematically and exhaustively (the publication of his political testament, to be sure, took thirty-two years). One year after his death 6,296 items of Leniniana had already been published in the Soviet Union. Forty years after his death Lenin as an authority on all things ideological – as well as on most other topics – is quoted far

[4] R. Fülop-Miller, *Lenin and Gandhi*, London, 1927, pp. 102–3.
[5] Lydia Seifulina, 'A Peasant Legend of Lenin', *Labour Literature*, March–April 1924.

more frequently than during his lifetime. In addition to the thousands of books about his life and work, there are dozens of films. Pictures of Lenin are in millions of offices and houses throughout the Soviet Union. His name has become a synonym for the revolution, the party, and the state – 'the greatest genius of all times and all nations, master of all the treasures of human knowledge and human culture'.[6]

Western students of Lenin have on the whole not been put off by the cult for the simple reason that his historical importance is indeed of the very greatest. He did not create the Russian revolutionary movement and his influence on it before 1917 was far from decisive. But he possessed an almost unfailing political instinct and it was mainly owing to this and to his characteristic tenacity, his supreme self confidence and single-mindedness, that the Bolsheviks prevailed over their rivals in 1917. Since that victory was the most important turning point in twentieth-century history, what does it matter if Lenin was not also – as some claim – the world's greatest philosopher, economist, and historian? There is remarkable unanimity between communists and non-communists about Lenin's historical role. Everyone agrees that it was of unique importance. The issues that continued to preoccupy non-communist historians were of a different character. They concerned the reasons for the Bolshevik victory in 1917, and Lenin's part in it, his ideas and methods, the question of continuity and break in Marxist thought. Above all, there was the question of Lenin's responsibility for the political and social developments that took place in the Soviet Union after his death.

The early biographers

The first biographical sketches of Lenin came from the circles most intimately concerned – his own party[7] – and from the new émigrés. What Lenin's comrades had to say often serves as valuable source material;[8] the émigrés evidence is of equal interest in so far as they had known Lenin. But few of them had; for the rest Lenin was as confusing a phenomenon as for most western observers. Marxism

[6] *Vladimir I. Lenin. A Political Biography*, prepared by the Marx–Engels–Lenin Institute, New York, 1943, p. 280.

[7] Krupskaya's *Memories of Lenin*; Zetkin's *Recollections of Lenin*; Trotsky's *Lenin*; Zinoviev's *Nicolai Lenin*, etc.

[8] The most interesting of which was M. A. Landau-Aldanov's *Lenin und der Bolschewismus*, Berlin, 1920. In this book Aldanov said that Lenin was devoid of all originality; subsequently he modified his views and wrote about Lenin's political genius.

was the key to it, or rather the impact of Marxism on Russia and its adaptation to local conditions. There were, of course, Russian experts in France and Britain, in America and Germany, but their political knowledge extended to 'official Russia'; they had not been interested in the *émigré* groups, in the left-wing underground, in Marxism and the international socialist movement. In consequence most of the early critical writing on Lenin and his régime was, with the exception of that emanating from socialist critics, on the level of 'I-was-a-prisoner-of-the-Cheka' or 'Jews-and-Freemasons-rule-Russia'. This sort of literature continued to appear throughout the twenties, and in some countries persisted up to the end of the second world war. A second wave of more serious Lenin literature began to appear only after the war.

The devotional literature, on the other hand, stressed Lenin's superhuman energy, his qualities as a political leader and also his gaiety and kindness; in the recollections of his contemporaries there was ample evidence of how Lenin had reacted to the 'Appassionata', how fond he was not only of children but of a political adversary like Martov (H. Guilbeaux). Another foreign admirer (writing in 1931) thought that it was too early to say with confidence whether Russia had in practice realized the Utopian state of plenty, liberty, and happiness. Nor was it possible to say that other countries might not reach a better state in speedier and less harsh ways. Perhaps mankind could make progress without struggle, violence, and widespread suffering. But history seemed to be on Lenin's side (Maxton). The perspective was still too short for final judgment, but there were already historical parallels: 'he was a man in the mould of Lincoln and Cromwell, very simple, very rugged, very great'; not a run-of-the-mill dictator, no one could have detested more the idea of a superman (Ralph Fox). Another biographer compared Lenin with Napoleon only to reject the parallel almost immediately, for Lenin was a great revolutionary, whereas Napoleon embodied counterrevolution. Lenin was the individual expression of the October revolution, the demagogue of the revolutionary assault *and* the first architect of socialist construction. There would be no Thermidor in Russia. The Russian revolution was only a transient stage of the world revolution, Lenin's message was intended for all countries (Prince Mirsky).[9]

[9] H. Guilbeaux, *Le Portrait authentique de Lénine*, Paris, 1924, p. 259, et seq.; James Maxton, *Lenin*, London, 1932, pp. 171–2; Ralph Fox, *Lenin*, London, 1933, pp. 309–10; D. S. Mirsky, *Lenin*, London, 1931, pp. 210–13.

This first group of western Lenin biographers was a curious one; Guilbeaux, the poet who had been close to Lenin during the first world war, an early communist who became deeply disappointed and moved perilously close to fascism; James Maxton, the Scottish labour leader who remained faithful to the Independent Labour Party to the end; Ralph Fox, poet, intellectual, and leading British communist, who was to die on the battlefield in Spain, and, perhaps the most interesting of them all, Mirsky, the Russian prince who became a communist in his London exile, returned to Moscow and disappeared in the purges of the thirties.

Some were attracted by his sheer force of personality; 'this was the most powerful magnet that drew us nearer and nearer to Leninism', Prince Mirsky wrote about the 'younger *émigrés* of good faith'. Others were fascinated by the purposefulness in Lenin's Russia, the revolutionary pathos in its arts and literature, the social engineering in economy and public life. It was, as a Marxist would say, no accident that the economic crisis of 1929 and the depression produced a whole crop of western Lenin biographies. Of the critical accounts George Vernadsky's *Lenin, Red Dictator*, published in 1931, was the only serious study. A Russian *émigré* who became an influential professor of history in the United States, he plumped for the Cromwell parallel (which incidentally had been first drawn by the Nestor of Soviet historians, Pokrovsky), only to reject it in the end; Cromwell had more respect than Lenin for man's individuality and historical traditions. Vernadsky was aware of Lenin's unique qualities – above all his will to power, so untypical of Russian intellectuals. He was inclined to regard the revolution as a great disaster; if judgment is based on the number of human lives destroyed by the government of Lenin, then it was impossible, he wrote, not to list Lenin among the most fearful tyrants history has known.[10] But Vernadsky the historian felt compelled to suspend judgment: history's estimate of Lenin depended upon the future role of Leninism in Russia. It was still impossible to say whether the system had been firmly established among the Russian people and whether it would extend throughout the world.

Beyond the camp of the admirers and critics there was in the nineteen-twenties yet a third school of non-partisan writers who regarded the life of Lenin as a fascinating subject for literary exercises, with, of course, a strong political undertone. The works of

[10] George Vernadsky, *Lenin, Red Dictator*, New Haven, 1931, p. 320.

Valeriu Marcu and René Fülop-Miller are the best known of this genre.[11] True, Fülop-Miller's comparison with Gandhi was far-fetched, and both books had all the weaknesses of the genre – the psychological biography of the twenties that was so fashionable at the time, hovering on the borderline between history and the historical novel. Nevertheless, they were, on the whole, well informed, more objective and of greater value than most partisan biographies. Marcu dealt mainly with Lenin's political career up to 1918, while Fülop-Miller's book provided a brief account of his whole life. Both writers were preoccupied with the problem of freedom and revolution. As a dictator, Marcu says, Lenin never abandoned the idea of force: freedom was bound to be harmful until the ideal state brought contentment to all, 'until happiness was as all-pervading and intoxicating as the perfume of a lemon grove'. Fülop-Miller, despite much admiration for Lenin, regrets his entanglement in the old traditions of Russian terrorism. The fact that Lenin even in his boldest dreams of a future classless world without hatred or oppression could see no other way of attaining his end but by brute force, was the most profoundly tragic thing in his peculiar destiny. If freedom had meant more to Lenin than a 'bourgeois prejudice', he would be remembered in history 'not only as an extraordinarily resolute and successful revolutionary but also as one of the greatest liberators of humanity'.[12] But how could freedom have prevailed in Russia at a time of such radical political and social transformation? This was the cardinal question and one to which there was no answer.

The second wave

After the second world war interest in Lenin was reawakened. The international importance of the Soviet Union had grown immensely, and with it the significance of Leninism. At the same time there had been an immense expansion of Soviet and communist studies in the West. I shall briefly introduce the authors of these biographies which, on the whole, are on a much higher level of sophistication than the works published in the twenties. This will be followed by a discussion of their views of the historical fortunes of Leninism in theory and practice.

David Shub (1948), Bertram Wolfe (1948), Louis Fischer (1964),

[11] Valeriu Marcu, *Lenin*, London, 1928, R. Fülop-Miller, *Lenin and Gandhi*, London, New York, 1927.
[12] Marcu, p. 395; Fülop-Miller, p. 123.

and Adam Ulam (1965) are the authors of the four major studies of Lenin.[13] Apart from the fact that they all live in the United States there is little in common between them; their works differ in scope and character. The books of Shub and, in particular, of Bertram Wolfe (the latter coming only up to 1914) are pioneering works based on much research and the extensive use of primary sources. Fischer's and Ulam's studies, while occasionally tapping some hitherto unused material, are by and large works of synthesis. Shub and Fischer confine themselves strictly to the life of Lenin, whereas Wolfe's book also covers the biography of Trotsky and Stalin before the first world war, and Ulam is concerned with the rise of the Bolshevik party in general, not merely the personal fortunes of its leader. David Shub is the oldest of this group of Lenin biographers. He joined the Russian Social-Democratic Party in 1903, participated in the first Russian revolution, and emigrated to America in 1908. He has been connected with the Mensheviks and has worked as a journalist in New York for many decades. He has, no doubt, a wider first-hand knowledge of the pre-war Russian revolutionary movement and its leaders than the other biographers, but he has not been back to the Soviet Union. His book is based on a wide selection of contemporary sources and is vividly written; direct speech is freely used even when the dialogue had to be reconstructed. Its strengths and its weaknesses are those of the journalistic approach.

Bertram Wolfe, born in Brooklyn in 1896, was an early leading member of the American Communist Party and at one time its representative in the Comintern. He lived for two years in Moscow in the nineteen-twenties and came to know many leaders of the Soviet party such as Trotsky and Stalin, though not Lenin. He broke with the party in 1929; in the thirties he wrote on Spanish and Latin-American culture. After 1939 Mr Wolfe returned to the Soviet field; *Three who made a Revolution* was written between 1939 and 1948. He has taught in several American universities, and worked for the State Department and the 'Voice of America' in the late forties and early fifties. Of the biographical studies of the communist leaders this is the one on the grandest scale, the most ambitious and the most difficult to write. It was received with almost universal acclaim and

---

[13] David Shub, *Lenin*, New York, 1948; Bertram Wolfe, *Three who made a Revolution*, New York, 1948; Louis Fischer, *The Life of Lenin*, New York, 1964; Adam Ulam, *The Bolsheviks*, New York, 1965.

has established itself as one of the *chefs d'œuvre* in the field of Soviet history. A sequel to this volume has not appeared.

Louis Fischer, distinguished foreign correspondent, has a more intimate knowledge of the Soviet Union than any other Lenin biographer. He first arrived in the Soviet capital in Lenin's day and left only in the late thirties. Never a member of the communist party, he was until the middle thirties sympathetically inclined towards the party line, especially on foreign affairs. He is the author of, among other books, a very detailed account of Soviet foreign policy in the nineteen-twenties. Fischer's main interest is in foreign affairs. (Chicherin, to give but one example, looms very large in the biography, but Axelrod is hardly mentioned.) He does not deal in commensurate detail with Lenin's thought, or with internal party and state developments; there is no attempt to sum-up the historical role of Lenin and Leninism. Generally speaking, Fischer's book is descriptive rather than analytical.

Adam Ulam, a Harvard professor, was born in Poland in 1922; he received his education in the United States and is the author of a number of books on socialist and communist thought. He is the only professional academic in this group (professor of government, not history), though both Wolfe and Fischer have held academic appointments. Ulam is not primarily concerned with Lenin's personal life, his family background, emotional involvements, intrigues or in general with character analysis. Lenin's ideas and policies are his main interest; on these Ulam's book is one of the most intelligent contributions as well as one of the best-written.

In this post-war literature there is much less controversy about Lenin's historical role than in previous decades. Almost all writers agree that he was a great political leader, and they are in accord in believing that had it not been for Lenin the Bolsheviks would not have come to power in 1917. Equally, there is full agreement that Lenin was quite unscrupulous in the means he used to promote his policies and attain his ends. Almost all historians recognize his modesty, lack of vanity, absence of personal ambition. The real problems emerge once one passes from the personal sphere to the assessment of Lenin's political role. Some of these questions are of interest mainly to the student of the history of ideas or of political theory. To what extent was Lenin original as the creator of a political party of a new type? Did his adaptation of Marxism to Russian conditions mark a break in the continuity of the doctrine? Other issues are of wider significance: from about 1903 Lenin pursued certain policies and adopted specific organizational methods. To what extent did each subsequent stage in his political career follow from the previous one? Was the doctrine of the 'dictatorship of the proletariat' bound to lead to the dictatorship of a single leader? Was the point of no return in this development reached in 1903 or in 1917 or in 1921? In other words: to what extent was Stalinism inherent in Leninism? Was Lenin aware of these dangers; did he regard them as a threat, or did he consider this an inevitable stage on the road to real political democracy? Did the development of Soviet Russia in the decades after Lenin's death proceed, more or less, in line with his expectations? These are the cardinal questions that have a direct bearing on the historical assessment of Lenin's ideas and policies. Before discussing some of the answers that have been provided, we shall have to deal, albeit briefly, with another set of problems that has increasingly preoccupied some writers. I mean Lenin's financial sources, his passage from Switzerland to Russia in 1917, and his sex life.

It had been known for a long time that the Bolsheviks, or at least some of them, engaged in 'expropriations' after the failure of the revolution of 1905. It was also common knowledge that other unorthodox means were used to replenish the party's depleted coffers. When the facts about the robberies and the hold-ups became known most western socialists and the Mensheviks were very indignant. Rosa Luxemburg wrote about the 'guerrilla struggle of the *lumpen-proletariat* against private property', which was harmful to the cause of the revolution. Lenin's attitude towards terror was, as Bertram Wolfe wrote, 'an unconscious heritage from the tradition of Russian conspirative technique and organization'.[14]

The essential facts about Lenin's journey to Petrograd in the famous sealed train have likewise been known almost since it happened. Lenin was attacked almost immediately by former comrades like Alexinsky, by Burtsev and by others as a German agent and spy; comments in the British and French press were in a similar vein. What was not known at the time, what was suspected but could not be proved, was that Lenin, through some trusted agents such as Hanecki and Kozlovsky (who were disavowed whenever necessary) maintained contact with men like Parvus and Keskuela, who combined socialist convictions and activities on behalf of

[14] B. Wolfe, op. cit., p. 424.

the German general staff and the German foreign ministry, with the aim of promoting revolution in Russia. As a result of the research by Messrs Katkov, Zeman, and Futtrell much new light has now been shed on these affairs.[15] What is the political importance of these revelations? Very limited indeed. The sums of money involved were fairly small; the fact that Lenin accepted them did not make him a German agent. There were no strings attached. Lenin did not undertake to pursue a policy other than his own. The 'sealed compartment' admittedly changed the course of history. Had the Germans not permitted Lenin to reach Petrograd there would have been no revolution. The Germans wanted to use Lenin to weaken the Russian war effort; Lenin used the Germans for his own, very different, purposes. There is no doubt who got the better bargain out of this deal. Should a revolutionary have accepted assistance from German imperialism? Few historians blame him in retrospect on these grounds; the Mensheviks after all followed in yet another such special train a few weeks later. These dealings prove that Lenin was not over-scrupulous in the means he employed to attain his political goals. But this was not exactly a new discovery; earlier, there had been more extreme manifestations.

Lenin's love-life has also received a fair amount of attention. One author has established that when Lenin took Inessa Armand to a little bistro near Longjumeau he drank beer while she had lemonade. It has also been found out that Lenin, when in hiding, spent between eighteen and twenty-five days in a house in Petrograd belonging to Margarita Fofanova, who was thirteen years his junior. There was an eerie quality about this interlude, says Professor Possony: perhaps he did feel the need to prove himself as the great conqueror during the Indian summer of his emotional life? Alas, we may never know. Before Professor Possony, David Shub had devoted attention and space to Lenin's alleged romance with Elizabeth K. 'a pretty and wealthy young woman' in Leningrad in 1905. This information was based on a little book by Beaucler and Alexinsky, published in Paris in 1937: *Les Amours secrètes de Lénine*.[16] Bertram Wolfe,

---

[15] George Katkov, *Russia 1917*, London, 1967; Z. A. B. Zeman, *Germany and the Revolution in Russia 1915–1918*, London, 1958; Michael Futtrell, *Northern Underground*, London, 1963.

[16] Possony, *Lenin*, pp. 271–2; David Shub, *Lenin*, pp. 81–2. Alexinsky's story was first published in *Illustrirovanaia Rossiya*, Paris, 31 October 1936; the Polish fiction writer Ossendowski had reported before that Lenin had used his lady friends to collect statistical material about the position of the working classes in Russia.

on a more serious level, has collected and sifted all the known material about Lenin's relations with Inessa Armand: a close comrade, a friend, and also an attractive woman.[17]

It is a truism that the biography of a public figure should not be studied in isolation from his private life. The non-Soviet biographer (as Professor Ulam says) has often an almost irresistible temptation to catch Lenin *in flagranti* – partly as a reaction against the official Soviet historiography which, having sanctified Lenin, would suppress such evidence. But all Lenin's contemporaries (including critics like Valentinov) attest that Lenin's personal moral standards were the highest; that as far as the moral code of his times and the revolutionary movement was concerned, he was a strict conformist. But what if there was a grain of truth in these stories? They would still be immaterial and irrelevant in a political biography of Lenin. The historian is obliged to take cognisance of the private life of his hero in so far as it helps to explain his public life. He will ignore the details of the private sphere if they have no such relevance; he is concerned, for instance, with Parvus the author of the theory of permanent revolution, not Parvus the womaniser – unless it can be proven that Parvus' dissolute way of life decisively affected his theoretical efforts. Lenin concerns him as the leader of the Bolsheviks and the Soviet state; the fact that Lenin met a number of women in his private and public life can be taken for granted.

Lenin was one of the very few leaders in modern times about whom it can be said without qualification that he was irreplaceable. In 1923 there were many candidates for the succession; it would, in all probability have made a great difference to Russia and the world if Bukharin or Trotsky or someone else had taken over. But the Bolsheviks were in power, the course of the new régime was set in broad outline, the freedom of choice was limited. In 1917, after the March revolution, all the big questions were as yet undecided. When Lenin returned from Switzerland in April of that year, he was almost alone in urging his party on to a more militant line – to seize power, and end the war. The situation in October, on the eve of the armed insurrection, was similar. On both occasions, with single-minded purpose, he won over his party to his own point of view. Sidney Hook, in an interesting study, has shown by this example to what extent a single individual can change history. The Bolshevik revolution in October 1917 was not inevitable; Lenin made it appear

[17] Bertram Wolfe, 'Lenin and Inessa Armand', *Slavic Review*, March 1963.

so in retrospect.[18] It is not certain whether this point had to be laboured, for there is now almost complete unanimity between communist and non-communist historians on this issue. The former have always stressed Lenin's unique genius and his absolute authority. Trotsky, who did not suffer from excessive modesty and who had a considerable share in the success of the revolution, wrote that one could by no means say with confidence that without Lenin the party would have found its way. There would have been a revolutionary crisis but it would not have lasted for ever:

> The conditions of war and revolution, however, would not allow the party a long period for fulfilling its mission. Thus it is by no means excluded that a disoriented and split party might have let slip the revolutionary opportunity for many years. The role of the personality arises before us here on a truly gigantic scale.[19]

There is similar agreement among historians about Lenin's methods. Bolshevik writers always praise his indomitable will, his hard, relentless fight against opponents resulting in their destruction – especially those in the socialist movement and in his own party. Critics have commented on Lenin's two standards of morality. Whatever benefited the party was permitted. The adjectives used by communists and their critics are not identical, but at bottom they mean the same. Having established this point, one might as well pass to the discussion of some more central and basic aspects of Lenin's policies.

The main issues dividing Russian social-democracy had existed, though not always very distinctly, since well before 1917. Lenin was firmly convinced that to bring about a revolution and a social transformation, special organizational preparation was needed and violence would have to be used. Squeamishness was tantamount to abdication; it meant renouncing all their aims; in a revolutionary situation waiting was a crime, procrastination in these circumstances was fatal. 'Great problems in the life of nations are decided only by force', he had written. His critics argued that Russia was not yet ready for a radical socialist revolution, that the use of undemocratic means, the establishment of a dictatorship, however well-meaning, would pervert the basic ideals of socialism; a social and political régime would emerge which would have nothing in common with the freer and more just order for which socialists had always fought.

[18] S. Hook, *The Hero in History*, Boston, 1955.
[19] L. Trotsky, *History of the Russian Revolution*, London, 1965, p. 343.

Most historians now trace the split back to 1903, the year of publication of *What is to be Done*, 'a primer of politics for the twentieth
century, a model for the movements – not only the Marxist ones –
that have increasingly displaced liberalism and democracy'.[20]

When *What is to be Done* was published, it seemed to be dealing
with a minor dispute about organizational problems. But Lenin was
right when he said that 'we quarrel only on organizational matters
but they are all-important'. These disagreements about organizational problems reflected different conceptions of the functions and
aims of a political party. They were disagreements at a deeper level,
reflecting political expectations and metapolitical attitudes, rather
than divergent interpretations of Marx.

Lenin's basic assumption was that, left to themselves the workers
do not develop a socialist consciousness; in its unaided efforts
and its spontaneous actions, the working class can develop only a
'trade-union consciousness'. A socialist consciousness can be brought
to the proletariat only from outside. This could be done only by
revolutionary intellectuals; not by intellectuals *per se*, certainly not
by the typical ineffectual Russian intellectual for whom Lenin had
nothing but contempt. It could be done only by a small band of
professional revolutionaries like himself joining forces with the
workers in a party of a new type.

This was certainly a novel conception. For Marx, the class consciousness of the workers, their striving for socialism, had been the
natural result of their economic conditions. Lenin, on the other
hand, thought that the worker had to have socialism beaten into his
head by the intelligentsia. This was a revision of the doctrine of the
master, not less extreme than that proposed by Bernstein, the
revisionist.[21] *What is to be Done* is both a theory and a panegyric of
the party:

> As yet this party existed only in Lenin's mind. It was to be composed of
> professional revolutionaries, but it was not a mere conspiracy. It was to
> enlist intellectuals, indeed from among them were to be sought its leaders,
> but it was to avoid the intellectuals' vices of continuous doctrinal dispute,
> indecision, humanitarian scruples and the like.[22]

The organizational scheme developed by Lenin vested the control
of party affairs in the editorial board of its central organ (*Iskra*).
The organization was to be strictly hierarchical; as Lenin's wife
wrote: Everyone could find a place, could become a cog in this

[20] A. Ulam, *The Bolsheviks*, p. 180.   [21] Ulam, p. 178.   [22] Ulam, p. 179.

73

revolutionary machine. Yet one question was left open: Who was going to be at the top of the hierarchy?

> Has not Lenin forgotten something? The party is to be like an army, but an army needs a general. Who is to decide which cogs are to fit various parts of the machinery? Unconsciously, Lenin has sketched a blueprint for a dictatorship. That it was unconscious, at least at this juncture, we need not doubt ... But the whole logic of *What is to be Done* cries out not only for leaders, but also for *the leader*, and that, in Russian revolutionary thought and tradition, was a vast novelty.[23]

It is admittedly much easier to discern this new trend in the perspective of several decades. At the time these seemed minor organizational disagreements. The Mensheviks and the Social-Revolutionaries agreed with the Bolsheviks that conspiratorial methods should be used for underground work in Russia, that strict discipline and therefore a hierarchical organization and a centralized apparatus were needed. There was no other way. Leonard Schapiro has pointed out that at the time all social-democrats accepted Lenin's dictatorial principles of party organization: 'Martov had no more than Lenin the remotest intention of allowing party organization to develop on democratic lines.'[24] It could be argued, in fact, that the illegal apparatus of the Bolsheviks in Russia before 1917 was not markedly different from other illegal party organizations and it certainly was not more efficient. True, the Bolsheviks were more extreme in their whole approach, but their influence was so small that this hardly mattered. They were even less responsible than the other illegal parties for the overthrow of Tsarism in March 1917. While Tsarism lasted, police repression made the spread of Bolshevik influence almost impossible. The situation changed only when the régime, weakened by defeats in the war, collapsed. The moment it broke down, the party built on the concepts Lenin had developed fifteen years before, gathered strength and began to overtake the others – in political influence, if not necessarily in numbers. The scheme that had originally been an adaptation to conditions of illegality became a great success only after the revolution of March 1917, when the Bolsheviks could for the first time operate legally, unhampered by police repression.

All this, however, was years ahead. It would be very wrong,

[23] Ulam, pp. 181–2

[24] Leonard Schapiro, *The Communist Party of the Soviet Union*, London, 1960, pp. 52–3.

Bertram Wolfe wrote, to regard the Lenin of that period as a budding conscious dictator, leader of a totalitarian party.

Lenin was a convinced democrat and the problem of political freedom concerned him deeply. Not only in these days but until he seized power in 1917. 'Not a single socialist', he wrote, for instance, in 1914, 'unless he pronounces the questions of political freedom and democracy of no consequence to him, in which case, of course, he ceases to be a socialist ...'[25]

A little later, in a polemic against Trotsky, he wrote that whoever wanted to approach socialism by any other path than political democracy would inevitably arrive at the most obscurantist and reactionary conclusions. Trotsky had been, if possible, even more outspoken about the dangers of dictatorship: the 'apparatus' of the party would take the place of the party itself, he had written in 1904; the central committee would replace the apparatus, and eventually a dictator would take the place of the central committee. And, eventually, assuming that such a party took over state power, the party would become synonymous with the state, the dictator of the party would be the only ruler of the state. Lenin countered by adding some safeguards to his blueprint – 'democratic centralism' – but, Wolfe says, it was not at all sure how much democracy and how much centralism would go into this compound, and whether the democracy would not be swallowed up by the centralism.

Lenin, according to most latter-day historians, was aware of the dangers inherent in his organizational scheme. But he was equally convinced that in a country like Russia, it was impossible to cling dogmatically to orthodox Marxist formulas that had been developed with West European conditions in mind. Lenin must have understood that his concept involved dangers and risks, perhaps great dangers and grave risks. But what was the alternative, except to wait passively until Russia had reached that degree of economic and social development which, according to the classical model, would make a proletarian revolution possible? Was there not a great danger that if they waited until then the Russian bourgeoisie would become too firmly entrenched and the kulaks and the middle peasants too strong? And was not the danger of a dictatorship minimal – he and his lieutenants, after all, were sincere and incorruptible revolutionaries, they did not strive for self-aggrandizement and personal power. Lenin's attitude is summarized by Bertram Wolfe as follows:

[25] B. Wolfe, *Three who made a Revolution*, p. 330.

Let's take power and then we'll see. This readiness to 'take power and then see' is the real core of 'Leninism', separating him by an abyss from the Mensheviks . . .' 'The seizure of power,' he wrote in 1917, 'is the point of the uprising. Its political task will be clarified after the seizure.' No one but Lenin among the Marxists could have written such a sentence. So, too, the last theoretical article he would ever write in his life would take as its text his favourite adage from Napoleon: *On s'engage et puis . . . on voit.*[26]

Underlying the doctrinal disputes between the Russian socialists, there emerge some basic differences in political temperament, instinct, and general orientation. The Mensheviks (to quote Wolfe again) were inclined towards the trade union, the mass organizations, the broad party of the working class. They kept their eyes fixed on the West and thought that their hour would come after more capitalist development and a bourgeois revolution. Lenin was more impatient, more militant, and thought in terms of the traditional Russian conspiracy:

> In a land which had been so long centralized every impulse had to come from above. His views were in the tradition of all past Russian movements for reform from the palace *coup d'état* to the *Narodnaya Volya*. All his hopes were concentrated on the speedy victory of a centralized uprising and then the organization and education of the working class and peasantry afterwards, from above, from the vantage point of the summits of power.[27]

The Mensheviks, after some initial shilly-shallying, had soon come to oppose the theory and practice of this new political party. Many years before the revolution, Martov accused Lenin of introducing a 'state of siege' in the Russian social-democracy. After 1917 (Ulam says) the psychology of the state of siege was imposed upon the communist party and then on Soviet society as a whole.[28] For Lenin the emergency was never to end – first there was the revolution, later on the achievements of the revolution were threatened by the White Armies, then there was the Kronstadt insurrection and the famine, with the whole national economy in a state of chaos. This was not the time for political opposition, not even for prolonged theoretical debates within the party. So much work had to be done before they could dream of restoring political freedom. Of course, Lenin had not abandoned in principle the ideal of political freedom. The state of emergency was to be of short duration only – eventually, the freest society on earth was to emerge. It was not to be bourgeois democracy, with freedom for the few, but a real popular democracy

²⁶ Wolfe, p. 336.   ²⁷ Wolfe, p. 415, p. 356.   ²⁸ Ulam, p. 466.

76

where cooks would run the affairs of state, or, to be precise, of society, for the state with its whole machinery of repression would wither away as Lenin had just forecast in *State and Revolution*. If anyone had called Lenin the dictator of Russia, even his most outspoken critic in the Communist party would have rejected this as vile slander. He pleaded with the party (to quote Ulam again), acknowledged mistakes, allowed himself to be outvoted, ruled through the party. 'But the essence of dictatorial power was certainly his; as long as he was well, no process short of a revolution could wrest the rule of Russia and Communism from his hands.'[29]

The heritage

After Lenin's death, the state of siege became an institution, was absorbed in the régime. True, there were no longer any immediate dangers inside the country menacing Soviet power. But the state was still isolated, the imperialist wolves were only waiting to devour the young socialist country; real and imaginary threats were used to justify the régime until, under Stalin, the disappearance, not only of all opposition, but also of inner party democracy, was accepted in the thirties, as the natural state of affairs. There was something paradoxical in the 'state of siege argument', Ulam notes, for in times of real crisis and emergency, there was usually more freedom in the country than when normal peaceful conditions prevailed.[30]

On most of these points concerning the emergency of Soviet rule and its specific character, non-communist historians have been, broadly speaking, in agreement. On details there have been differences of opinion: some of them here argued that the development towards absolute dictatorship was more or less inevitable, given Lenin's radicalism, his unwillingness to share power, and, of course, Russia's general backwardness. Others believe that while this trend was admittedly very strong, it was, in the beginning, not irreversible. There were various turning points (or points of no return) in this development – the dissolution of the Constituent Assembly in 1918, for instance, or the continuation of dictatorial rule after the end of the civil war in 1921. Both these occasions provided an opportunity to return to normal conditions, to invite other parties to share responsibility and power. Some Bolsheviks realized this, but they were overruled by Lenin.

[29] Ulam, p. 465.   [30] Ulam, p. 466.

Only two biographies of Lenin published since the second world war were written by communists: Pospelov's official biography (Moscow, 1960) and Christopher Hill's little volume *Lenin and the Russian Revolution* (London, 1947). P.N.Pospelov is a high Soviet official, a member of the Central Committee of the Party, a former editor of *Pravda*, director of the Marx-Engels-Lenin Institute. The biography was actually prepared by a group of authors working under his supervision. Professor Hill is now master of Balliol College, Oxford; his little volume was also written from the communist point of view, but there are in it traces of unorthodox attitudes which eventually took the author out of the Communist party.

This can be seen, for instance, in the frequent comparisons with Cromwell, or the admission, unusual for a communist in 1947, that it may not be necessary in future to copy the Soviet régime in all details in Western Europe and North America. All other biographies of Lenin are critical in spirit; some treat the October revolution as a major disaster, others regard it as one of the alternatives open in 1917 to restore order and modernize the country. But they, too, do not share the belief in Lenin's basic tenets and fail therefore to view 7 November 1917 as the red letter day *par excellence* in the history of mankind. The liberal and socialist critics of Lenin are convinced that the price that had to be paid by the Bolsheviks for seizing and retaining state power was too high, that socialism without freedom would, as Lenin predicted, have 'obscurantist and reactionary results'.

Inevitably, these works on Lenin were written to a large extent with an eye to events in the Soviet Union after his death. The main criterion they employ is not industrial production or military strength, nor even the survival of the Soviet state; success and failure are measured in terms of the original aspirations of the Bolsheviks and the traditional libertarian programme of the revolutionary movement. The risks inherent in the suppression of freedom and the establishment of a dictatorship were not altogether unknown to Lenin – just as they were clear to those writers who at the time sympathized with him and later came to oppose his policies (Souvarine, Bertram Wolfe, to a certain extent Louis Fischer, and others). If so, why did the Bolsheviks and their followers abroad run these risks? Because, no doubt, at the time it seemed the only way out. The tremendous impact of the first world war, the senseless slaughter of millions of people, the enormous material destruction had created a revolutionary situation. The duty of preventing a repetition of such a disaster was higher and more urgent than all other considerations. A radical transformation of the social order seemed the most effective way to prevent war in future.

The Bolsheviks came to power in Russia as the party of peace. Abroad, too, they attracted most of their support under this banner. To understand Lenin, it may be useful to make the otherwise obvious point that 1917 was not 1907, that the old order had broken down in chaos, that the Provisional Government was incapable of action. Political life in Russia (and throughout Europe) had been brutalized by the war. After July 1917 (Ulam says) there could have been no democratic way of arresting the trend of events leading to catastrophe. It is not just the character and doctrine of the Bolsheviks and of Lenin himself which determined subsequent developments. There was more to it than that, and not all of it was the responsibility of the Bolsheviks.

Most of Lenin's old comrades in the Soviet Union perished in the purges or were eliminated from political life. Most of his early followers abroad ceased to be communists and turned into critics. Yet there were others who had opposed him in 1917 and during the first years of the Bolshevik régime but came to realize, under Stalin, that he had been right after all; Mensheviks like Dan, aristocratic émigrés like Mirsky, British liberals like Bernard Pares. The great bourgeois press, too, became much more respectful; for *The Times*, Lenin had been the scum of the earth: 'with such a movement there is no question of peace, but only the kind of war that must be waged against it.'[31] Twenty-five years later, there were long paeans of praise for Lenin's immortal work and Russia's great achievements under his successor. No one had been more extreme in his anti-Bolshevism than Churchill; he had compared Lenin to a snake creeping along on its slimy stomach and then suddenly striking at its prey. Twenty-five years later Churchill went to Moscow and praised his great ally's war effort. Could there have been a more complete vindication of Lenin, a more complete refutation of the prophecies that Bolshevism would not work, that it was economically disastrous that the régime would collapse at the slightest test? Had not Lenin's behest to preserve a strong united party been fulfilled?

The party, under the guidance of its leader, in an uncompromising struggle with opportunists of all hues, preserved the purity of the teachings

[31] 5 January 1920.

79

of Marx and Lenin, and continued to develop these teachings. The further elaboration by Stalin of Lenin's teachings on the Party, on the building of socialism in one country, on the dictatorship of the proletariat, on the national question, on the agrarian question, especially on all-round collectivization and the wiping-out of the kulaks as a class on this basis, on socialism and communism, and many other questions – is a worthy continuation of the theoretical work of Lenin ... The Party, as a result of its solidarity and strength, was able to undertake successfully the fulfilment of Lenin's plan for building socialism.[32]

About Stalin's great theoretical contributions there was less enthusiasm in 1967 than in 1937. But the growth of Soviet power, industrial and military, was undisputable. So was the spread of Communism in Eastern Europe and above all in Asia. Could there be a greater triumph for Lenin's ideas and policies? What other figure in recent history had made such a lasting and radical impact on both his own generation and posterity? Lenin's critics apply different criteria to judge his policies. Most of them contend that, in the perspective of fifty years, the outcome has not justified the effort, the enthusiasm, the sacrifices, and the many victims that went into the realization of the great dream. Lenin's aim, they argue, was to establish a higher social order, not merely to modernize Russia and expand its heavy industry. Autocracy had been overthrown in Russia before Lenin came, and democracy would have prevailed had it not been for the Bolshevik seizure of power. The industrialization and modernization of that enormous country would have taken place anyway. Similar achievements would have been reached at much less cost. There would not have been the immense pressure and frantic haste to prepare for war; fascism, after all, gathered strength mainly as a reaction to communism. Would Mussolini and Hitler ever have come to power but for the Bolshevik victory in 1917?

At this stage the argument has, of necessity, become largely speculative. Lenin's admirers will argue that, capitalism being doomed, a revolutionary socialist had to act as Lenin did in 1917. There was no other way out for Russia, and for that reason alone the various 'might have beens' are irrelevant. Was it as senseless as asking what good had come to mankind as the result of the first world war? Lenin's critics will not, of course, accept this analogy. For mankind stumbled into the first world war, whereas October 1917 was a deliberate attempt to change the course of history

<hr>

[32] P. Kerzhentsev, *Life of Lenin*, Moscow, 1937, p. 326.

according to a preconceived plan. The achievements of the revolution must then be judged not as a series of spontaneous events, but as a development deliberately willed. Unless one considers the Soviet Union of 1967 at least a qualified success in terms of freedom and social justice, Lenin's decision in 1917 was a mistake which ended in failure – whatever its incidental consequences, such as the enhancement of Russia's place in the world. (The anti-socialist will regard it as a disaster in any case, since he did not share Lenin's premises in the first place.)

We have reached the last stage of the argument. History, Lenin's apologists will answer, is a dialectical process. Under Lenin and his successors, the material basis for communism was created. Lenin had hoped that the revolution would soon spread to the rest of the world. This process has taken much longer than originally assumed. Russia was for a long time in a state of siege; its policies and its economy were affected, and human rights had to be restricted in the transition period. But with the further growth of Soviet power and with the development of communist régimes elsewhere, the road is now open to pass on to that higher stage of social development which Marx, Engels, and Lenin had envisaged. There is no exploitation in a socialist society; soon the other forms of compulsion will disappear too, and with the return of political freedom the Soviet system will emerge as in every way superior to all other political and social systems.

The critics do not share this optimism. Each state, each society, develops according to certain laws; the circumstances in which it came into being and developed are of decisive importance. Dictatorships have, in the course of time, become milder; occasionally they have mellowed into some form of democratic rule. But this refers only to the old-established forms of autocratic rule. The Soviet Union constitutes a novel phenomenon; a new type of régime; planning, control, and regimentation are far stronger than in any régime in the past. The state apparatus is the most powerful in history. These are formidable obstacles on the road to the restoration of freedom. Arbitrary rule and the lack of democratic initiative are ingrained in this régime, just as the planned economy is an inherent part of it. Under enlightened rulers, such a régime will behave in a relatively enlightened way, but this does not mean that the régime itself will change its character and that the whole repressive apparatus can be dismantled. With the spread of polycentrism, will a measure of

81

freedom return with the emergence of factions within the various communist movements? A basic democratic transformation is not impossible in the sense that there are no absolute impossibilities in history, but at present it seems unlikely that such an initiative can succeed in the near future. It may be a long drawn-out evolutionary process, or it may come in the wake of violent disturbances and crises; at present it is difficult even to imagine it.

The debate continues, and is likely to go on for a long time. But at this point it concerns the future of the Soviet Union rather than its past, and for the historian it is time to take leave. It was in many ways easier to assess Robespierre's role in 1840 than Lenin's in 1960. Robespierre's rule was a brief interlude; the French Revolution had lasted altogether five years, it was finished even if its repercussions were to be felt for decades to come. Lenin's revolution may have lost some, or much, or all of its original impetus, its character and significance may have changed greatly. But there is enough continuity to regard it as a historical process whose end is not yet in sight. Historians, on the whole, find it difficult enough to interpret the past; their ambitions do not extend to comment on the future.

Stalin: For and Against

Stalin is a subject for courageous people. During his lifetime his very name sufficed to provoke the most violent reactions. He was the wisest and kindest of men and the greatest of revolutionary leaders to some people, and a Byzantine despot and mass murderer to others. To the non-communist left he was the betrayer, *par excellence*, of the elementary principles of socialism. Those who were not of the left found it easier to regard Stalin with less personal involvement, but their views, too, were often highly ambivalent and changed frequently: in the West Stalin was in turn evil incarnate and esteemed honourable ally. Hitler was impressed by him but (except for 1939–41) Nazi propagandists had standing orders to depict him as the most hideous monster the world had ever known. Stalin was grossly underrated by his early biographers, who failed to understand how a man of mediocre gifts in most respects, one who had not been among the foremost heroes of the revolution, came to succeed Lenin and ultimately to concentrate in his hands much more power than Lenin, or any other contemporary ruler, had ever wielded. Beginning with the late twenties a Stalin legend was systematically created in the Soviet Union, the like of which had not been seen before in modern history. Pliant historians made Stalin into Lenin's closest comrade in arms and his best pupil, almost equal to Lenin in the October revolution and the early years of Soviet power. Subsequently the glorification of Stalin went even further: in a host of history books, plays, films and pictures, not to mention millions of newspaper articles, radio broadcasts, and other forms of propaganda, Stalin became the greatest military leader, a master of science, the most profound philosopher, the most original economist, and, generally speaking, the greatest genius of all ages and peoples.

No one, not even the extreme anti-Stalinist, remained quite unaffected by this unprecedented build-up of a political leader;

admirers helped to spread the legend, opponents felt themselves obliged to do their bit to destroy it. The official catalogue of Stalin's virtues and achievements was so ludicrous by European standards that outside Russia it was often counter-productive. It provoked hilarity and ridicule, and it often made outside critics forget that, when all was said and done, the Soviet Union continued to be one of the world's great powers, and one that was steadily growing in power, and that Stalin remained its undisputed ruler, while the leaders of other nations came and went. The official legend thus distorted Stalin's image both inside the Soviet Union and abroad.

The fluctuations in the features of this image after his death are known and need not be retold in detail. Half-hearted de-Stalinization and modest attempts to restore the 'historical balance' followed each other and, for all one knows, may continue for a long time to come. A clear, complete break with the past was impossible; it would have fatally undermined the legitimacy and continuity of Soviet power. It was equally impossible to perpetuate the legend.

In the West the need was felt after Stalin's death for a fresh study of his life and policies and perhaps for a new approach. But the most elementary prerequisite for this did not exist; there had been some revelations about the Stalin era at the 20th party congress in 1956, mostly imprecise in character and anecdotal. But the archives remained closed; unless one believes that Stalin's actions speak for themselves, there is not what most historians would regard as a basis for historical research. Every scrap of writing by Lenin has by now been published; as far as Stalin is concerned the publication even of his *Collected Works*, that most unrevealing of series, has been discontinued. (Ironically, the last 3 volumes of his works have been published in America [R. McNeal, ed., Stanford, 1967] but not in the Soviet Union.) We know in broad outline what Stalin did; his policies are common knowledge. But it is not known why he acted in a given situation as he did. As for what happened inside the Kremlin during the Stalin era there is now, as there was then, virtually only one source, namely *Pravda*.

There is no period in modern history – nor even in medieval history – shrouded in secrecy to the same extent as the Stalin era. Yet Stalin was a key figure of the twentieth century, and the quest for an historical assessment of his role will continue undiminished. Was he, as his apologists have maintained, cruel by necessity, but playing a progressive role, sending Russia to school, turning it into a great industrial power, leading it to victory in the second world war? Or are his achievements outweighed by the relapse into barbarism? Could not the same successes have been achieved at a far smaller price? Did the Soviet Union prevail in the war because or despite of him? And is the negative part of his legacy not likely to be more lasting and more pernicious than whatever good he may have done, wittingly or unwittingly, in his lifetime?

The early biographies

The first Stalin biographies were journalistic accounts and appeared in the early thirties. With two exceptions they are of no particular interest in this context, whatever their other merits.[1] Isaac Don Levine's and Henri Barbusse's books should be singled out, however, because each in its way constituted a first landmark in the writing of the history of the Stalin era.

Mr Levine's published work on Russia spans many years. His first book, an account of the February Revolution of 1917 and its prehistory, was written before Lenin came to power, his last (for the time being) came out the year Khrushchev fell from power.[2] Levine is Russian-born; his books betray the strong influence of the school of American journalism: short, sometimes staccato sentences; no abstract reflections but plenty of colour, anecdotes, human interest stories. For all that, we owe to Mr Levine the first serious Stalin biography in any language: even though it appeared at a time when Stalin had just emerged as sole ruler from the relative obscurity of the Politburo. It is based on a wide variety of Russian sources.

Mr Levine's Stalin is a dictator of the unobtrusive variety , a man who does not believe in hero worship, who does not seek honours and loathes pomp. In fact, Mr Levine's Stalin resembles more an American super-boss than a traditional European dictator with his urge for personal aggrandizement. This boss is quite sympathetically drawn: a man without vices, virtuous and modest in his domestic life, impressively self-sufficient, widely informed and well read, with a good sense of humour. He is single-tracked rather than

[1] Among them, Stephen Graham, *Stalin, An impartial study of the life and work of Joseph Stalin*, London, 1931, and 'Essad Bey', *Stalin*, Berlin, 1931, English translation, London, 1932. Nor will reference be made in what follows to biographies published during the second world war (Nikolaus Basseches, Eugene Lyons, Emil Ludwig, and others), or after (Louis Fischer, J. T. Murphy).

[2] I. D. Levine, *The Russian Revolution*, New York, 1917. I. D. Levine, *I rediscover Russia*, New York, 1964.

imaginative or brilliant, but in Stalin's position, Levine says, these may be sources of strength. He is not, nor does he want to be, a Nero or Napoleon. His only ambition is to help create a new order as outlined by Lenin and to bring happiness to the Russian people. With all these favourable impressions of the new Soviet leader Mr Don Levine is more than doubtful about his system: the seeds of political Bolshevism, 'carried from a century of western revolutionary movements into the soil of Russia, developed there into a grotesque and misshapen plant'. He is doubtful about the success of the five-year plan and comments on the early signs of political corruption he detects in the system – despite Stalin's personal incorruptibility and his professions that he does not want to be a dictator: 'In a backward and primitive continent like Eurasia [this system] inevitably breeds subserviency, servility, arbitrary rule and all the other inescapable fungi of dictatorship.'[3]

Henri Barbusse

Barbusse, the author of the most famous anti-war novel of this century, joined the communist movement in the twenties and made several visits to the Soviet Union. His Stalin biography, published in 1935, was translated into many languages; it set the pattern for the communist literature about Stalin outside the Soviet Union for the next twenty years. It should be mentioned in passing that it is not certain how much of the book was actually written by Barbusse himself: it was apparently co-authored, if not ghosted, by a leading German communist, Alfred Kurella.

It is panegyric, but Barbusse-Kurella say that it is not they but reality which sings Russia's and Stalin's praise. In seventeen years the most wretched country of Europe has become the most civilized one in every respect.[4] Stalin's story is a series of successes in the face of unheard of difficulties. Stalin is a man of iron and steel and of tremendous common sense: 'he has the wisdom and the caution of a lion.' He is a man of the widest knowledge, of passionate purity, of unshakable resolution – he is the Lenin of the age. The authors imply that he is in fact, greater than Lenin, for Lenin had to be an agitator, whereas Stalin is above all the statesman. Another

[3] I. D. Levine, *Stalin*, London, 1931, p. 256.
[4] Henri Barbusse, *Stalin. Eine neue Welt*, Paris, 1935, p. 218. I have used the German edition because it is probably the authentic original text.

outstanding feature is his 'terrible patience'. At the same time he is most modest of men. He takes care of everything, and has only one secretary (unlike Lloyd George who has thirty-two). Stalin writes his speeches himself, and answers all his mail. He laughs like a child and loves children. The Soviet leader never tries to shine, prefers always to stay in the background. It is his simplicity and the fact that he is so uncomplicated that makes it sometimes so difficult to understand Stalin. He is motivated not by personal vanity but by his conviction and faith. Stalin believes in the masses as the masses believe in him. He is the most important of all contemporaries. The other Soviet leaders love him, believe in him, and need him. In this way he towers with all his greatness over Europe and Asia, over yesterday and today at the same time. The book ends with an apotheosis on Red Square:

> Whoever you are your fate lies in the hand of him who is awake even now and works for you; the man with the head of a scholar, the face of a worker, and the dress of a simple soldier.[5]

Barbusse died in the year that the book was published; Kurella lived to become minister of culture in East Germany. Reviewing Barbusse's writings in 1962 the *Short Soviet Literary Encyclopedia* said about his *Stalin* that it was written under the strong influence of the cult of the personality.

Trotsky on Stalin

In his Mexican exile, during the last years of his life, Trotsky began work on a Stalin biography. When he was killed in August 1940 seven chapters were finished, with drafts for five more sections which would have brought the narrative up to the middle twenties. In this incomplete state the book was ready for publication by the time of Pearl Harbor, but the publisher decided that it would not have helped the war effort and it did not appear until 1946. Trotsky's view of the Stalin phenomenon is summarized in his introduction:

> Stalin represents a phenomenon utterly exceptional. He is neither a thinker, a writer nor an orator. He took possession of power before the masses had learned to distinguish his figure from others during the triumphal processions along Red Square. Stalin took possession of power, not with the aid of personal qualities, but with the aid of an impersonal

[5] H. Barbusse, *Stalin*, pp. 8, 286

machine. And it was not he who created the machine but the machine that created him ...

The machine was the bearer of the idea before it became an end in itself

... [For taking possession of the machine] exceptional and special qualities were necessary. But they were not the qualities of the historic initiator, thinker, writer or orator. The machine had grown out of ideas. Stalin's first qualification was a contemptuous attitude towards ideas.[6]

Trotsky is aware of Stalin's strong points – his tenacity, iron will, common sense. But his main concern is to prove (which is not too difficult) that before 1917 Stalin did not belong to the Bolshevik central leadership, that in fact hardly anyone knew him, and that after 1917 he succeeded mainly owing to ambition, scheming, and hunger for power. Stalin was the leader of the Soviet Thermidor, the conservative-bureaucratic reaction, a trend which even Lenin could not have stemmed had he lived longer. But the bloody purges had loosened the social and political foundations of Soviet Bonapartism: 'An open revolutionary conflict between the people and the new despotism is inevitable. Stalin's régime is doomed. Will a capitalist counter-revolution or worker's democracy replace it?'[7]

In the heat of polemic Trotsky, like some other former party members in the twenties and thirties, tried to prove too much. For his book was above all a polemic as well as an *apologia pro vita sua*, a detailed refutation of the new official Soviet party history. Trotsky attempted to explain his own failure in 1923–4 and the subsequent development of the Communist party and the Soviet Union by reference to 'objective' economic, social and political trends, and simultaneously by making Stalin personally responsible for the treachery, degeneracy and despotism connected with it. Mr Deutscher was right when he called Trotsky's fragment not a biography but an indictment of Stalin.[8] It was Trotsky's answer to the Moscow Trials and the campaign of vilification against him. It was no doubt a psychological and political necessity for him, but it was not history. Except for being true?

[6] Leon Trotsky, *Stalin: an appraisal of the man and his influence*, New York, 1941, p. xv.

[7] Trotsky, *I Stake My life*, New York, 1937, p. 21.

[8] I. Deutscher: 'Trotsky on Stalin', in *Heretics and Renegades*, London, 1955, p. 79. For a critique of Trotsky's views of Stalin and Stalin's Russia, as well as his analogies with the French Revolution, see also S. Bahne in *Survey*, No. 41, 1962; L. Gottschalk in the *American Journal of Sociology*, 1938, p. 33; R. D. Watkin, *The Journal of Modern History*, 1948, p. 27.

The official biography

While Trotsky was writing his life of Stalin, the finishing touches were being given at the Marx-Engels-Lenin Institute in Moscow to a short official biography.[9] It begins by stating the one fact that has not been in dispute so far between biographers – that Stalin was born in Gori in December 1879. It ends with several incantations: long live our great Stalin, long live the great, invincible banner of Marx-Engels-Lenin-Stalin!

This little book of some eighty-odd pages does not really contain anything over and above what can be found in the official party textbook (the *Short Course*) that was published two years previously. It is mentioned here mainly because it was at the time – and for a dozen years to follow – published and translated in many millions of copies all over the globe. There is the usual praise in the style of the epoch of Stalin the leader and teacher of the party, the great strategist of the socialist revolution, the omniscient genius. Everyone, it says, knows the irresistible, crushing strength of the Stalinist logic, the crystal clarity of his mind, his steely will, his devotion to the party, his burning belief in the people and his love of the people: 'Everyone knows his modesty, his simpleness, his delicacy towards people and his lack of mercy *vis-à-vis* the enemies of the people.'[10]

Boris Souvarine

A contemporary observer, not a Bolshevik, wrote in 1917 that Stalin at the time of the October revolution impressed him (and not him alone) as a colourless, dull personage acting sometimes in an evasive way: 'In fact, there was little more to say about him.' Ten years later Stalin had emerged as the strongest man in the Soviet leadership. But the Stalin cult had not yet begun. Little was known about him outside the Communist Party leadership; accounts in the foreign press were brief and often misleading. By the middle thirties, with the collectivization of agriculture virtually accomplished, the second five-year plan under way, and with the growing tension in European politics, the name of the 'colourless personage' of 1917 was in everyone's mouth. Following the world economic crisis and

[9] *Iosif Vissarionovich Stalin*, Kratkaia biografya, Moscow, 1940; translated into English as *Joseph Stalin, a short biography*, London, 1940.
[10] I. V. Stalin, p. 74.

the rise of Nazism, but following also the reports about the great social reconstruction in the USSR, conflicting reports admittedly but fascinating none the less, the importance of the Soviet Union in western eyes (and with it the stature of its ruler) had grown by leaps and bounds. At this time there appeared the first of the two major Stalin biographies that exist. Its author, Boris Souvarine (Lifchitz), was born in Kiev in 1895, came to France with his parents at an early age, was wounded in the first world war. Previously a socialist, he was one of the early converts to communism, and a leader of the French Communist Party. He was also a member of the Executive of the Communist International, and in this capacity lived in Moscow for some eighteen months in the early twenties. Souvarine was excluded from the party in 1924, mainly for supporting Trotsky against Zinoviev, the then secretary-general of the Comintern. He continued to lead a French communist opposition group for some years, but gradually left active politics. He has contributed frequently to the French press on Soviet politics, and is the editor of journals devoted to communist affairs and social history.

The emphasis in the first part of M. Souvarine's book is on the history of Bolshevism, on Lenin, the revolution and the civil war. Though there is a detailed and authoritative account of Stalin's youth, and his career before 1917, the author devotes even more attention to the growth of the revolutionary movement. Souvarine compares Lenin in 1905 (and in 1917) with George Washington, who could not really trust his lieutenants: 'Without Lenin there would have been no Bolshevism.'[11] He describes the political education of Stalin during revolution and civil war: 'He emerged . . . matured and tempered. He had won no notoriety, but under Lenin he had acquired the technique of government, a modicum of empirical political science and confidence in himself.' Souvarine notes that the trend towards a one-man dictatorship existed under Lenin, though Lenin himself was not inclined to personal power or violence. But once having opted for the dictatorship of a single party, he yielded to the force of circumstances. And thus power passed from the party to its Central Committee, from the Central Committee to the Politbureau, and ultimately into the hands of one man. Viewing the Russian Revolution in a perspective of almost twenty years, Souvarine concludes (following Rosa Luxemburg) that in Russia the

---

[11] B. Souvarine, *Stalin: a critical survey of Bolshevism*, London, 1940, p. 77.

problem of building socialism could be posed – but it could not be resolved. Bolshevism was a Russian simplification of Marxism, its adaptation to the conditions of a vast, predominantly rural country. And so, under the pressure of circumstances, Lenin had after his victory gradually to purge Bolshevism of its original character. His death therefore merely hastened' a development that had begun much earlier; between the old Bolshevism and the new Leninism ('socialism in one country'), which Souvarine views as a reactionary development, there was therefore properly speaking no breach of continuity.[12]

M. Souvarine, once a follower, albeit never an uncritical one, of Trotsky, censures the policies of the opposition after 1923: they competed with one another in dogmatic Leninism, with avalanches of quotations from the scriptures and unintelligible pamphlets on China. If they attracted any sympathies at all it was not for their views but for their courage in defying the dictatorship. The opposition was thus defeated above all by its own faults and, in particular, by its lamentable lack of common sense. In an aside, M. Souvarine throws out a sociological theory of the revolution: the best men of the revolution had been absorbed into the minor, intellectual offices of the State, by reason of their capabilities. The most mediocre, those otherwise useless, became the top layer of Soviet society: every Bolshevik who showed himself unfit for responsibility in one of the vital spheres of work finished up by finding a place in the hierarchy of the party secretaries.[13]

M. Souvarine regards collectivization as a colossal failure and super-industrialization as a myth; he records the effects of the growing police terror, as sad consequences in Russian cultural life, the growing Byzantism in public life. His judgment of Stalin's policies and character, never very high, becomes more and more negative.

There is nothing equal to Stalin's dictatorship in world history. In some respects Stalin is ideally fitted for this post: he has an iron will, he is exceedingly patient, meticulous, wary of illusions. Above

---

[12] Souvarine, pp. 356–7. Souvarine had voiced similar fears in November 1917, following the news about the revolution in Petrograd. Not yet a communist, he wrote in *Le Populaire* that it was to be feared that for Lenin and his friends the 'dictatorship of the proletariat' meant the dictatorship of the Bolsheviks and their chief, which would be a disaster for Russia's working class and, consequently, for the world proletariat. *Ce qu'il faut dire*, 17 November 1917.

[13] Souvarine, pp. 473–4.

all he has a strong contempt for people and lacks principles and scruples. But with all his new majesty he is the product of circumstances. He has never been far-sighted except on the level of personal relations and when his power is at stake. He is supposed to be physically brave but lacks moral courage. He has no friend, no confidant. He loves nobody, and nobody loves him.

Souvarine knows about the limitations of historical analogies. But like all other biographers of Stalin he is for ever looking for parallels in the history of Russia and other countries. He compares Stalin with Peter the Great (not a true but an imitative genius, building an immense edifice on weak foundations), with Fouché (a man in the middle ground between revolution and counter-revolution; intrigues, police methods, but also 'curious psychological and temperamental concordances'), with Bismarck ('never had a trace of a political idea, but this narrowness was fortunate for him. Without it he would never have been able to consider universal history from the point of view specifically Russian'). But the most frequent parallel is with Ivan the Terrible, the *Oprichnina*, the massacre of the Boyars, the reforms undertaken by that Tsar. Yet

the barbarity excusable in Ivan, explicable in Peter which was characteristic of their time if we take account of the backwardness of Russia, is an enormous anachronism in Stalin and therefore inexcusable . . . The use of 'barbarian methods', as Lenin said, to force industrialization is not enough to render 'great' an industrializing Tsar, when civilized methods exist . . .[14]

Souvarine's book ends with melancholy reflections about the historical fate of the Russian Revolution. For Marx and Engels as well as for Lenin it had been self-evident that civilization, democracy, and socialism were inseparable. For Lenin it was obvious that socialism was impossible without democracy, and that Russia was not yet civilized enough to pass directly to socialism. Stalin had never understood this.

The English translation of Souvarine's book appeared in 1939, in the same month as the outbreak of war in Europe, and had therefore only a limited impact. But it included an eighty-page postscript entitled The Counter Revolution, a detailed account of the trials and purges. Souvarine feels that things cannot get much worse. Stalin feels most at ease in this new milieu, characterized by

that bestiality of the strong, that humility of the weak, the real abuses of the one, the false confessions of the other, in the absence of all normal

[14] Souvarine, p. 644.

expressions of political thought and individual needs, of all respect for human personality and for any moral rule.[15]

The miscarriage of Bolshevism in Russia is complete: Lenin's optimistic forecasts about the gradual evolution of a superior democracy as well as Trotsky's theses have all been contradicted by the force of things and the behaviour of men.

Less than two years later Hitler attacked the Soviet Union and Stalin became one of the pillars of the anti-Nazi coalition. Souvarine's book was not reprinted during the war, nor did the author try to bring his biography up to date after the war.

For the period it covers, Souvarine's *Stalin* is the fullest biography; it is unlikely to be superseded before the opening of the Soviet archives. About Russian history and Russian literature Souvarine knows more than all other biographers of Stalin; in contrast to them he also knew personally most of the Soviet leaders. He writes well; he is among other things a master of invective. He was of course deeply involved because he knew most of the actors and victims in the unfolding drama, and because he cared deeply about the political and moral issues at stake.

His book was written in the middle thirties under the impression of the establishment of totalitarian rule with all its abuses, and with no achievements as yet to show in terms of industrial production or military might. There were the statistics of the five-year plans; but who could believe these figures in the light of the general mendacity of official propaganda? Precisely because he cared so deeply about what he considered the betrayal of all socialist and democratic ideals, Souvarine's condemnation of Stalin and his régime is extreme in both form and substance. It was bound to appear too extreme to those who felt less deeply about the fate of socialism and the Soviet Union. Souvarine's passionate involvement makes him feel the agony of it all the more acutely, it gives his biography a sense of immediacy and an insight which other biographers lack – or for which they try to compensate by giving free rein to their imagination. But it also led him into inconsistencies and mistaken appraisals.

Souvarine's biography is a massive indictment of Stalin. Yet at the same time developments after 1917 are described as if there was a certain inevitability about them. If the trend towards the absolute dictatorship goes back to Lenin, if there is no break of continuity between the Old Bolsheviks and the new Leninism (Stalinism), if

[15] Ibid., p. 648.

93

Russia was not yet civilized enough to pass directly to socialism, if the bureaucrats and the mediocrities were bound to emerge on top in the new régime – why blame Stalin for developments which were largely preordained and over which he had but limited control? Souvarine's dilemma was similar to the one facing Trotsky, despite all the differences of opinion between them. If it was impossible to build socialism as he understood it (socialism with democracy and civilization) in a backward country, then the October revolution had been, at best, premature. But M. Souvarine did not think so at the time and his appraisal of Lenin's role is ambiguous; someone, obviously, committed a big mistake, but it is never made quite clear who did so, and why and when.

Souvarine underrated Russia's strength, or, to be precise, the power of resistance of the people, the national economy, the army, their ability to overcome the chaos of the thirties. He predicted that there was every evidence that Stalin's régime, if forced to rely on its own strength, could not withstand the supreme test of war any better than Tsarism had done. Neither industry nor agriculture nor transport was ready to sustain the high tension of a modern war. Elsewhere he said that eternal Russia could hold out a long time in a defensive war but the régime would have to be transformed or to disappear in a war which threatened its vital centres. (Another possibility, it is true, was also once mentioned: that in a common victory won by the arms and resources of her allies and ending in general exhaustion one of Marx's main fears would come true – the rejuvenation of Europe by means of the knout ...) The assumption that Russia had been fatally weakened by the purges was shared by most observers outside the Soviet Union. We shall perhaps never know exactly how much damage was done in economic and military terms in the nineteen-thirties and how near Russia was as a result to breaking point in 1941–2. All that Souvarine says about Stalin's weaknesses and mistakes and crimes may be correct but it did not necessarily mean his doom. There is no good reason to assume that in politics the genius, the far-sighted statesman, the great intellect necessarily prevails over the cautious mediocrity. (Where, anyway, were the geniuses among Stalin's rivals and adversaries?) The tendency to overrate the immediate impact of the purges was psychologically intelligible; after all, it affected most of the people one knew. But it was incorrect; it concerned only the top layer of society. Factory workers and kolkhoz peasants went on with their work as before, and the Red Army soldiers continued to be drilled even if many of their officers disappeared. Russia in the thirties had not yet reached a high level of sophistication in its structure; the state and economic machinery were not yet dislocated beyond redemption by the violent, sudden, and frequent changes at the top. In many fields, such as industrial production, progress continued; the Soviet *élite* was to some extent expendable.

On the basis of the experience of the thirties communists could argue that while Stalin committed many mistakes, his tremendous achievements in building up Soviet power were in historical perspective really more decisive. If the Soviet régime was to last it had to catch up with the advanced industrial countries within a very short time and this could be achieved only by the application of strongly dictatorial methods. The greatness of the Marxist idea, and the strength of the fabric of the Soviet state and society were such that even Stalin's abuses did not do them lasting harm. For the decisive test came with the second world war and the expansion of communist power after 1945.

Stalin's critics are convinced that the same results (viewing the course of history from the Soviet point of view) could have been achieved with far less suffering and far fewer victims. Seen in broader perspective, they believe that Stalin's policy was disastrous inasmuch as it was a contributory cause of the second world war. Nor could the 'mistakes of the thirties' be shrugged off from the point of view of world communism, for they contained the seeds of the quarrels and the dissension that was to plague the communist camp in the fifties and the sixties, and which eventually shattered its unity. Had Stalin really helped the spread of communism in a long-term view – or had he perhaps done permanent harm to its cause by perverting the idea and compromising socialist aspirations? The purges of the thirties, with which M. Souvarine deals at such length, had not brought Russia to ruin. But was this a sign of Stalin's greatness or did it simply show that the policies of a modern dictator, however criminal, stupid, and destructive, are not likely to destroy his country unless he actually involves it in a disastrous major war. Does not historical experience show that, unless a dictator manages to reduce significantly the population as well as its output, a big power is likely to remain a big power regardless of doctrines and policies? These questions are likely to be debated for a long time; in a way the discussion has hardly begun. Souvarine concluded his book in the late thirties with reflections on the miscarriage of Bolshevism in Russia, the irremediable failure of the Communist International, and the death agony of socialist hopes in the world which had opened up an immeasurable ideological crisis. However, victory in the second world war greatly strengthened the position of the Soviet Union and with it Stalin's own. True, the Comintern was dissolved; but there were now some eighty communist parties all over the world with millions of members; communist régimes had taken over in Eastern Europe and in the Far East. Souvarine's biography was written at the height of the crisis of Stalin's régime; this affected his perspective, but it would be rash to say that it invalidated his general assessment of Stalin and his policies.

We shall now turn to the other major Stalin biography—the one conceived and written in the hour of Stalin's triumph.

Isaac Deutscher

If Mr Carr is the Thiers of Soviet historiography, Mr Deutscher is in the tradition of Carlyle. Combining a solid knowledge of the period with great persuasiveness in presentation, he is the author of biographies of Stalin and Trotsky. His books have had a great success in many countries owing both to their readability and to the author's patent desire not to be influenced in his judgment by current fashions of communist apologetics and cold war propaganda. When in the post-war years many other authors either glorified Stalin or relegated him to deepest hell, Mr Deutscher in his biography made an attempt to do justice to this most controversial of all contemporary leaders. It was a brave attempt, and a successful one, as the author says in the Preface to a new edition in 1960; in this he has made no changes, and he is convinced that for the time being his interpretation of Stalin and Stalinism has stood the test of time. Many critics disagree; Mr Deutscher has been one of the most controversial of historians of the Soviet Union, perhaps above all because he tried to combine so many things that seemed incompatible to his contemporaries. A convinced historical materialist (he would no doubt indignantly reject any comparison with Carlyle), there is in him nevertheless a strong romantic vein; he has devoted all his important works to individual heroes rather than to economic or social history. A Marxist-Leninist, militantly involved in current politics, he yet claims for himself a measure of objectivity and detachment (in contrast to the 'subjectivism' of others) that is not generally accorded to those so deeply involved in current political controversies.

Mr Deutscher was born in Galicia in 1907. A journalist by profession, he joined the Communist Party in the middle twenties but was expelled in 1932 for a series of articles in which he criticized the Communist Party line in Germany, where the main attack was directed at the time against the Social Democrats rather than the rising Nazi tide. He continued to work for Jewish non-communist literary periodicals in Poland. Some months before the outbreak of war he moved to London. After a spell in the Polish army he became a regular contributor to English periodicals. Since 1950 most of his time has been devoted to the series of biographies of communist leaders; he has continued, however, to comment in press and radio on current developments and earlier happenings in the Soviet Union.

Stalin, the book which made Deutscher famous, appeared in 1949; it had been written in 1946-8 under the impression of the Soviet victory and the subsequent spread of the Soviet sphere of influence through Eastern Europe. The first part deals with Stalin's Caucasian background, his youth and adolescence, and his political career before 1917. Deutscher agrees with Souvarine that Stalin's role before the revolution was a minor one by any standard and that in the actual uprising Trotsky played much more important a part than Stalin, even though Soviet historiography invested great efforts in later years in rewriting this particular chapter of Russian history. In fact Mr Deutscher detects in Stalin the pent-up frustration of a man whose peculiar gifts were such that they had not yet earned him a great name despite the fact that he was reaching the threshold of power.[16] Yet his rise was to begin soon – with the Civil War, and, in particular, with the transformation of the revolutionary party into a bureaucratic machine. The author intersperses some observations on the general law of revolutions, or at any rate on the general trends common to all of them; the anti-climax that comes sooner or later, the inability of the leaders to fulfil their promises, the subsequent growing division between the cold autocracy and the will of the people.

Mr Deutscher's account of the period is written from the point of view of the party of the revolution. But this is not done obtrusively;

[16] I. Deutscher, *Stalin*, p. 171.

97

the general course of events is never questioned and appears there-fore perfectly natural. As general secretary of the party Stalin became more and more powerful, but he was still playing a waiting game; there was much talk about a Thermidor in 1923–4, but the mask of Napoleon might have fitted any personality with the excep-tion of Stalin – 'in this lay part of his strength'.[17] There are no major factual differences between Deutscher and the other Stalin biographers with regard to the presentation and assessment of the factional struggles of the twenties. But Deutscher takes Stalin's doctrine of 'socialism in one country' far more seriously than his predecessors. Stalin may not have been a great thinker, and the old Bolsheviks, many of whom were professional ideologists, regarded him with amusement and contempt. But they were quite wrong in dismissing the new doctrine, for it summed up a powerful and hitherto inarticulate trend of opinion. Stalin's vision might at first have been a mere trial balloon[18] but it corresponded to things that were latent in many other minds. Having opted for the new course, Stalin was bound to pursue a policy of violent social change; the peasants threatened to starve the towns and so (Deutscher says) Stalin was precipitated into collectivization. But industrialization got top priority. In a famous and often quoted speech, Stalin said: 'We are fifty or a hundred years behind the advanced countries. We must make good this lag in ten years. Either we do it or they crush us.' Follies and cruelties attended Stalin's 'great change', yet at the same time it marked a tremendous progress in the history of mankind, opening a new and not unhopeful epoch of civilization (p. 343). We now reach, under Mr Deutscher's guidance, one of the most obscure and macabre chapters in Stalin's life. Stalin, our guide says, continued to be the guardian and the trustee of the revolution; his social programme was progressive. But the technique of govern-ment, the means with which he implemented his programme, were in line with the cruel traditions of Russian history. Stalin, Deutscher contends, needed the purges and mass executions because in case of an attack on the Soviet Union, an opposition against him might have arisen in the hour of defeat. He probably did not act from sheer cruelty or lust for power but was sincerely convinced that he served the interests of the revolution (p. 378).

About Stalin's foreign policy during the twenties and thirties his biographer has greater misgivings. All independent minds were

[17] Deutscher, p. 273.   [18] Deutscher, pp. 291–3.

squeezed out of the Comintern, which came to shine with the reflected light of the Russian party. There was defeat in China and then in Germany, elsewhere the Communist International on Stalin's orders engaged in a wholly futile ultra-radical line. Stalin was quite unaware of the significance and the destructive character of Nazism; instead he played up the bogey of a French-led anti-Soviet crusade. Later on, during the middle thirties, he made a genuine effort to achieve a *rapprochement* with France and Britain, but it did not work and so he decided in favour of a pact with Nazi Germany. Stalin was aware of the results of his 'friendship' with Hitler but he assumed that they were of little importance in comparison with the tangible advantages he gained – in time, in space, and in morale. It may have been a mistaken calculation, but it was not a personal error of judgment; 'his policy had behind it a powerful current of popular feeling' (p. 460). The Soviet people needed peace. Then, in June 1941, the Nazis attacked. Stalin was not unprepared for the emergency. It was his finest hour. He had armed his country and reorganized its military forces. He took all final decisions personally.

He was in effect his own commander-in-chief, his own minister of defence, his own quartermaster, his own minister of supply, his own foreign minister, and even his own *chef de protocol*. From his desk in the Kremlin he directed not only all military operations but also industrial and agricultural production and took political decisions . . . Thus he went on, day after day, throughout four years of hostilities – a prodigy of patience, tenacity, and vigilance, almost omnipresent, almost omniscient (pp. 966–7).

His will to victory had an heroic, almost superhuman quality; but it was not based on blind fanaticism. The ideas he indicated to his generals were founded on an exceptional knowledge of all aspects of the situation, economic, political, and military.

Victory helped Stalin to make Eastern Europe into a Soviet sphere of influence, but there was no blueprint, no grand design, it happened almost in a fit of absent-mindedness. His intentions were extremely contradictory, the result of nationalism and communism, of domestic and foreign pressures. As for the East European countries, the takeover was probably the best that could happen to them. It may well be that for these people the only way out of the impasse lay in a *coup de force* such as that to which Stalin had goaded them. Ruled by archaic cliques, their lives had been bogged down in savage poverty and darkness (p. 535).

At the end of the war Stalin was at the height of his glory, in the full blaze of popular recognition and gratitude. But these feelings were spontaneous, genuine, not engineered by official propaganda. The people were willing to forgive him his misdeeds, Deutscher says, and remembered only his better efforts (p. 550). Yet victory again contained the seeds of dialectical contradictions – above all, between a nationalist and a revolutionary policy. If despite themselves Napoleon and Bismarck played a progressive role, the former in carrying the revolution to Europe, the latter in destroying the remnants of feudalism in Germany, Stalin the inspirer of the 'revolution from above' also helped to transform the European social and political scene. The 'Iron Curtain', Deutscher thinks, also fulfilled a dual function, progressive and reactionary at the same time: behind it the revolution found safety and Stalin could go ahead with his projects of industrialization and modernization. At the same time, it shielded Stalin's autocracy and his despotism (p. 559).

The narrative ends in 1945–6 with an attempt to assess Stalin's role in historical perspective. Stalin belongs, Deutscher thinks, to the breed of great revolutionary despots such as Cromwell, Robespierre and Napoleon. His inhuman despotism vitiated much of his achievement, but he was a great revolutionary leader and the progressive social performance of his régime will survive. There is a basic difference between him and Hitler. Hitler was the head of a sterile counter-revolution, his record one of absolute futility and worthlessness. Stalin was of a different mould and filled a different historical role. Like Cromwell he embodied the continuity of the revolution through all its phases; like Napoleon he carried the revolution beyond the frontiers of his country:

> The better parts of Stalin's works are certain to outlast Stalin himself as the better parts of the work of Cromwell and Napoleon have outlasted them. But in order to save it for the future and in order to give to it its full value, history may yet have to re-cleanse and reshape Stalin's work as sternly as it once cleansed and reshaped the work of the English revolution after Cromwell and of the French after Napoleon.[19]

Deutscher's biography appeared in 1949; his comments on the last years of Stalin's reign are given in two subsequent books. In the interval, Deutscher says, the element of primitive magic in it became gradually stronger. The cult of the leader assumed unthought of proportions and a nightmarish quality and there was a bizarre

[19] Deutscher, pp. 565–70.

unreality over the nationalist orgy of the last years. But did these antics affect its basic social and political role? Mr Deutscher does not think so. The West had its eyes fixed on the witch hunt and the purges but this was not the most important aspect.

Stalinism had persistently and ruthlessly destroyed the soil in which it had grown, that primitive, semi-Asiatic society on whose sap it fed. By its barbarous methods it had succeeded in driving out of Russia most of the barbarism from which it had drawn its strength.[20]

With the dictator's death a whole era came to an end and the stage was now set for a return to democracy and freedom, a new epoch which might bring a breathtaking reversal of the process by which the Soviet democracy of the early days was transformed into an autocracy.

So much for Isaac Deutscher. He has continued to comment since – on Beria and Malenkov, Khruschchev and Mao, always cheerful and full of optimism, a ray of hope in an otherwise not too sanguine world. But I am here concerned mainly with his book on Stalin, which from the literary point of view is the most imaginative, the most readable, now in existence of all Stalin biographies. Written with deep feeling and sympathy for the cause of the revolution and the Soviet people, its sufferings and triumphs, it is replete with brilliant formulations, psychological insights, and attractive arguments. The style is forceful, the pathos not artificial, attention never flags, and there are striking historical analogies and literary allusions. It makes Stalin the leader and his whole era come to life as no other book has done. In some respects it is a model biography. Considering Mr Deutscher's own involvement in communist politics and quarrels it is a remarkable feat. With all his sympathy for Trotsky, Deutscher realizes that in the middle twenties Stalin became the chosen instrument of the revolutionary *Weltgeist*. He does not therefore go along with Trotsky in his vituperation of Stalin, but tries, from a lofty standpoint, to do justice to both his heroes. Considering the heat of the passions generated by the Stalin–Trotsky controversy in the twenties and thirties, this is indeed an impressive achievement. Mr Deutscher's indestructible optimism is another attractive, if occasionally slightly comic, feature of his writing; whatever happens in the Soviet Union or the communist bloc, be it the outbreak of the second world war, or the victory over Nazism, the ascendancy of Beria or the rise of Malenkov, or the

[20] Deutscher, *Russia after Stalin*, London, 1953, p. 54.

101

Chinese revolution, it always opens great and promising vistas. Mr Deutscher may often be mistaken, but on a subject that is so often conducive to cynicism, and to which so many commentators reacted sourly, a surfeit of optimism has its uses if only as a countervailing factor. An East European and communist background such as Mr Deutscher's often makes for various intellectual qualities. But extremist views breed more easily on this background than a spirit of tolerance and balanced judgment. Here too Deutscher's book seems to score fairly highly, considering that it is written on the basis of what may be broadly defined as a Marxist-Leninist world view. There is none of the narrow dogmatism which so often disfigures and vitiates the writings of the more orthodox adepts of that school. How to explain, then, that with all these achievements and virtues, Deutscher's book generated perhaps more controversies and heated polemics than any other work on Soviet history? It could not be his views alone; books that were more extreme in approach one way or the other did not provoke a similar storm. Some of the reasons were probably extraneous; Deutscher, as I have mentioned, is the author not only of biographies but also of current political commentaries. His writings in this latter field do not always display (to put it cautiously) the virtues he commands as a historian; the contradiction which they often attracted was thus transferred to the appraisal of Deutscher's historical work. But there are other reasons for the controversy about his *Stalin*; some concern the presentation, others are basic questions of approach. What were the main accusations? Deutscher, to begin with, has repeatedly been accused of tampering with the facts, of selecting them in accordance with his bias. His account of the purges was said to be, at best, only half true. His interpretation of the murder of Kirov and of Tukhachevsky's conspiracy against Stalin, to give but one example, while more or less in accordance with the contemporary Stalinist version, is most certainly incorrect.[21] If there was still a shadow of doubt in 1949, there could be none after the twentieth party congress. Yet in the 1960 edition Mr Deutscher, in the face of all the evidence, continued to stick to his old version.[22]

---

[21] F. Borkenau, 'Stalin im Schafspelz', *Der Monat*, November 1949, pp. 207–8.

[22] Only in a new edition of *Stalin* in 1966 did the author modify his account of the Tukhachevsky affair. But he still maintains that there was a plot against Stalin (p. 375); Mr Deutscher is a hard man when it comes to the admission of mistakes. This new (Penguin) edition also includes a long epilogue, 'Stalin's last years', written in a more critical vein than either *Stalin* or Deutscher's essays of 1953–4:

This brings us to two other specific features of the work that have provoked much criticism. One is Deutscher's seemingly unshakable confidence in himself and his hypotheses, a belief untouched by that healthy scepticism which all historians need and in particular those dealing with a subject on which there is such a paucity of reliable evidence. A readiness to re-examine and revise his conclusions is not one of Mr Deutscher's characteristics; he seems reluctant to admit that he has ever been wrong in his appraisal of any major issue, or at any rate of any specific topic. His books abound with statements such as 'far from refuting my prognostications events have confirmed them', which, even if true, need substantiation which he does not provide.

These are perhaps minor irritants, but they touch upon more serious issues. Much of *Stalin* is imaginative writing at its best. In a different context Mr Deutscher once wrote that there are several legitimate ways of writing history, although the best histories are those that are works of imaginative insight and art as well as science. This is absolutely true, but it raises certain problems: nothing is perhaps more difficult than writing a history that combines imagination with scrupulous adherence to accepted standards of scholarship. Mr Deutscher's vivid imagination, which is that of a gifted writer is not – how to put it? – always restrained by such discipline. At this point, the romantic and the historian in Mr Deutscher fall out – and the former seems to get on top.

The reader is told in persuasive detail what went on in Stalin's mind, without it being made clear that these are Mr Deutscher's assumptions, for which there is no other warrant than his creative

'Like a drug addict, he craved the incense burned for him and administered it to himself in ever-increasing doses . . . He struck at the very roots of the idea by which the revolution, the party and the state had lived; he was destroying the birth certificate and the ideological title deeds even of his own régime. By this act Stalinism was committing suicide even before its author was dead.' Mr Deutscher is still convinced that the better part of Stalin's work will outlast Stalin himself, as have the better parts of the work of Cromwell and Napoleon. But he adds that in Stalin's last years the worst features of his rule were aggravated and magnified (p. 612). What had caused Deutscher to adopt in 1966 a sterner line towards the hero of his book? The basic facts about the late Stalin period had been known, after all, in the West all along; the revelations of the 20th and 22nd Soviet party congress did not come as a great surprise to most Western observers. But there is an important difference; had Mr Deutscher echoed the western denunciation of Stalin before, say, 1960, he would, no doubt, have been guilty in his own conscience of Cold War propaganda. The Soviet revelations made a shift of emphasis possible, if not imperative – another illustration of the impact of the *Zeitgeist* even on a historian who had always emphasized that the Cold War was not his war and who had so often stressed the virtues of the Olympian approach.

imagination. It may be a brilliant flash of insight – and it may be utter rubbish. We do not know, nor does he, and we only have his great confidence to rely upon. There is in *Stalin* an imaginary conversation between the ghost of Nicolai II and Stalin which, of course, is a legitimate device for a biographer, for it is fairly generally believed that ghosts do not talk. But there are also devices which are illegitimate in serious historical writing; in one of his essays, for instance, Mr Deutscher gives in quotation marks the exchanges that took place at a Politburo meeting, at which, to the best of our knowledge, Mr Deutscher was not present. ('Khrushchev, pointing to Kaganovitch and Molotov, exclaimed: "Your hands are stained with the blood of our party leaders and of innumerable innocent Bolsheviks." "So are yours", Molotov and Kaganovitch shouted back at him', etc., etc.) It is magnificent, but it is not history. These lapses are probably the more serious because Mr Deutscher's first-hand knowledge of the Soviet Union is slighter than that of most other writers on Soviet affairs. Imagination can never entirely compensate for direct knowledge and for that understanding of the quality of life and the imponderabilia which only a prolonged stay in a country gives. Mr Deutscher spent a few weeks in Russia in the late twenties or early thirties. He does not know the Russia of the purges, or wartime, or post-war Russia, and he has not been to the country in the post-Stalin era. He obviously reads *Pravda* assiduously and he has a certain image of the Soviet Union, based on his study of Marxism-Leninism and his experience in the communist movement in the twenties. Such lack of immediacy and first-hand knowledge may not be of great importance as far as Stalin's decision-making is concerned, for no one knows about this anyway. But it does make for rigidity and a dogmatic attitude. *Stalin* and Deutscher's other books abound with sweeping statements about the impact and the consequences of Stalin's policies – such as the progress of industrialization, the mood among the young generation, the purges of the early fifties – which are not correct and which he might not have made had he had closer access to Soviet realities. The question of what facts and sources to use is a difficult one in this case. When Mr Carr was criticized for using almost exclusively Soviet sources, Deutscher wrote that the historian should

of course listen to *altera pars*. But when that other side consists of *émigrés* who could watch the growth of Soviet institutions and policies with no more facility than any outsider, and who have often been prevented by circumstances and bias from watching even as much, what shall the historian do? Shall he, in order to save the appearances of impartiality, quote authorities that in truth are no authorities at all?[23]

The issue, as I have said, is complicated. Should a history of Nazi Germany in 1939 be written mainly with reference to official sources, ignoring the German *émigrés*? Mr Deutscher incidentally has been criticized both for using the wrong kind of *émigré* literature (memoirs of Stalin's non-existent nephew, Budu Svanidze) and for ignoring much of the genuinely scholarly work on the Communist Party and the Soviet Union put out by Western students. But this is a side issue. The real problem is the clash in Mr Deutscher's work between artistic truth (imagination) and real truth. As one of Deutscher's critics put it:

> The first obligation of the historian is accuracy. Not dramatic effect, not wistful improvisation, not tidiness in constructing a story, not a passionate expression of hope, despair, or even of inner understanding, but the cool and sceptical discovery of evidence. Unless he distinguishes between fact and supposition, not after deliberation but as a mental habit, his literary flair will betray him, and the line between history and fiction will be blurred.[24]

It is a strong case against Deutscher's approach, but it is not unanswerable. Deutscher could argue that more and more historians over the last hundred years have come to regard history as a proto-science, that they have realized that insight, empathy, understanding, *nacherleben* are of decisive importance. After all, Deutscher's attempt to reconstruct what went on in Stalin's mind in September 1935 or what Khrushchev and Molotov said at a Politbureau meeting may be approximately correct and, anyway, we have no other way of finding out for the time being. It could also be argued that political biography is a distinct genre, not subject to all the laws and taboos of historiography in general. Some of the greatest historical studies have been written in a partisan spirit. Bias *per se*, if the dose is not excessive, is not a disqualification. But Mr Deutscher, with an avowedly partisan study, nevertheless claims for himself the disinterestedness of the true scientific spirit. He regards Lenin as his model of a 'critical student in the laboratory of thought' – a 'free and disinterested mind'. It is a model of the disinterested mind that will

[23] *International Affairs*, April 1951, p. 205.
[24] Leo Labedz, 'Deutscher as Historian and Prophet', see below.

not be universally accepted. He makes no secret of his political convictions: *Stalin*, when all is said and done, is an apologia for its hero and to some extent as we know now an idealization. It is not a naïve all-out defence; Deutscher does not hide the negative features of Stalin's régime, his errors and mistakes. The word 'crime' is used sparingly, if at all. When hard pressed, Deutscher will prefer the term 'scandal'. (A scandal is defined by *The Concise Oxford Dictionary* as a general feeling of outrage or indignation, especially as expressed in common talk as malicious gossip and (legally) a public affront, an irrelevant abusive statement in court. The purges, the executions of the fifties, the case of the Kremlin doctors, were thus scandals, not crimes.) Of all these things the author is aware, but he is firmly convinced that, all considered, Stalin has played a progressive role, that in the long run this will be recognized and that he will enter history, properly cleansed, as a great hero.

Deutscher's critics agree that this indeed is one possibility. With the passing of time indignation about the Stalin years may be blunted and may make the crimes appear inevitable or even statesmanlike:

> No generation is really very much concerned with the horrors of the past and although they register in the memory of humanity, they are not comparable to the horrors of the present. We all look at St Bartholomew's night and the Smyrna massacres with a much greater degree of detachment than did their contemporaries ... there must be something in Deutscher's historical perspective: Genghis Khan is a hero of modern Mongolia.[25]

To anticipate posterity's judgment is always risky, if only because there may be various judgments and they may continue to change. Perhaps it will be thought at some future date that there was some truth in both Deutscher's and Souvarine's assessment of Stalin. Extenuating circumstances will be found for Stalin in the period that preceded him and in some ways paved the way for his rule. But it will still be asked by what qualities was Stalin great – except by the dimensions of the historical stage that he occupied? Could not a better job have been done (from whatever angle approached) by thousands of others, provided they had been equally ambitious and equally lucky? Did Stalin not stumble into success rather than prevail owing to a far-sighted policy? Should our judgment of a political leader really depend so much on the dimensions of the stage he occupied? Deutscher is very much concerned with Stalin's

[25] Labedz manuscript.

106

progressive legacy; his errors, he seems to believe, will be forgotten but his achievements (literacy, rise in industrial production) will survive and form the basis for a development towards a really free, socialist, and democratic society such as the world has never seen. But the rate of literacy and industrial production would have gone up in the Soviet Union anyway, whereas Stalin's methods may have done fatal damage to the cause he stood for. Following Marx, Deutscher compares revolutionary violence with the midwife who merely helps the baby to leave the mother's womb when the time has come. With Stalin as midwife is it not possible that irreparable harm has been done to the baby? And lastly, is it not a little disingenuous to talk about history 'having sternly to cleanse' Stalin's work. (In Mr Deutscher's view history is a very independent goddess; Lenin, he says, 'died at a moment when history had overtaken him'.[26]) But is history really a detergent, or is it not that some historians, claiming to speak on behalf of Clio, volunteer for cleansing operations?

These are some of the questions arising out of the discussion around this Stalin biography. The time that has passed and the events that have taken place since the book was first published do not confirm Mr Deutscher's confidence that his version, and his version alone, is the correct one. But neither can it be argued that Mr Deutscher's thesis has been refuted – the perspective is far too short for final judgments. What can be said without much fear of contradiction is that Deutscher's *Stalin*, quite apart from its intrinsic value, served a valuable function in provoking an important debate. True, it bore strong traces of the specific period in which it was written, as do all such books. Of course, it was a partisan work; without the pretence of being strictly objective, it would not have stirred controversy.[27] It is too early to say whether it will be the better

---

[26] *Russia after Stalin*, p. 25.

[27] Deutscher the historian, it was said at the beginning of this chapter, is in the tradition of Michelet and Carlyle. I think of the revolutionary pathos and the unflinching optimism of the former, the concentration on individual heroes by the latter. But a comparison with Lamartine obtrudes itself perhaps even more strongly. Like Lamartine, Deutscher began as a poet, his books had a similar popular success notwithstanding all criticism. Like Lamartine, Deutscher is fond of historical abstractions that have their own life and personality distinct and apart from the struggles of men. The Revolution (or History) decides, justifies, cleanses, forgives, accuses, is understood or misunderstood. A sentence such as 'The shocks and the crimes do not detract from the holiness of the Revolution; they were due to the imperfections of men' could be the motto of *Stalin*. Lamartine's predilection for the Girondists and Danton does not prevent him from admiring Robespierre. He abhors the terror but invokes *le salut public* and revolutionary necessity whether it concerns the execution of Danton or the

107

parts of Stalin's work, properly cleansed, that will outlast him. Historiography is more liberal than history; the better parts of Deutscher's biography will, in all probability, survive – with or without that famous cleansing operation.

Was Stalin really necessary?

The question whether Stalin was really necessary is likely to be debated for a long time. Hardly anyone now maintains as inevitable the purges of the thirties or the 'cult of the individual', with all its grotesque manifestations. But it has been persuasively argued that Stalinism in the nineteen-twenties was largely situation-determined. The dilemma facing Stalin, as it would have faced any other ruler, or group of rulers, was very briefly this: for political, military, as well as economic reasons, the Bolsheviks were dissatisfied with the relatively slow progress that was being made at the time. They felt themselves threatened by imperialist intervention and thought that a new world war might break out soon. Priority had to be given to heavy industry because it alone provided the basis for an arms industry. Rapid industrialization (the first five-year plan) could be financed only by levying tribute on the peasant (primitive accumulation). This could have been done by encouraging the better-off peasants (the *kulaks*) to expand; they were the more efficient producers and could supply the off-market surplus. But this solution was unacceptable to the Bolsheviks for political reasons. The alternative was forcible collectivization. Collectivization, Professor Nove has argued, could not be voluntary. Rapid industrialization, especially with priority for heavy industry, meant a reduction in living standards, despite contrary promises in the first five-year plans. This meant a sharp increase in the degree of coercion, in the powers of the police, in the unpopularity of the régime. The interests of the bulk of the population were bound to clash with the aims of the party, and it was this that made necessary the 'revolution from above'; the party was the one body that could carry out a policy requiring complete subordination. It also required an extremely tough supreme leader. The decision to move fast, once taken, had radical

terror in general. He is firmly convinced that Robespierre died for the future of mankind and that, purified by History from shortcomings and excesses, the Jacobin spirit will guide the way to a better future for France and all mankind. Historical parallels are never perfect. But the similarities in this case are very striking indeed.

consequences.[28] This argument has not been universally accepted. Though Stalin may have felt in 1929–30 that 'squeezing agriculture' was necessary to build industry quickly, it does not seem at all certain, more than three decades later, that he was right on grounds of economic rationality. Other roads to industrialization could have been chosen, as emerged from the great debate about industrialization that raged in Russia in the nineteen-twenties. For Stalin (as Professor A. Ehrlich has said), industrialization and collectivization were not merely devices of economic policy but means of extending the direct control of the totalitarian state over the largest possible number within the shortest time. The economic perspective, moreover, is not the only one: what may appear economically necessary may not be 'really necessary' if the price in human life and welfare is too high. The price of collectivization was very high. It made it possible to attain the goals of the first five-year plans. But it also caused extreme disaffection and not only among the peasants; the logic of police rule led to the great purge. If it strengthened the Soviet Union in some respects, it weakened it in others.

In 1945 the debate seemed to be settled. The Soviet Union under Stalin's leadership had emerged triumphantly from the second world war, and this was taken as history's endorsement of Stalin's approach. Whether the same aims could have been attained through different policies seemed at the time immaterial. But as the years passed the debate was resumed because it appeared more and more clearly that Stalin had not merely industrialized the Soviet Union and socialized its agriculture; his policies had a lasting effect on the Soviet political system and on Soviet society. Some observers thought that in the last resort only the economic progress mattered, since Stalin's political system would wither away or be discarded once it became a hindrance to further advance. It is far too early to say whether these hopes will be fulfilled in the near future. In the meantime the debate continues as to whether Stalin was really necessary – not as a question of moral approval, but as the only choice open to the Bolshevik party if it wanted to continue to rule the Soviet Union.

Professor Robert Tucker believes that it was not predestined that

---

[28] See the debate between Professor A. Nove and Mr L. Labedz following the publication of Mr Nove's 'Was Stalin really necessary?' in *Encounter*, April 1962. Also *Encounter*, August 1962; November 1962; and Harry G. Shaffer, *The Soviet System*, New York, 1965, p. 81 et seq. for Labedz's second rejoinder.

the Leninist party dictatorship would be transformed into a Stalinist-type totalitarian autocracy; it did happen but it was not a foregone conclusion. For the 'pathological personality of Stalin was a critically important factor in the outcome'.[29] In Tucker's eyes Stalin was a twentieth-century Ivan the Terrible, for George Kennan 'criminality enthroned', while Carr attributes little importance to his personality, pathological or not: 'Few great men have been so conspicuously as Stalin the product of the time and the place in which they lived.' Only when the Soviet archives are opened shall we know what remains of Stalin's foresight and organizational genius, of his iron will, his steely nerves, and his tenacity. The essential qualities to reach the top in a dictatorship – will to power, self-confidence, and single-mindedness – are not uncommon. To stay in power luck is often of decisive importance – trivial as it may sound. Stalin was very lucky indeed.

[29] Robert C. Tucker, *The Soviet Political Mind*, New York, 1963, pp. 37 et seq.

« 6 »

E. H. Carr

There is in the vast literature on Bolshevism and the Soviet Union no work comparable in size, and in the prodigious amount of research that went into it, to E.H.Carr's *History of Soviet Russia*. Professor Carr began his work in 1945; the first volume appeared in 1950. By 1964 eight books totalling four thousand pages had been published and there are several more to follow. When completed, the work will span the whole period from the revolution to 1929–30.

The mere physical effort involved in doing such research, in planning and writing a history on such a scale, the wealth of the source material perused, is awe-inspiring. Carr's work has had considerable influence in shaping the image of Soviet Russia held by a whole generation in England and in America; a discussion of his work is therefore of cardinal importance. If, as he says in the preface to his first volume, 'the temerity of an attempt to write a history of Russia since 1917 will be obvious to everyone', it is no less audacious to try to do justice to a work of such magnitude in a brief account.

In his Trevelyan lectures delivered at the University of Cambridge in 1961, Carr strongly advised his listeners to

study the historian before you begin studying the facts . . . [this] is already done by the intelligent undergraduate who, when recommended to read a work by that great scholar Jones of St Jude's, goes round to a friend at St Jude's to ask what sort of chap Jones is, and what bees he has in his bonnet. When you read a work of history, always listen out for the buzzing. If you can detect none, either you are tone deaf, or your historian is a dull dog.

Mr Carr is certainly not a dull dog; there is a lot of buzzing even if frequently in a low key. What sort of chap is he? What bees does he have in his bonnet? Born in 1892, educated at Merchant Taylors School, London, and Trinity College, Cambridge, his formative

111

years were spent before the first world war in that world of the long weekend, less beset by doubts and uncertainties than any since. During the first world war Mr Carr joined the Foreign Office; he was, in a junior capacity, a member of the British delegation at the Versailles peace conference. His main interests were divided between Eastern Europe and the League of Nations; he spent some years in Riga and was subsequently an adviser on League of Nations affairs. His interests were, however, by no means confined to the contemporary scene, as his excellent biographical studies of nineteenth-century Russians and German exiles show (Bakunin, Dostoevsky, Herzen, Marx and Herwegh). The undertone of these books is one of irony; Mr Carr seems to have been fascinated by his characters, but he does not take them terribly seriously. In 1936 he resigned from the Foreign Office and joined the University of Wales; between 1941 and 1946 he was assistant editor of *The Times*. Since then he has been based in Oxford and Cambridge and most of his time has been devoted to his *History of Soviet Russia*.

Although largely shrouded by the anonymity of the Foreign Office and *The Times*, what did become known of his views provoked harsh comments from some quarters. This was true above all in regard to Germany, Italy, and 'appeasement', which is only of indirect concern in the present context. More relevant is the shaping of Mr Carr's basic political philosophy in the twenties and thirties.

His views are usually not easy to retrace; his training as a diplomat, superimposed on the natural reticence of the highly educated Englishman of that generation, often make it difficult to unravel Mr Carr's own ideas, whether he is writing about Machiavelli or Lenin, Hitler or Neville Chamberlain. No doubt he has strong views on a great variety of subjects, but they are only seldom emphatically stated; for the most part they appear by implication. Not for him the sweeping phrase, the extreme statement, the colourful stroke; Mr Carr always prefers the low key, the deliberately unemotional approach. With perhaps exaggerated modesty, he says in his introduction to the *History* that he has neither a Marxist nor a Russian background; this of course is true in the sense that he was not born in Russia and never belonged to the communist party. But even a cursory glance at his publications before 1950 shows that Russia, and to a lesser extent Marxism and communism, had for long held a strong fascination for him. His decision to write the *History* came after years of study of nineteenth- and twentieth-century Russian history; which English writer before 1939, who was not of the extreme left, would have read and quoted Lenin (let alone George Lukacs) in his books?

In his *Karl Marx, a study in fanaticism*, Carr pays respect to the founder of scientific socialism, his immense intellect, his gift for masterly political analysis. He had no doubt about Marx's place in history: Marx was perhaps the first man since Luther whose life constituted a turning point in human history, the protagonist of the whole twentieth-century revolution in thought. Yet his appraisal of Marx (as the very title of the book indicates) is almost purely negative. Not merely of Marx the man, but above all of Marx the political thinker. 'Marx was the genius of destruction, not of construction.' Marxism is an act of faith, Mr Carr says; one cannot reason with it. Dialectical materialism is nonsense, the 'unity of thought and action' so much mumbo-jumbo, the labour theory of value unoriginal and dogmatic. The driving force in Marx and Marxism is class hatred; how utopian of Marx to have thought that class hatred was destined to lead mankind into the perfect communist commonwealth. Mr Carr is, if possible, even more sarcastic about the pseudo-Marxist: 'The pseudo-Marxist is a pathetic figure. He knows that Marxism is moonshine; but he still nourishes the hope of finding in it a gleam to follow.' As for the fascist dictatorships in Europe, 'the only difference between the so-called "dictatorship of the proletariat" and the dictatorships which prefer to hoist other flags is that the one proclaims its Marxist paternity whereas the others deny it'. The book was written in 1933–4; at that time socialism and communism had suffered grave setbacks in Central Europe; the Soviet Union had not yet emerged as a world power.

So much, then, for Carr's views on Marxism in the thirties. His general comments on the long-range trends in world affairs emerge from *The Twenty Years Crisis*, a study of international relations written two years before the outbreak of the second world war. Here again his own opinions cannot easily be reconstructed, for much of the work is given over to describing the 'realist' and the 'utopian' schools of thought in world affairs. The general impression is that Mr Carr feels himself nearer to the realists than to the utopians; but it is not at all easy to pin him down. What clearly emerges, however, is that Mr Carr would not attribute the catastrophe of 1939 solely to the ambitions and arrogance of a small group of men. It simply was not true that, as Professor Toynbee believed, 'we are living in an exceptionally wicked age'. Criticizing Churchill's vigorous denunc-ations of the wickedness of the national-socialists, Mr Carr wrote:

> The realist will have no difficulty in recognizing the pragmatic, though no doubt unconscious adjustment of Mr Churchill's judgments to his policy of the moment.[1]

Neville Chamberlain's policy in the late thirties is described as a reaction of realism to utopianism. The writer's thoughts can be summarized as follows: the liberal nineteenth-century theory of the harmony of interests was wrong. There is a clash of interest between haves and have-nots, a sort of class struggle on the international level. Germany had suffered an injustice at Versailles; there had been need for peaceful change but this change never came. It might not have been too late to make concessions to Germany in 1935-6; even about Munich it could be said that the change itself corresponded both to a change in the European equilibrium of forces and the accepted canons of international morality. Was not the warmongering of the dissatisfied powers the 'natural cynical reaction' to the sentimental and platitudinizing response of the satisfied powers on the common interest in peace?[2]

Hitler's demands for more *Lebensraum* were an authentic echo of the Marxist denial of a community of interest between haves and have-nots, and of the Marxist exposure of the interested character of bourgeois morality. About Soviet policies there is little in this pre-war work, apart from some observations to the effect that the group in power in Moscow was more and more discarding theory in favour of practice; but then history had been teaching all along that left-wing parties and politicians, when brought in contact with reality through the assumption of political office, tend to abandon their doctrinaire utopianism. The teachings of the realist school are very briefly these: there can be no reality outside the historical process. Condemnation of the past on ethical grounds has no meaning. What was is right. History cannot be judged except by historical standards. Nothing succeeds like success. 'World history is the World Court.' The popular paraphrase 'Might is Right' is misleading only if too restricted a meaning is attached to the word 'might'. History creates rights, and therefore right. The doctrine of the survival of the fittest proves that the survivor was, in fact, the fittest to survive.[3]

This somewhat unsophisticated 'realism' is not quite identical with

---

The Twenty Years Crisis.   [2] Ibid., p. 106.   [3] Ibid., p. 85-6.

Mr Carr's own philosophy of history; he is clearly aware of its limitations. The weapons of realism, he thinks, should be used to demolish the current utopias, but sound political thought for the future ought to be based on elements of both utopia and reality. Pure realism empties thought of purpose, condemns man to passive contemplation, and in practical politics offers nothing but a naked struggle for power which makes any kind of international society impossible:

> Having demolished the current utopia with weapons of realism we still need to build a new utopia of our own, which will fall to the same weapons.[4]

In his thoughts about the future society (a subject which very much preoccupied him during the war years) he preaches a synthesis of realism and utopianism. But as a historian, as a destroyer of myths, his bias is towards the realist school – towards Marx, Mannheim, and Machiavelli.

This then was Mr Carr's basic approach to politics (and history) on the eve of the second world war. In his Trevelyan lectures, published in 1961, he said that if anyone took the trouble to peruse some of the things he wrote before, during, and after the war he would have no difficulty in finding contradictions and inconsistencies. He did not amplify this remark but it is obvious that during the second world war he had, to a certain extent, modified some of his attitudes, for instance to Marxism. At the same time there was considerable consistency in Carr's thought; his belief that history can be judged only by historical standards goes back to well before the second world war, as does his antipathy to sentimentalism in historiography, his unwillingness to pronounce moral judgments, his fascination by power and those wielding it. There was also, all along, his belief that events in another country cannot be understood by British or American analogies and should certainly not be judged in accordance with them. In 1950 Mr Carr complained that this had been the case with regard to the policies and institutions of France, Italy, and Germany – they had been judged by false analogies. As for the Soviet Union:

> No sensible person will be tempted to measure the Russia of Lenin, Trotsky and Stalin by any yardstick borrowed from the Britain of Mac-Donald, Baldwin and Churchill, or the America of Wilson, Hoover or Franklin Roosevelt.[5]

[4] Ibid., p. 118.   [5] *The Bolshevik Revolution*, preface, p. v.

Ten years later he was much more pessimistic:

> Much of what has been written in the English speaking countries during the last ten years about the Soviet Union . . . has been vitiated by this inability to achieve even the most elementary measure of imaginative understanding of what goes on in the mind of the other party . . .[6]

Mr Carr's ideal historian is not the one who (in Croce's words) bustles about as a judge on the plea of narrating history, condemning here and giving absolution there; he emphatically rejects the notion of the historian as hanging judge. His ideal historian must above all strive for imaginative understanding. *In Cold Blood* had not yet been published, otherwise Mr Carr might have mentioned Truman Capote as a writer worthy of emulation.

A History of Soviet Russia

The structure of the *History* is very briefly as follows: the first three volumes (published in 1950, 1952, and 1953 respectively) constitute an entity called 'The Bolshevik Revolution'. This is, partly at least, a misnomer; the reader will look in vain for an account of the revolution and the civil war. It was the intention of the author (as he says in his preface) to write the history not of the events of the revolution, but of the political, social, and economic order which emerged from it; the events of the revolution had, after all, been chronicled by many other hands.

The first volume opens with a brief discussion of the foundations of Bolshevism. Lenin, Mr Carr says, was a great revolutionary, perhaps the greatest of all time, a man of immense learning and unique stature. His genius was far more constructive than destructive, an appraisal in strong contrast to Carr's assessment of Marx. His contribution and that of his party to the overthrow of Tsarism was negligible, and it is only in an 'external sense' that they can be held responsible for the overthrow of the Provisional Government in 1917. From July of that year its downfall had become inevitable; Bolshevism succeeded to a vacant throne. Lenin's major achievement came after the bloodless victory of the revolution in October 1917.[7]

Though not free from inner contradictions, the Bolsheviks took far more account of the specific local circumstances than the Mensheviks, who were alienated from Russian conditions and seemed unable to

[6] *What is History?*, p. 24.   [7] *The Bolshevik Revolution*, vol. I, p. 25.

grasp that the Russian social and political order provided none of the soil in which a bourgeois democratic régime could prosper. The Mensheviks, like the German Social Democrats, failed to realize that there had been an error in the original Marxist model: far from prevailing in the most developed capitalist countries, the revolution would find its target in the nascent capitalism which did not yet represent the interests of strong social forces. However, the fact that Bolshevism came to power in one of the most backward European countries also committed its leaders from the very beginning to certain policies; they had to try to bridge the gap (Mr Carr says) between autocracy and socialist democracy without the long experience and training in citizenship which bourgeois democracy, with all its faults, had afforded in the West. Economically, it meant that the Bolsheviks had to bear the handicap of being a régime of scarcity rather than, as had been expected, a régime of abundance.[8] There were endless debates among socialists as to whether the course adopted by Lenin could and would lead to socialism. Ultimately it turned on a point of interpretation: what was meant by socialism? Mr Carr does not give us his own answer, but he seems to imply in his *History* that a socialist régime may assume a different character in each country in accordance with its historical traditions, and its degree of social and political development.

The first volume of the *History* describes in some detail how the machinery of the new Soviet régime came into being. It discusses the new constitution and deals at length with the nationality question ('self determination in practice'). Bolshevism, it will be recalled, was bound by its programme to grant to all minorities the right of self determination. Mr Carr, in drawing the balance sheet, regards the reassembly of nearly all the former dominions of the Tsar (the main exceptions being Poland and Finland) as one of Lenin's 'astonishing achievements'.

Economic development during the first years after the revolution, 'War Communism', and the beginning of NEP (New Economic Policy) are the subject of the second volume of Mr Carr's history, Russia's relations with the outside world is the topic of the third. In his economic work Marx had provided an analysis of capitalist society; but what exactly was going to replace capitalism? There was general agreement that it would be socialism, and most socialists believed, in general terms, in a planned economy. But there was no

[8] Ibid., pp. 44 and 100.

blueprint for the economic policies of the transition period through which the revolution would have to pass after its victory. War and civil war had caused tremendous ravages and the Bolshevik leaders had to feel their way by trial and error, their most immediate aim being to restore agricultural and industrial production. On coming to power, the Russian communists believed that the world revolution was a matter of weeks, if not of days. That being so, there was little sense in re-establishing a foreign ministry after October 1917; for what could the new minister possibly do apart from publishing a few secret documents from the archives – and then close shop? Yet gradually it came to be realized that world revolution was not that near after all; the new masters had to negotiate with the Germans at Brest Litovsk and, later on, with the Allies. Meanwhile the Communist International, founded in 1919, developed its activities in Central Europe and, to a lesser extent, in Asia. The Comintern, too, was bound to suffer disappointment, for, as Mr Carr puts it, granted that the Russian workers in 1917 had nothing to lose but their chains, the majority of workers of Western Europe had standards which were worth defending: too many had too much to lose to abandon lightly the legality of 'bourgeois democracy'. Despite all these setbacks and difficulties in domestic and foreign politics, it was generally realized in 1922 that the revolution in Russia had come to stay. And with this turning point, *The Bolshevik Revolution* ends.

Mr Carr's first trilogy was originally to be succeeded by another series provisionally called *The Struggle for Power 1923-1928*; in the process of doing his research and organizing his material, however, Mr Carr decided to change his plan. His history became, as happens so often, much longer than originally intended; instead of immediately proceeding with his narrative to the period after Lenin's death, he wrote a single volume about the *Interregnum* (1923-4) which was then followed by a new trilogy (*Socialism in one Country*); this, albeit consisting of four volumes, comes only to 1926, not to 1928 as initially planned.

Most critics thought the first trilogy, and in particular the very first volume, the weakest part in Mr Carr's *History*. His decision not to deal with the revolution and the civil war was, in retrospect, not a happy one. It leaves a sense of imbalance that persists throughout the subsequent volumes: a history of Soviet Russia which does not provide an account of revolution and civil war, which, to give but a few examples, devotes merely a few lines to Kronstadt, but in subsequent volumes deals in incommensurate detail with such subjects as the Swedish and Yugoslav Communist Parties, the situation in Korea, Mongolia, and Afghanistan, is bound to provoke criticism. But it is not only a question of organization. It is very difficult to shed light on the political and social institutions that emerged after 1917 without constant reference to the revolution that had given birth to the new order. The way the Provisional Government was overthrown and the Civil War fought shaped the character of the Bolshevik party and the Soviet state for decades to come; an analytic account of how Soviet power was established is indispensable for an understanding of its dynamics in later years.

There is in the first volumes little if anything of the stirring passions and the drama of the early revolutionary 'heroic' period. Mr Carr's approach is matter of fact, almost impersonal; there is a great deal about legal issues and constitutions, as if these things greatly mattered in a revolutionary era. But there is no colour, no excitement; there are no reflections on the general course of events. It is a history of decrees and institutions – not political history. It is not just that the *dramatis personae* do not come alive; there are hardly any human beings at all in these volumes. And there are certainly no surprises. The reader who wants to know about the men who led the revolution and those who fought against it will be disappointed. There is nothing about their suffering and triumphs, nothing about the life of the Russian people in that period. As one reviewer (R. Pipes) noted: 'Who were the Bolsheviks, what did they want, why did some follow them and others resist? What was the intellectual and moral atmosphere in which all these events occurred?' Questions of this sort the author does not answer. All this is somewhat surprising, since Mr Carr's style is as a rule anything but flat, and his interest in people, as his previous books show, at least as pronounced as his interest in institutions.

Various explanations have been offered for these shortcomings in the first volumes of the *History*. With all his interest in revolutionary leaders and movements, there are obvious difficulties (Mr Deutscher once mentioned the 'peculiar limitations of the diplomatic mind' in this context) in understanding people and doctrines so utterly remote from Mr Carr's own background and professional training. However strong his belief in the doom of the world of liberalism, however sympathetically inclined he is towards revolutionary change, his basic interest is with the post-revolutionary order. Revolutionary phrases and actions call forth little response in him; they are after all purely destructive, and they conflict with good sense and order. Revolution may be historically necessary, but it is a necessary evil. Like Thomas Mann's bourgeois, Mr Carr has a strong dislike of *Unordnung*; the professional revolutionaries in his books, from Marx and Ogarev to Trotsky are, everything considered, pathetic figures and slightly ridiculous. His real heroes are the post-revolutionary ones; Carr, as I have said, always stresses Lenin's positive, constructive role as a builder of the new order rather than as a destroyer of the old one. He also tends, in Deutscher's phrase, to exaggerate the Stalin in Lenin. Disdain for Marx and admiration for Stalin are from this position not incompatible attitudes. There may be other reasons for Mr Carr's reluctance to tackle revolution and civil war. A revolution evokes overwhelming passions and conflicts and makes the task of the historian notoriously complicated. The passions stirred up in times like these make it exceedingly difficult to maintain the detachment necessary for writing history; they may also tend to obscure the trends that in the long run may be of decisive importance. People, after all, have suffered and been used as cannon fodder by all kinds of religions and doctrines, or simply by ambitious rulers, throughout known history. But new social orders have come into being only infrequently; should the historian in these circumstances not concentrate on what is unique and may have a lasting impact, rather than on the ephemeral aspects of the revolution, however large they may loom at the time? Trotsky once (with evident disapproval) quoted Madelin, who had asserted that the historian ought to stand upon the wall of the besieged city and behold at the same time the besiegers and the besieged. Mr Carr would perhaps prefer to watch such a siege from some height; as for the actual fighting (or the revolution), one need not watch it too closely, for the historian can tackle his subject only after some order has again been restored, some new pattern has evolved in the chaotic anthill down below.

There are weighty arguments against detachment of this kind. It has been argued that such neutrality, if analysed more closely, only too often conceals partiality towards one side. From a moral point of view it denotes the absence of sympathy and compassion, even of humanity. And to disregard moral considerations and judgments may not be the ideal approach to writing history. For history, as *inter alia* Marx has taught, is what human beings do; once one moves too far away from human beings, their hopes and fears, and the *condition humaine* in general, history becomes abstract. One can write a history of laws and institutions on such a basis, but it will be, at most, only one aspect of the far richer and more complicated general flow of history.

There are two more possible explanations for Mr Carr's approach in his first volumes. A diplomat should recognize every government that functions more or less properly. Rival groups do not exist for him, unless and until they accede to power. From a legal point of view this assumption is absolutely correct. But there is the danger of a *déformation professionelle* – namely, that the diplomat will gradually assume that every government wielding effective power is not only legal, but by definition good and reasonable and worthy of respect. Mr Carr, it will be recalled, was a diplomat for many years – a training and an experience that is no doubt a great asset in some respects, and the source of weakness and misunderstandings in others. Lastly, one has to consider these books in the context of their time. The first three volumes of the history appeared in 1950, 1952, and 1953 respectively. No historian can deliberately shut himself off from newspapers and radio, cut himself off from communication with the outside world, escape 'contamination' by current events. The late Stalin period provided an inclement climate for historians both within the Soviet Union and outside. It is not merely that the shadow of Stalin always looms somewhere in the background of Mr Carr's first volumes; the writer's whole approach and even style were affected. Whatever the explanation, with the publication of the fourth and fifth volumes (1954 and 1958 respectively), there is a palpable break; Mr Carr, as it were, is shifting gears; he becomes more relaxed, surer and more outspoken in his own judgment.

We have now reached the year 1923–4, and Lenin's last illness. Important problems were to be faced, especially on the economic front, the interregnum made the adoption of important decisions difficult if not impossible. Factional disputes within the party had reached a climax. The struggle for power, as Carr says, had assumed a naked form, 'personalities rather than principles were at stake'. The Trotskyite opposition was bound to fail not only because Stalin was a superior organizer and tactician, but because it lacked any broad basis of support within the party. Among the triumvirs who took over after Lenin's death, Stalin, self-effacing, cunning, and infinitely patient, was the most powerful and the most ambitious. He made no original contributions to Soviet policy (rapid industrialization, was, after all, Trotsky's rather than Stalin's idea), but he was vigorous and ruthless in its execution. Carr sees his historical role as paradoxical and to a certain extent contradictory. He was a great executor of the Marxist testament and a great westernizer, yet the goal and the method adopted seemed to be in flagrant contradiction.[9] Thus Stalin was both emancipator and tyrant, a man devoted to his cause and a personal dictator. Carr believes that the key to these contradictions cannot be found in the man himself, who only reflected the general dilemma of the revolution in a backward country: 'Few great men have been so conspicuously as Stalin the product of the time and place in which they lived.'

Trotsky, on the other hand, towered above all other Bolshevik leaders by sheer force of intellect; but this was not matched by the tact and sense of timing which are essential in statecraft. Many of his colleagues continued to think of him as a latecomer to the Bolshevik cause, if not as an intruder. His arrogance made not a few enemies and his efficiency, while universally admired, did not endear him to anyone. Ultimately, the general course of events greatly contributed to his downfall. Theory was beginning to matter much less, the need for highly gifted individual leaders was giving way to fear and suspicion of potential Bonapartes: 'Trotsky was a hero of the revolution. He fell when the heroic age was over.'[10]

The fifth volume, inaugurating the series *Socialism in One Country*, opens with a number of general reflections such as historians usually (but not invariably) publish at the very beginning of their work. They deal with the tension between continuity and change in Soviet Russia. While the inspiration of the Russian revolution had come from Western Europe, and while it had been conceived by its leaders primarily as the first step in a world-wide revolution, it also took the form of a national restoration. Russian national interests began to play an ever expanding role; seen in the perspective of Russian history, the revolution represented an attempt of the Russian national tradition to reassert itself against the encroachments of the West. Similarly, 'revolution in one country' (proclaimed by Stalin in 1924) was in Carr's view merely a repetition of what had happened countless times before in Russian history: the reabsorption of Western inspiration in a national setting, the Petrine reforms at a higher stage of development. 'But, as the cause of Russia and the cause of Bolshevism began to coalesce into a single undifferentiated whole, the

---

[9] *Socialism in One Country*, vol. 1, p. 186. [10] Ibid., p. 152.

resulting amalgam showed clear traces of both the original components out of which it had been formed.'[11] Yet socialism in one country was not the Russian 'Thermidor'; the revolutionary elements in it were perfectly real. The Russian revolution had gone much further in destroying the social and institutional fabric of the old régime than its French predecessor; the society that was to emerge was bound to be essentially new; there could be no return to an *ancien régime*. This also made it easier to preserve revolutionary dynamism, to impose on society a permanent 'revolution from above'. When Stalin first propounded this doctrine in a polemic against Trotsky in winter 1924–5, he was (Mr Carr believes) only dimly aware of its potential importance. It was a flash of originality, a quality otherwise rare in Stalin. But it enabled him to appear before the party and the country as offering a constructive policy, whereas his opponents had nothing to offer but scepticism,[12] thus laying themselves open to the charge that Russia would have to wait with folded arms for the success of the revolution in other parts of the world before any substantial progress in the Soviet Union could be achieved. By implication this was a belated negation of the October revolution; for what was the purpose of the revolution if the country could not forge ahead? They also exposed themselves to charges of adventurism, the reverse side of the lack of belief in the strength of the Russian revolution.

It was easy, on the basis of the new doctrine, to depict Stalin as the true expositor of Bolshevism and Leninism and his opponents as the heirs of those who had resisted Lenin and denied the Bolshevik creed in the past. Unwittingly Stalin had forged for himself an instrument of enormous power. Once forged, he was quick to discover its strength, and wielded it with masterful skill and ruthlessness.[13]

The second volume of *Socialism in One Country* describes in detail developments well known to students of Soviet history: how the rift in the triumvirate occurred and how Zinoviev and Kamenev were outmanœuvred by Stalin with the greatest of ease. At the fourteenth party Congress in December 1925 the opposition was routed; a rigid discipline was imposed – the Communist Party became monolithic. Administrative decisions by the party machine replaced inner-party discussion: and the party machine and thus supreme power was from now on concentrated in the hands of one man.

At this point, Carr interrupts his narrative to survey the changes

---

[11] *Socialism in One Country*, vol. 1, pp. 8, 21–2.
[12] *Socialism in One Country*, vol. II, pp. 36, 38, 51.   [13] Ibid., II, p. 51.

that had taken place in domestic and foreign policy since the death of Lenin. Detailed sections discuss the constitution of the USSR, regionalization, the attempts to 'revitalize the Soviets'. The author reviews the development of the Red Army from the end of the Civil War and the transformation of the character and functions of the security organs. The OGPU had been originally conceived as turned against enemies outside the party. By the middle twenties the opponents of Bolshevism inside Russia had ceased to be a real danger: 'The repressive powers of the OGPU were henceforth directed primarily against opposition in the party, which was the only effective form of opposition in the state.'[14]

Lastly, foreign affairs. Two volumes, more than a thousand pages, deal with the activities of the Soviet Foreign commissariat and the Comintern. Their length exceeded (as he says) the author's intentions and expectations. But he felt that since this period set the pattern for relations between the Soviet government and the outside world, and since so little spade work had been done by other students in this field, a detailed investigation was called for. Carr deals at length with the Locarno pact, the post-Locarno situation in Europe, and the revolution in China. He reviews the situation in the various European Communist parties, as well as Comintern activities. He describes the structure of the Communist International and its various auxiliary bodies. This was the period when the *détente* between the Soviet Union and the outside world seemed to be near its end and when communist party activities, after the defeats of 1922–3, were limited in scale, with no immediate revolutionary prospects in sight. It was, in retrospect, both in Soviet domestic and foreign politics a comparatively quiet period and it is no doubt a convenient point to conclude the second trilogy, *Socialism in One Country*. Work on the next set of volumes, to be entitled *Foundation of a Planned Economy* covering the late twenties is still in progress.

From the publication of the first volume, *A History of Soviet Russia* attracted a greal deal of attention – not only among students of Soviet history. The first three volumes (the *Bolshevik Revolution* series) were, as we have already stressed, more controversial in character than the subsequent volumes and were subjected to much criticism. But even the most severe critics of the early volumes paid homage to Mr Carr's scholarship, his standards of exposition, his

[14] *Socialism in One Country*, vol. II, p. 454.

unrivalled gift for presenting a vast mass of material with crystal clarity. If one critic wrote after the publication of the first volume that there was nothing in it that had not been said before, this was strictly speaking correct, but it was not really relevant. For it had not been Mr Carr's intention to write a history of the Soviet Union based mainly on hitherto untapped sources. He wanted, above all, to survey the enormous mass of known and published evidence and to weave it into a connected narrative. Fresh ground is occasionally broken in some of the later volumes, notably the ones on foreign affairs in the middle twenties, which are partly based on the files from the recently opened German archives. But on the whole, the *History* was not, and could not be, conceived as a pioneering work in this sense; it is above all a work of synthesis. Since the Soviet archives remain closed, it is unrealistic in present circumstances to expect any new facts and elucidations about Soviet history, except perhaps in regard to some minute segment to which the student devotes an inordinate amount of time and effort. The main charges brought against Mr Carr's first volumes were very briefly these: that at least some of the sections of the first volume (notably the one on Lenin) had been written from the standpoint of orthodox Leninism. 'The work is scrupulously honest and thorough in detail, but the perspective of the whole remains that of a restrained but admiring recording secretary of the Leninist Central Committee' (James Billington: 'Six Views on the Russian Revolution', in *World Politics*, April 1966, p. 463).

Carr (one critic argued) had shown himself in his previous books a born mocker; the pose of the panegyrist did not really fit him. It was also said that he had ignored the basically new (conspiratorial) character of the party organization as propagated by Lenin, that he had taken 'democratic centralism' seriously, that with all his criticism of Marx's fanaticism he disregarded Lenin's fanaticism and showed blindness to the possible far-reaching effects of his dictatorial policies. If on occasion he did express some scepticism with regard to Lenin's utopianism (concerning, for instance, the 'withering away of the state'), the reason was only to show it in contrast to the realities of Stalin's régime which, cleansed of the remnants of Lenin's utopianism, evoked his admiration. There were other charges pertaining to matters both of fact and of interpretation which are, however, not particularly relevant in this context. Some critics tried to provide a political-psychological explanation: Carr, they said, did not think highly of the future of democracy in industrial society; he accepted Michels' dictum that real democracy was incompatible with modern mass society. Hence his belief in the necessity of a bureaucratic dictatorship and the inevitability of despotism, and hence his 'ambiguous record' *vis-à-vis* fascism and national-socialism in the thirties and his 'admiration' for Stalin's Russia in the nineteen-fifties. Hence his obtuseness *vis-à-vis* political crime: 'Human suffering he seems to say, is not a historical factor; Carr belongs to those very cold people who always believe they think and act with the iciest calculation and therefore fail to understand why they are mistaken in their calculations time and time again.'[15]

Both Mr Carr's early work and the attacks on it were published in the early fifties. He did not answer his critics directly, but his Trevelyan lectures of 1961 repeatedly touch on some of the issues raised, albeit in a somewhat general form, and incidentally provide a brief exposition of his philosophy of history. Carr reiterated his conviction that there are no universal standards of morality, that events in each country can be judged only in their specific context. Quoting Carlyle on the French revolution, he regrets that the history of both the French and the Russian revolutions has generally been written in hysterical terms: 'Exaggeration abounds, execration, wailing, and on the whole darkness.' And on the terror: 'Horrible in lands that had known equal justice – not so unnatural in lands that had never known it.' Two other points of interest here concern the question of inevitability in history and of the historian as judge. Mr Carr's dispute with Sir Isaiah Berlin about historical inevitability is known and need not be retold. He is somewhat annoyed with the constant harping of his critics on this subject; he thinks the charges of inevitability barren and pointless.[16]

Why do people not cease once and for all to ask whether the Russian Revolution was inevitable? If anyone wished to discuss whether the Wars of the Roses were inevitable, it would rightly be considered a joke. Carr thinks that his critics' charges that he had not fully considered what might have happened had it not been for the revolution, reflect the emotionalism of people who had suffered

[15] Franz Borkenau, 'Der Spoetter als Panegyriker', in *Der Monat*, No. 36, September 1951, p. 614.

[16] He mentions that he once used in his history the 'offending word' when writing about the inevitable clash between Bolshevism and the Orthodox Church. Mr Carr overlooked at least one more important instance – when he wrote at the beginning of his first volume that the downfall of the provisional government in 1917 was inevitable.

'directly or vicariously from the results of the Bolshevik victory, or still fear its remoter consequences'.[17] Who would want to reverse the results of the Norman conquest or the American revolution, and who would blame the historian for considering these events closed chapters?

Mr Carr's illustrations are perhaps not entirely convincing; there is after all a difference between the significance in world history of a dynastic squabble like the Wars of the Roses and the Russian Revolution; nor was the Norman conquest conceived and carried out in accordance with an ideological blueprint. The questions may not be as idle as Mr Carr thinks, for the historical significance of the Russian Revolution can be assessed only if we measure its achievements and failures against the original intentions of its leaders, and if we compare them with both the situation in Russia on the eve of the revolution, and developments in other parts of the world during the last five decades.

This brings up the other important issue – judgment in writing history. Carr makes it quite clear that he sees little point in pronouncing moral judgments on the private lives of historical figures. What if Stalin treated his first wife badly? The historian has more important matters to attend to. Is not the denunciation of Hitler's wickedness a convenient alibi? Does it not exempt the Germans from blaming the society that had produced him? Was not such a society much more to blame than the individual leader? Mr Carr probably misinterprets his critics' charges on this point; they were concerned not about his evaluation of Hitler's and Stalin's private lives, but about his judgment (or lack of it) on the institutions of National Socialism and Stalinism.

Mr Carr does not think that it is the duty of the historian to judge Charlemagne or Napoleon or Hitler or Stalin harshly for their massacres. The latter two cannot really be judged because they are too near us; Napoleon and Charlemagne, on the other hand, are too remote – what profit is there today in denouncing their sins? And in any case what are the absolute values according to which they should be judged? 'The serious historian is the one who recognizes the historically conditioned character of all values, not the one who claims for his own values an objectivity beyond history.'[18] Freedom and liberty are abstract terms, the content put into them has varied throughout history from time to time and from place to place – each

---

[17] *What is History?*, p. 97.   [18] *What is History?*, p. 84.

127

group has its own values, rooted in its history; there is no super-historical standard of value. The discussion about values and moral relativism is not exactly a new issue between historians and philosophers of history. Mr Carr is aware of certain weaknesses in his argument; he does not leave it at that. Historians, he continues, tend to express their moral judgments in words of a comparative nature like 'progressive' and 'reactionary' rather than in uncompromising absolutes like 'good' and 'bad'. The historian ought therefore to devote his time and energy to finding out which historical developments are progressive and which reactionary. If the industrial revolution, for instance, is considered desirable and necessary, and if its long-term consequences are beneficial, its costs in human suffering – in Britain and Russia alike – will have to be considered unavoidable. The historian thus has no more of an answer to human suffering than the theologian; he has to fall back on the thesis of lesser evil and greater good. Ivan Karamazov's famous gesture of defiance is a heroic fallacy. We are born into society, we are born into history.[19] And we cannot opt out.

The debate on historicism is interesting and important; on the continent it has been in progress for more than a century. Acton held it against Ranke that he refused to call a spade a spade in the field of morality: 'Ranke (Acton wrote) spoke of transactions and occurrences where it would have been safe to speak of turpitude and crime.'[20] But it is only partly germane to the subject of this study, which is to give an exposition of the views of Mr Carr as an historian of the Soviet Union, to find out more about the underlying assumptions of his work and to assess the strength and weakness of his approach in relation to those of other historians of the same period. Mr Carr, to begin with, is emotionally less involved in Soviet and communist affairs than most historians of the period. Some are true believers, quite a few sympathized with communism in the past and, suffering disappointment, broke away; some belonged to communist or socialist opposition groups, others again were born in Eastern Europe but had to leave as the result of the political events of the last five decades. The fact that someone was born in Russia or that he belonged at one time to the communist movement does not, of course, predetermine his subsequent attitudes; but it does point to an element of emotional involvement that is absent in the case of Mr Carr, who

[19] *What is History?* p. 81.
[20] Theodor von Laue, *Leopold von Ranke: the Formative Years*, Princeton, 1950, p. 107.

was never a socialist, let alone a Marxist, who never took part in active politics, who, it would seem, never had much hope and was therefore only rarely disappointed: his God never failed. His involvement is intellectual and academic: such engagement, as experience shows, can be habit-forming too, but its manifestations are somewhat different. The advantages of the unemotional approach need hardly be spelled out in detail; it imparts a sense of proportion and balance often absent in those emotionally engaged. Yet while it is conducive to a more realistic appraisal in certain respects, non-involvement makes it exceedingly difficult to understand some aspects of history and human behaviour, and particularly those apparent in a revolutionary movement and régime. What impulses move the revolutionaries? What is the quality of life at a time of revolution or in a dictatorship? These are the imponderables which the detached academic historian will find it difficult to recapture however hard he tries. It is easy to write about the millions who died as a result of famine or terror, for such figures are meaningless; it is a very different thing to starve or to experience fear or imprisonment. These considerations affect the historical perspective. Mr Carr in several of his books has quoted Lenin to the effect that politics is where the masses are. If millions starve or are terrorized this experience is unlikely to remain restricted to one group or generation; it shapes the character of the régime and of the society for many years to come. It may have a lasting effect. History that has no feeling for these realities is likely to be lifeless and therefore untrue.

It is this that led Mr Carr, in his first volume, to devote almost one-third of his space to constitutional questions, to the neglect of the social background and the political history of the period. A Marxist training has its shortcomings but it does immunize its adepts against such legal hypertrophy. Mr Carr's lack of familiarity with the inner springs of revolutionary movements and régimes shows on other occasions. This may be connected with the fact that he was in a way a late comer to the study of Soviet history. He wrote, for instance, in 1949 that only now do 'we dimly perceive that the revolution of 1917 was a turning point in world history' and 'the significance of Lenin's work is just coming into focus' (*Studies in Revolution*). These generalizations are based on his personal experience; most serious students of Soviet affairs had agreed already in the nineteen-twenties about the importance of Lenin and the world significance of the Russian Revolution. Both friendly and hostile critics of his work agree that he mistakenly views the Russian Revolution almost entirely as a national, Russian phenomenon. He thinks that the Bolsheviks were not at all serious about world revolution but that this 'was in fact imposed upon the régime not so much by doctrinal orthodoxy, as by the desperate plight of the civil war'.

Both Bertram Wolfe and Isaac Deutscher, who otherwise have little in common (their own work on Soviet history is discussed elsewhere) stress emphatically that this is a misreading of Bolshevik intentions and hopes during the early years after the revolution. Mr Wolfe says that 'Mr Carr believes that the revolution was right for Russia. But he cannot quite make himself believe that in the matter of world revolution, this power-concentrated, dogmatic man [Lenin] was in deadly earnest.'[21] Mr Deutscher comments: 'Perhaps the main weakness of Mr Carr's conception is that he sees the Russian Revolution as virtually a national phenomenon only . . . he treats it as a historical process essentially national in character and self-sufficient within the national framework. He thinks in terms of statecraft and statecraft is national. His Lenin is a Russian super-Bismarck.'[22] Critics of different persuasion agree that there are other serious flaws in the first volumes of the *History*. The habits of thought of Stalinism, says a friendly critic, colour the approach of a historian like Mr Carr, whose interest in Marxism is only secondary to his study of Lenin's and Stalin's Russia. Hostile critics, putting it more bluntly, called the first volumes an apologia for the régime of the day.

Historians of the contemporary world are never *au dessus de la mêlée* – and Mr Carr is no exception; the impact of current events is, as we said, palpably stronger in the first volumes of his history than in the subsequent ones. Somewhere in *What is History?* Carr mentions Pieter Geyl's *Napoleon: For and Against*, in which the distinguished Dutch historian showed how the judgment of successive historians on Napoleon depended to a considerable extent on the character of their own time. Equally fascinating changes can take place, as Mr Carr's work shows, in the lifetime of one historian. His views on such subjects as Marx, Bolshevism, Lenin, and Stalin changed between 1935 and 1950, and his historical perspective was again modified, it would appear, between 1950 and 1960. There is, of

[21] Bertram D. Wolfe, 'The Persuasiveness of Power', in *Problems of Communism*, No. 2, 1955, p. 47.

[22] Isaac Deutscher, 'Mr E. H. Carr as Historian of Soviet Russia', in *Soviet Studies*, April, 1955, p. 347.

course, continuity in many respects but equally striking is the change in others. If Mr Carr is perhaps less a prisoner of the past than other historians, his perspective is probably more affected by what he considers the wave of the future. Moral judgments can be made without reference to future developments, but if the judgment of the historian depends mainly on whether a certain historical development is progressive or reactionary, the quest for the wave of the future is of paramount importance. In this case, historical perspective and judgment may have to be adjusted from time to time; today's victor may be tomorrow's loser, or a victorious régime may in its triumph revert to the old order; centuries may sometimes be needed to disentangle the paths of progress and reaction. One hundred and fifty years after Napoleon there is no general consensus of opinion about his place in history; the role of Charlemagne is still controversial; and Genghis Khan has his admirers in China.

Mr Carr, we have said, is more interested in trends than in individuals. Mention has been made of his views on these subjects in the nineteen-thirties. In a series of lectures in 1945-6 (*The Soviet Impact on the Western World*) he expressed his credo for the post-war world: 'the trend away from individualism and towards totalitarianism is everywhere unmistakeable'. Marxism was the most consistently totalitarian of modern movements; it had the widest appeal and Russia had dazzled the world by its immense industrial progress, the spirit of its people, and the rapid development of its power. Only the 'blind and incurable' refused to acknowledge this trend. Mr Carr did not explicitly identify himself with this wave of the future, but he could not ignore it. We have to assume therefore that the first three volumes of the *History* were written on the basis of the belief in the coming victory of totalitarianism. This is never stated in so many words, but it shows on many occasions: in the description of controversies we usually get only Lenin's side of them. (Often it is, admittedly, not clear whether the exposition is of Lenin's views or Mr Carr's.) It is reflected in the often uncritical acceptance of the vocabulary of the victorious party. It is shown, moreover, in the lack of interest in the causes of things; everything happens because it was bound to happen – the opposition lost because it had to lose, the Bolsheviks triumphed because it was predestined that they should prevail.

The author's approach in the volumes of the *History* published after 1953 is different. There is more detachment, less identification between the author and his subject and heroes. He is now preoccupied not only with the description of the course of events but also investigates their causes. He deals less with institutions and more with political and social history. If most critics agreed about the shortcomings in his first volume, there is similar agreement about the masterly sketches of Stalin and Trotsky, Zinoviev and Bukharin, at the time of the interregnum. We can only guess what produced this change, for Mr Carr has not yet given us his credo for the post-Stalinist era. But it would probably be safe to assume that he is now less certain than he was in 1945 of the coming victory of totalitarianism; it may come and then it may not. Meanwhile the historian will probably fare best if he tempers his own prophecies and predilections with a dose of healthy scepticism.

A History of Soviet Russia has been compared by one reviewer in a brief aside with Thiers' *Histoire du Consulat et de l'Empire*. It is, with all the customary reservations, a useful comparison; there are some striking parallels between the two. The first volume of Thiers' *Histoire* appeared in 1845, the twentieth and last in 1862 (like Carr's series it was originally planned on a much smaller scale). There is a high standard of exposition throughout, but in some respects the later volumes are better than the earlier. Events caused M. Thiers to modify his approach midway; the revolution of 1848 induced him to stress more than before the dangers of dictatorship. (His credo appears not in the introduction to the whole series but in the preface to the 12th volume; Carr's is contained in the opening of the fifth volume.)

Thiers made use of all the immense documentation that was already available and also included material that had not been open to his predecessors. His history was a great success, in virtue of its logical arrangement, its lucid presentation of a mass of material that almost seemed to defy organization in a readable way. Thiers said that he had approached his subject without any preconceived idea, simply to explore the '*verité des faits eux-mêmes*'. But is truth contained in the facts *per se*? Thiers takes a favourable view of Napoleon and the leaders of the French Revolution; his attitude becomes slightly critical whenever their chain of success is broken, but on the whole the dominant motif is admiration; when the faults of the hero have to be discussed, Pieter Geyl says, it is done more in sorrow than in anger.

Thiers' history was attacked for reasons and with arguments

similar to those that were brought against Carr's first volumes. Lanfrey wrote: 'His book is the *épopée* of his subject', charging Thiers with uncritical glorification of power in general. 'He only recognizes evil-doing if it is punished by adversity', wrote Lamartine. Another critic thought his judgments about people and actions 'void or without force and profundity; for M. Thiers does not have the sense of the good and evil which creates the urge to judge. It is sufficient for him to explain how things were, how the facts were interconnected and how they succeeded each other' (Prosper de Baraute). The central charge against Thiers was that his work, for all its grandiose scale and its other accomplishments, lacked profundity; that Thiers preferred, in Geyl's words, to evade the ultimate questions. It is tempting to speculate about the historical fate of Carr's *History*. All historians are influenced by what happens around them. There would be no final and definite histories even if all the relevant facts about a given age and country were known. With these obvious limitations in mind, will Mr Carr's *History* be accepted as great history, as the ultimate achievement of its age, revealing the maximum detachment on a subject that was conducive to anything but detachment? Will its impact be limited to the fifties and sixties, or will it continue to influence thinking for a long time to come? Or will it merely be remembered as a series of long and detailed volumes, useful as a compilation but lacking a central vision, ill-proportioned and fragmentary, unduly influenced by the *Zeitgeist*? Such speculation should be resisted at least until the last volume is published, possibly for a longer time. The boldness of the author in tackling this vast and complicated subject on a grand scale, the effort that has gone into it, will no doubt continue to evoke admiration and should be a source of inspiration to future historians. There will also be general agreement that as the volumes continue to appear a certain mellowing in Mr Carr's approach can be detected; largely, no doubt, under the impact of the events of the last two decades, partly perhaps under the influence of his own researches. The firm belief in a wave of the future which only the blind and the incurable fail to see has given way to a declaration of faith in the future of society and the future of history, in short, faith in history as progress. This in itself is perhaps an indication of historical progress; the forecasting of waves is a notoriously tricky endeavour, even more difficult in human affairs than in oceanography. Not everyone shares the belief in history as progress. But it is a legitimate working hypothesis.

133

« 7 »

Soviet Historiography

Soviet contemporary history is the Cinderella of the Soviet arts and sciences – and not by accident, to use an overworked phrase from the professional vocabulary. Soviet science has a great many achievements to its credit, and even the harshest critic will find something to admire in Soviet literature and music. Soviet philosophy and economics have been the subject of serious discussion by communists and non-communists alike all over the world. The performance of Soviet contemporary history over most of the past five decades has been unsatisfactory in communist eyes; non-communists by and large have refused to take it seriously, regarding it as little more than propaganda. Propaganda, everyone agrees, is a legitimate activity, it may be interesting, it may even coincide with truth. But it is not history.

How justified is this attitude? It is easier to give a summary account of Soviet historiography than of Western literature on the Soviet Union. In contrast to the bewildering multitude of conflicting views and interpretations in the West, there has been, and is, in Soviet historical writing only one official view at any given time, and there are no unofficial, individual comments. About the distant past there may be differences of opinion among Soviet historians; within the general Marxist framework there is room for discussion and even disagreement. But our concern is with the post-revolutionary, the Soviet period of Russian history, and in this context a Soviet historian is guided not merely by Marxism-Leninism, but above all by *raison d'état* and *raison du parti*. The writings of historians must not be in conflict with the party line – and there can be only one party line. Histories of the Soviet period, and in particular of the Communist Party, are therefore official policy statements that can be made only by the highest political authority.

A review of Soviet historiography is made easier for yet another reason: there is comparatively little of it. True, tens of thousands of books and booklets have been published since 1917 about the Russian Revolution, the development of the State, and the history of the party. However, all but a handful deal with specialized aspects, are either local history, collections of documents, monographs, or popular editions of the few standard works. A history of the Soviet Union does not exist other than a one-volume school textbook. There are no biographies of Lenin, Stalin, and other revolutionary leaders comparable to the books published in the West. Nor are there systematic histories of the Soviet economy, or of intellectual life in the Soviet period.

Soviet historians maintain that Western historians have at best been able to collect interesting factual material, but are unable to produce works of a systematic coherent character – that they are afraid to generalize boldly. That there is such a tendency cannot be denied. But with all their self-doubts about approach and methodology, some Western historians have not been afraid to tackle big subjects in Soviet history. Soviet historians, with all their enthusiasm for generalization, have usually been unable to do so. We have mentioned the absence to this day of a history of the Soviet Union other than a college text. Party histories there have been, but all have been withdrawn, often shortly after publication. Only in 1964 was the attempt first made to produce a party history on a big scale; all previous efforts were 'General Outlines', 'Short Courses', 'Concise Histories', etc., that did not go into detail.

The function of history and the task of the historian are conceived differently in the Soviet Union from that in the West. Lenin's views on the subject remain mandatory to this day. History, according to Lenin, has to be scientifically objective and devoid of exaggeration; it has to correspond strictly with the realities of a given period, which implies that the historian must study the historical process as it developed; to transfer present-day concepts to the past and to measure the past by contemporary standards, to 'modernize the past', is to perpetrate a major distortion.

So far, Western students of history will find little to disagree within these basic concepts. But history is and remains in the Soviet view a party science (*partiinaya nauka*), unlike, for instance, mineralogy or gynaecology. According to Lenin, there can be no impartial social science in a class society; no human being can refrain from choosing the side of one class or the other; he cannot help rejoicing at the

135

success of his class, or regretting its defeats. The historian, therefore, is not a dispassionate recorder of events, but a fighter. Historical science is a battleground for the communist transformation of society, an arena of sharp struggle against non-communist, bourgeois ideology. How to combine the demand for objective research with *partiinost*? All historiography is partisan in the communist view; a historiography reflecting the views and interests of reactionary social forces will necessarily be subjective and reactionary in character. But historical study that identifies itself with the progressive forces will be objective: 'The *partiinost* of history and its scientific character can coincide only when history reflects the interests of the working class.'[1]

Many Western historians will agree that there exists a nexus between historiography and class, that all historical writing is based on preconceived ideological concepts. Few would accept the view that the historian is motivated entirely by the interests of the class to which he belongs or with which he identifies himself. Different conclusions, at any rate, will be drawn from this insight about the relativity of historical thought. The communist historian will identify himself more closely with the working class, as personified by the presidium of the Central Committee of the Communist Party, because only such close identification ensures objectivity. The non-communist scholar, if he is worth his salt, will try to attain objectivity by trying to free himself from prejudice; recognizing his involvement in it, he will attempt to rise above his social and historical situation.

The strengths and the weaknesses of the communist approach have been discussed frequently and no attempt will be made here to reiterate the arguments. Nor is this the place to debate whether historical materialism can be a useful approach to the study of, say, the social history of the Middle Ages. The only relevant question in the context of contemporary history is whether Soviet historiography has been successful in attaining the targets that were set for it, whether it has produced scholarly works of lasting value. Has it, on the non-academic level, produced books that fill Soviet people with 'legitimate pride in their great party and in its epoch-making victories'? Has it helped them to 'apply the rich experience of the party in solving new problems and has it engendered the creative energy required for building Communism?'[2] For these were, and are, the main assignments of Soviet history.

[1] *Sovetskaya Istoricheskaya Entsiklopedia*, vol. 6, p. 587.
[2] *History of the Communist Party of the Soviet Union*, Moscow, 1960, p. 15.

All communist historians past and present agree on a number of basic tenets: that the revolutionary struggle grew in intensity in Tsarist Russia, that with the rise of Social-Democracy and, more specifically, with the founding of the Bolshevik party a new era began in the fight against oppression and exploitation. They agree furthermore that in Lenin, with his theory of the party as the principal weapon of the working class in its struggle for the dictatorship of the proletariat, a leader of genius appeared. Lenin, according to the general consensus of opinion, adapted Marxism to Russian conditions and created a party of a 'new type' – he was the architect of victory. The revolution of 1905 showed how weak Tsarism was, but since all other opposition parties betrayed the people, and since the Bolsheviks were not yet strong enough to clinch the victory, it was bound to end in failure. The next decade was a difficult one, but the party was steeled in its fight against deviationists. When the inner contradictions of imperialism caused the imperialist world war in 1914, the Bolsheviks were the only political party to take a consistent stand against it. The war further weakened Tsarism, which even before had been the weakest link in the imperialist chain. The revolution of March 1917 was bourgeois-democratic in character, marking the conversion of the imperialist war into a civil war. Under the leadership of Lenin, the Bolsheviks stood for the transfer of all power to the Soviets, fought Menshevism and the Socialist-Revolutionaries, called the masses to struggle for peace and bread, and thus proved that they were the only force that could abolish capitalism and lead the way to a socialist revolution. Responding to the call of the party, the masses rose in November 1917, and their revolution ushered in a new era in the history of mankind. After this victory the Communist party led the country out of the imperialist war and saved it from economic disaster. It fought against internal enemies and foreign interventionists. Under the leadership of Lenin it adopted the New Economic Policy, as the only correct line for the transition from capitalism to socialism. At the same time it continued its struggle against the capitalist elements in the country and thus paved the way for the new phase of socialist construction.

So far there is general unanimity; even Trotsky agreed with the picture as drawn here in general outline. After Lenin's death, there was dissension, but communist historians throughout the world usually agree that the aim of the party in the nineteen-twenties was, broadly speaking, to overcome the age-old backwardness of the country and to transform it into a mighty industrial power. The main problem, to accumulate funds for building a heavy industry, was successfully overcome. 1929 was the year of the great change; agriculture was reconstructed on socialist lines, the peasants joined the collective farms. The targets of the first five-year plan were fulfilled ahead of time, the Soviet Union was converted within the span of a few years from an agrarian into a strong industrial power.

This briefest of all outlines of an agreed version of Soviet history could without undue difficulty be brought up to the more recent past, though, of course, the nearer we move to the present time, the more contentious the issues become. The real difficulties begin once the attempt is made to fill out this skeleton with flesh and blood and to write a history that is more detailed. For at this stage the communist historian has to ask whether a certain policy was carried out at the right time and in the right way; he has to consider whether mistakes were made, whether the price for certain achievements was not too high, whether alternative policies were not possible in both domestic and foreign affairs. And he has above all to begin to mention names.

At this point, the writing of contemporary history in the Soviet Union becomes exceedingly difficult. It is one thing to write Russian history from a Marxist-Leninist point of view: a historian dealing with, say, the Kievan period of Russian history will not be unduly affected by current political events. Once every twenty years there may be a far-reaching ideological reorientation which he will not be able to ignore, but he need not be troubled by the daily political fluctuations; even the fall of Khrushchev or the adoption of Libermanism will not normally have an impact on his work. His colleague specializing in the revolutionary and post-revolutionary period is in a very different position: the changing political line, the often sudden changes at the top, are of immediate concern to him. For yesterday's hero may overnight become a villain or an unperson; his policies, that were the subject of adulation, may be subjected to heavy attack. Since the historian of the Soviet state or the Communist Party does not express his own individual views, the histories have to be adjusted immediately. In the case of a radical break (Stalin's victory over his opponents, or the rediscovery of some of the traditional heroes in Russian history), the old history books will have to be scrapped altogether. At other times it may suffice to publish revised editions, if all that is required is the deletion of the names of some former leaders now fallen into disgrace. The 'Short Course' is the textbook that lasted longest – with minor modifications for almost fifteen years. It is now criticized for serious theoretical and factual distortions, about which more below. All other such history books have lasted only a few years; some were already obsolete before they appeared.

The writing of Soviet and party history would no doubt benefit from more continuity, less violent change in the top party leadership. But the basic predicament of contemporary Soviet history will remain: the historians have to react to all the vicissitudes of the changing party line.

These are the inbuilt difficulties of contemporary history as an academic discipline in the Soviet Union. But it is also not certain that Soviet historical literature has fulfilled its function as an instrument of political education. To be effective, a history of the Soviet state and the Communist Party ought to be consistent, but the frequent changes introduce a great deal of uncertainty. A serious student of Soviet and party history will have to consult not only the current version; he will want to look also at previous histories and, of course, at the original documents. He will discover wide discrepancies which are bound to shake his belief in official histories; if yesterday's truth has been found wanting, what certainty is there that the present version will not be rejected at some future date?

A few illustrations will indicate the kind of question that is likely to arise from even a superficial preoccupation with the history of the CPSU. Trotsky, of course, is a typical example: he played a central role in 1917 and the early years after the revolution. All histories published since 1927 say that he sabotaged the revolution. But the record shows that he was the first People's Commissar for Foreign Affairs and later Commissar for the Army, despite the fact that he was a comparative newcomer among the Bolsheviks. If Trotsky was indeed a wrecker, part of the blame has to be put on Lenin, for his gullibility, his failure to remove from his immediate neighbourhood an enemy of the revolution and the Communist party. It is, of course, a problem that concerns not Trotsky alone, but the great majority of Lenin's closest aides, excepting only those who died in the twenties (Sverdlov, Dzerzhinsky) and were thus not involved in the purges of the thirties. There are two possibilities: that Lenin carried out the revolution not merely single-handed, but against the opposition of the majority of the party leadership. This is not really plausible, for how can a revolutionary party succeed if its general staff tries to sabotage and betray the revolution? The second possibility seems more likely, that the versions which have prevailed since 1927 are false.

Until well after Stalin's death, it was impossible for anyone but the professional specialist to compare the various consecutive versions of party history. They had been withdrawn from circulation, together with the protocols of the party congresses from 1917 to 1934, and the early editions of Lenin's works. All other publications, including Stalin's own works, had been censored. Since the late fifties, some of this early material, especially the protocols of the party congresses, have been reprinted. Some material is still kept in limbo, not even mentioned in bibliographies prepared for and by specialists. The writings of a White Russian general like Denikin, of Milyukov, Nabokov, or Rodzianko, or of a right-wing extremist like Shulgin, are freely mentioned and even quoted, but never Trotsky's history of the revolution, or Shlyapnikov's *1917*. The bibliographies of the history of the communist parties mention hundreds of trivial and insignificant works, but not Zinoviev's history, published in 1923. Whatever the intrinsic value of the books of Stalin's opponents, they were widely read at the time and are part of the historical record. Soviet history has never been able to find a satisfactory solution for dealing with losers – from the Old Bolsheviks, through the majority of the Central Committee that was purged in the thirties, to the 'anti-party group' of 1957, and up to Khrushchev. The prevailing version of Soviet and party history always *a priori* justifies the current party leadership. The historians show that these leaders act in the true spirit of Leninism, they prove that the current line is the only correct one, and they thus provide the necessary legitimacy. This no doubt assists political education; but invariably changes take place, often drastic changes, and it becomes necessary to rewrite history. This, in the long run, vitiates most of this kind of work, for it appears that the only certain historical law is the law of change. It has happened time and time again over a period of several decades; most outside observers have commented in a spirit of incomprehension and derision. The conviction has grown among them that since Soviet party historiography fulfils a function different from the writing of history in a non-communist régime, discussion and polemics are fruitless. Western students of history (as one of them has put it) regard historical events as unique and interesting because humanly meaningful in themselves; they also want to find a rational explanation for the sequence of events, their causes and consequences. The

Soviet historian cannot approach his material with a genuine query, because the fundamental answers are already furnished by the ideological framework in which he operates. Therefore to him history is less an attempt at understanding, at finding causes and explanations, than an illustration 'on the basis of concrete, factual material' (as they are fond of saying) of the accepted interpretation of the general scheme. In this sense Soviet historical writing is much closer to the histories written in Europe in the seventeenth century and before (Bossuet), or even to the Biblical Chronicles, than history as understood today in the West.[3] Some Western students do not think that this judgment applies to all Soviet historical writing, and therefore deny that there can be no communication between Western and Soviet historians, because they mean something different by writing history. A doctrinaire history is likely to ask only certain questions – those allowed by the doctrine. But, as Professor Richard Lowenthal has argued, it could still be fruitful if it asked these questions genuinely and within the sphere in which they applied, provided, of course, it is not bound by the necessity to produce specific political results but is based on a general concept of laws.[4] The discussions about the so-called Asian mode of production could be mentioned as an instance in this context.

Party history, however, has to produce specific political results, as even the briefest survey of these textbooks shows. The two earliest party histories, by Lyadov and Baturin, both published in 1906, need not be discussed here since they were written before the revolution. They deal with Russian Social-Democracy in general rather than with the Bolshevik faction that had just come into being. The very early post-revolutionary histories (Zinoviev 1923, V. I. Nevsky 1923, A. S. Bubnov 1924) were still relatively liberal in spirit; they reflected inner-party democracy as it existed before Lenin's death. Of course, they justified the Bolshevik revolution, which they describe as a popular upsurge. They attack not only Tsarism and the 'bourgeois' parties, but also the Social Revolutionaries and the Mensheviks without, however, entirely denying their revolutionary merits in the past. In 1923–4, open warfare erupted inside the party and the history of the party and, particularly, the 'lessons of October' (following Trotsky's book with that title) became one of the main weapons

[3] Marc Raeff, in *Contemporary History in the Soviet Mirror* (ed. John Keep), London, 1964, p. 148–9.
[4] Ibid., p. 150.

in the ideological struggle between the warring factions. With the publication of the first histories of N. N. Popov (1925) and E. Yaroslavsky (1926), and particularly Bubnov's *VKPB* (1930), party histories were shaped to prove that Stalin's enemies were not merely wrong at the time of writing but had been mistaken all along. Soviet historians now take a favourable view of the work done by their predecessors in the late twenties: party historiography (we are told) was inseparably connected with the ideological work of the party, the sharp struggle against Trotskyism. It fought for the Leninist theory of socialist revolution, against the Trotskyite concept of permanent revolution. According to the present view, Soviet party history had achieved much in that period: many documents had been collected, edited, and published, quite a few monographs had been written, a definite step forward towards the writing of a scientific history had been taken; this advance continued during the early thirties, when the main emphasis was on the clarification of some basic ideological questions: the character of the social and economic prerequisites of the October revolution and its moving forces, the transformation of the bourgeois-democratic revolution into a proletarian revolution. Unfortunately, the negative impact of the 'Cult of the Individual' (about which more below) became more palpable in that period and had a detrimental influence on the writing of party history.[5] A Western critic takes a less positive view of that era:

> Histories succeeded one another at a faster and faster rate, as if they were being consumed by a more and more irritable gigantic chain smoker who lit the first page of each new work with the last page of the old. Histories, and a little later historians, disappeared without trace.

> Sometimes the first volume of a new series was published, then the whole work was scrapped, and a new history was begun by the very same author. All these histories were designed for the glorification of Stalin, and the political destruction of his opponents.

> The heroes of one work became the dubious weaklings of the next and the villains and traitors of the third. Persons of one work became unpersons in the next; the stature and single-handed achievements of Stalin became so much larger from one year to the next that each earlier version had to disappear, lest, rising from oblivion, it might bear witness against its successor.[6]

[5] *Sovetskaya Istoricheskaya Entsiklopedia*, vol. 7, pp. 716–17.
[6] B. Wolfe in *Contemporary History in the Soviet Mirror*, loc. cit., p. 48.

It is not denied in the Soviet Union now that things were moving in the wrong direction at the time: 'The materials published in *Pravda* on the occasion of Stalin's fiftieth birthday in 1929 were permeated with the spirit of glorification of the supreme leader.' Yaroslavsky, the editor of a four-volume history of the CPSU (1926–30) and his collaborators were charged with the falsification of history and the smuggling in of Trotskyite contraband, because they had incidentally mentioned that Stalin had not always been right in 1917.[7] Stalin himself, we are now told, began to give personal instructions to the historians about how exactly his role should be described.

Since all these efforts made by individual historians and groups of authors were considered unsatisfactory, the *Short Course* was published in 1938 to settle the problem of party history once and for ever. Its authorship is uncertain to this day. Originally it was announced that one chapter in this book had been written by Stalin; later the whole was ascribed to him. The *Short Course* was launched with a great fanfare by means of a special decree of the Central Committee. It was scheduled from the very beginning to become the main instrument of political education in the country and the communist movement as a whole. It aimed to show, as it said in the introduction, that the history of the CPSU, 'the struggle of our party against all enemies of Marxism-Leninism, against all enemies of the working people, helps us to master Bolshevism and sharpens our political vigilance'; to arm its readers with a knowledge of the laws of social development and the motive force of the revolution. At the end of each chapter there is a brief summary. The one dealing with the opposition of the twenties says:

Defeated ideaologically by the Bolshevik party and having lost all support among the working class, the Trotskyites ceased to be a political trend and became an unprincipled careerist clique of political swindlers, a gang of political double-dealers.

The main lessons of party history are summarized at the end of the book under six headings, each beginning: 'The history of the party teaches us . . .' One of these, the fifth, says, that the history of the party 'teaches us that unless the petty-bourgeois parties which are active within the ranks of the working class and which push the backward sections of the working class into the arms of the bourgeoisie, thus splitting the working class, are smashed, the victory of proletarian revolution is impossible'. The language of the *Short Course* is nothing

[7] Details in *Sovetskaya Istoricheskaya Entsiklopedia*, vol. 7, p. 718.

if not outspoken. The victims of the purges and trials of 1936–8 are described as 'these whiteguard pigmies, whose strength was no more than a gnat'. Elsewhere they appear as 'whiteguard insects' and 'contemptible lackeys of the Fascists'. 'They forgot that the Soviet people had only to move a finger, and not a trace of them would be left . . . The Soviet court sentenced the Bukharin-Trotsky fiends to be shot. The People's Commissariat of the Interior carried out the sentence. The Soviet people approved the annihilation of the Bukharin-Trotsky gang and passed on to the next business . . . '

The *Short Course* was printed in fifty million copies and for fifteen years it was the basic ideological document of the CPSU and the catechism of all other communist parties. Since Stalin's death it has not been reprinted, and it is now subjected to criticism for its 'serious theoretical and factual distortions'.[8] Among these the following are mentioned: the problem of the predecessors of the Bolsheviks, the exclusion of the names of many leading Bolshevik figures who had become 'enemies of the people', the role of Stalin during the civil war, the playing down of the role of Lenin and other Old Bolsheviks. Other criticisms now voiced refer to Stalin's policy in 1917–20, the multitude of unending quotations from Stalin in the *Short Course*, and the fact that virtually all the political, military, economic, and cultural achievements of the Soviet people are either attributed to Stalin personally, or at least somehow connected with his name. It is a long list of shortcomings, but according to present-day Soviet sources, the indirect impact of the book was even more unfortunate: the archives were practically inaccessible, history could be written only by way of illustrating the *Short Course*. Dogmatism, a scholastic attitude, and the language of (Stalin) quotations prevailed; references to source material could hardly ever be given. Instead, millions of brochures were printed, extolling the person of Stalin. But the picture, as Soviet observers now see it, is not one of unrelieved gloom: even under the influence of the 'Cult of the Personality', party history continued to develop. Local party histories were written and the Marxist-Leninist classics were often reprinted.

With Stalin's death, his history disappeared. From 1953 to 1959, the Soviet Communist Party had no official history. A document of some 7,000 words, published in *Pravda* in July 1953 ('Theses on Fifty Years of the Communist Party of the Soviet Union') stated the party line during this interim period. Lenin was mentioned eighty-three

---

[8] Details in *Sovetskaya Istoricheskaya Entsiklopedia*, vol. 7, p. 716.

times in this statement, Stalin only four. The general trend was unmistakable. When the new party history came out in June 1959, it was twice as long as the *Short Course*, but it was given much less publicity than its predecessor. This 1959 *History* (a second edition appeared in 1962) was printed in several millions of copies and it had, of course, official blessing. But it was not very often quoted; it was apparently regarded from the very beginning as a work of a transitional character. The lessons of the *Short Course* were, after all, quite fresh. After Khrushchev's fall, the 1959 *History* was not withdrawn, but as far as can be ascertained, it was not reprinted. The stage was set for a definitive five-volume history of the party. Of this, at the time of writing (summer 1966), only the first volume has appeared.

The 1959 *History* is similar in didactic structure to the *Short Course* of 1938, with its summaries and conclusions. It is to a certain extent identical; on occasion, entire pages have been taken over. Some of the contributors (Ponomarev, Mints) had a hand in the writing of the *Short Course* and previous party histories in the thirties. Of course, the new *History* takes a different line towards Stalin. It carries the narrative up to the fifties, whereas the *Short Course* had stopped in the late thirties. The purges of the thirties (to give but one example) are dealt with very briefly in the 1959 *History*; the trials are not mentioned at all. It says that Stalin was right in keeping a watchful eye on the intrigues of Trotsky, Bukharin, and other such enemies; they had deceived the party more than once, violated Soviet legality, and were often in league with counter-revolutionary elements. For this reason, the State security organs were compelled to take the necessary measures against them. The *History* does not specify what the necessary measures were, but apparently Stalin went too far; for since they had already been routed ideologically it was not necessary to apply mass repressions against the party's ideological enemies. We learn that many honest party members and non-communists, not guilty of any offence, became victims of these repressions. It was largely the fault of Yezhov (who 'played a despicable role') and of Beria (a 'political adventurer and scoundrel') who took advantage of Stalin's personal shortcomings.

This debunking of Stalin had been preceded by the twentieth party congress (1956), particularly by Khrushchev's famous speech, which has not, however, been published in the Soviet Union to this day. The hero of the 1959 *History* is the Communist Party itself, rather than any individual leader – certainly not Stalin. But even if Stalin

was criticized and downgraded, the overall assessment of his historical role was not negative. He had played a leading part in the destruction of the Party's external and internal enemies. Under his leadership,
heavy industry had been built up, agriculture collectivized, socialism constructed in the Soviet Union. He had done much to
extend Soviet power. His general political line had been correct up
to the middle thirties, though he had not been altogether blameless.
In the thirties he made some serious mistakes, violating basic principles of inner-party democracy. Some of his actions as a war leader
were also criticized; he had misjudged the political situation on the
eve of the war. And finally there were some negative aspects 'resulting
from the personality cult', 'during the last years of his life'. But even
so his achievements outweigh his failings, according to the 1959
version: under the leadership of the Communist Party and the
Central Committee in which Stalin played a leading role, the Soviet
Union achieved enormous, world-wide successes. Stalin had done
much that was beneficial to the Soviet Union, to the CPSU, and to
the whole international working-class movement.

Since 1959, there have been further fluctuations: there was more
sweeping debunking at the twenty-second party congress (1961);
this was reflected mainly in novels describing the general climate of
the thirties and forties, only to a lesser extent in historical literature.
But there were also warnings against excessive de-Stalinization, and
the wholesale condemnation of an entire period in which, it was
argued, great things had, after all, been accomplished.

Many victims of the purges were rehabilitated in the fifties, the
names of about eighty more or less prominent Old Bolsheviks have
been mentioned in the press during the last decade. In some cases the
victims were fully exonerated (Krestinsky, Faisula Khodjaev). The
more prominent ones such as Bukharin, Zinoviev, Kamenev, Rykov
were personally rehabilitated, the charges of having been spies and
traitors were tacitly dropped. But they were still considered to have
been enemies of the party; their rehabilitation was juridical, not
political. Little publicity was given to these rehabilitations; often
they emerged by implication rather than specific announcement. A
drastic reappraisal was politically impossible; it would have been a
source of embarrassment (or worse) to those who had made their
political career under Stalin, and it would have fatally weakened the
continuity of the party tradition.

Some daring spirits tried in 1956–7 to reappraise not only the Old

Bolsheviks but also the role of the Mensheviks and the Socialist-Revolutionaries before October 1917. According to the Stalin version, these left-wing parties had been as much part of the reactionary camp as the extreme right, enemies of the revolution all along. Burdzhalov, Pankratova, and other professional historians maintained in the more relaxed atmosphere of 1956–7 that these left-wing groups had some revolutionary merits after all, especially in 1905 and at the time of the overthrow of Tsarism. But these heresies were almost immediately condemned. According to the post-Stalin official version the Narodniki of the eighteen-eighties had indeed fulfilled a progressive role; Stalin's *Short Course* had erred by denying them revolutionary spirit altogether. But this referred to the early period in Russian revolutionary history: after 1903 there was no progressive force in Russia but the Bolshevik party.

Since Stalin's death it has become easier to be a Soviet contemporary historian in some respects, more difficult in others. The burden of repeating parrot-like the grotesque distortions of the Stalin era has been lifted; but to write history has not become easier since now even more persons and events have become unpersons and un-events. In the *Short Course* of 1938 there was but one great hero and only one arch villain. Stalin's role in the Civil War – to give one illustration – was magnified with scant respect for the historical record. Trotsky's part was described in an entirely negative way. Twenty years later, Trotsky, as a hero of the Civil War, has not been rehabilitated, Stalin's part has been severely downgraded, and the names of other Civil War heroes of 1938 have been eliminated (Molotov, Kaganovich, Shshadenko, Shkiryatov, etc.).

The historian is faced by the danger of being left without heroes and villains altogether. The *Short Course* of 1938 gave a mendacious account of the purge trials of 1936–8 – the 1959 *History* does not mention them. Rehabilitation has been slow and incomplete, and has only seldom reached the official textbooks. Since the list of the important un-persons has grown, the historian of the CPSU has now scarcely anyone but Lenin to fall back on – and this is not of much help for the period after 1924. The 1959 *History* no longer mentions Molotov, Kaganovich, Malenkov, Bulganin and the other members of the 'anti-party group' – apart from a very few negative references referring to their dismissal. In the next history Khrushchev will no doubt be missing, but his enemies will not be restored. As a result the party histories have more and more to describe the course of events in terms of institutions rather than people. The Central Committee is very often mentioned, the index of names is exceedingly brief.

Such a history has much to commend it. For if one disregards personalities the writing of Soviet history becomes a much easier assignment, and permits greater continuity because the basic appraisal of the main trends in Soviet history since the middle twenties has not changed substantially. Trotsky and Stalin were, after all, at bottom in agreement about the November Revolution; they both condemned the Mensheviks and the Social-Revolutionaries to the dustbin of history. Nor was there disagreement between Stalin and Trotsky in 1939 about the conquest of the Baltic countries, Eastern Poland, and the Finnish war. There were several beliefs common to both Stalinists and deviationists – despite the polemics, the bitter denunciations, and even the executions. There is much continuity between the *Short Course* and the 1959 *History*: of the six conclusions of the *Short Course*, five reappear with little change in the new history of 1959; victory is impossible without the Communist party, there can be no victory without Marxist-Leninist theory, the party must be self-critical, the party must wage a struggle against opportunists in its ranks, the party must maintain close links with the masses.[9] All this, of course, in considerably greater detail. There is no unanimity about the individual role of certain leaders. But Communists of whatever persuasion agree in broad outline in their appraisal of pre-revolutionary history, of 1917, of the Civil War. Even when he attacked Stalin severely, Khrushchev did not for a moment doubt the wisdom of the German-Soviet pact of 1939, or of the Soviet advance into Eastern and Central Europe after 1945, and of a great many other decisions taken by his predecessor. The rapid turnover continues in party history as far as individual leaders are concerned, and certain aspects of past history come in for reappraisal, but on the general lines of development there is a larger area of common ground than is often assumed. The collective wisdom and the courage of the party is not doubted. Individuals acting on behalf of the party may have erred and have had their failings, but the party as such has always been right. Future party histories will no doubt be written on these lines; difficulties will occur mainly in the more specialized works in which the writers will have to go into detail about certain periods, policies, and persons. Such studies will be read by a limited audience

[9] See L. Schapiro's comparison between the two party histories in *Contemporary History*, etc., p. 81.

of specialists only, and it is not excluded that in the course of time greater concessions will be made than hitherto to historical truth in this kind of literature.

It is exceedingly difficult to draw a clear dividing line between party history and Soviet history in general, even though the latter is a separate discipline. For the party has been the guiding force and the prime mover in all fields of political, social, economic, and cultural endeavour since 1917. Among the Bolsheviks of pre-1917 vintage there were a few historians, some of them even professionals. By and large, historians are not strongly represented in revolutionary movements. In the French revolution they belonged to the Gironde and came to grief; they were more numerous in Germany before 1848, but alas, without great effect. In Russia after the revolution these men were given various important organizational assignments; they had no time to write the history of their time. When Arthur Ransome, the *Manchester Guardian* correspondent, went to see Professor Pokrovsky, the Bolsheviks' chief authority on Russian history, who had been made a deputy commisar of education in February 1919, he found him reorganizing elementary education rather than developing his theories about the origins of the Muscovite State. Not the least of Pokrovsky's worries was to feed the children ('if under these conditions we forced the children to go through all their lessons we should have corpses to teach, not children . . .'). After 1917 he could spare only half an evening weekly for historical research, he once wrote. There were historians of the older school who remained in the Soviet Union, but none of them was a Marxist and none, for obvious reasons, was much interested in contemporary history. The few major works about the revolution in the early twenties were written almost exclusively by eye witnesses who were not Bolsheviks (Sukhanov), or by oppositionists who took an enforced rest from political life (Shlyapnikov). Pokrovsky and his assistants tried during the early period of Soviet power to pave the way for subsequent studies by creating the organizational framework for the development of historical studies: the Socialist Academy was founded in 1918, the *Istpart* (Commission for the study of the party and the revolution) in 1920, the Institute of Red Professors and the Association for the study of the social sciences (RANION) in 1921. New periodicals came into being, such as *Krasny Arkhiv*, *Proletarskaia Revoliutsia*, *Istorik Marksist*, devoted largely to the collection and editing of archival materials, pertaining mainly to the pre-revolutionary period.

Perhaps most noteworthy among these collections was the multi-volume series about the *Fall of the Tsarist Régime*, based on the interrogations of Tsarist officials throughout 1917, the *Chronicle of the Revolution in 1917* published by the *Istpart* (in five volumes, 1923–6), and the series *1917 in Documents and Materials*, under the editorship of Pokrovsky and Yakovlev. A collection of essays on the October revolution written by Pokrovsky and some of his pupils at the Institute of Red Professors (1929) was the most valuable attempt at analysis from a communist angle undertaken in the nineteen-twenties.

No one tried his hand at a general history of the revolution and the post-revolutionary period, other than the briefest popular outlines. The old Bolsheviks felt that it was more important to make the revolution than to describe it; the time for writing history had not yet come; in any case the preconditions did not yet exist, a new generation of Marxist scholars had not yet come into being. There was also the conviction, especially on the part of Pokrovsky, the most influential by far of the official historians, that traditional history was bunk and should no longer be taught in schools and universities. It was not enough, in his view, to replace Klyuchevsky and the other pre-Marxist standard works with new textbooks. Pokrovsky advocated the replacement of the study of history by the study of 'socio-economic formations'. As a result, history was for some years not taught in Russian schools, its place being taken by some ill-defined sociological subjects. The study of 'formations', Pokrovsky thought, would provide the key not only to the historical laws of the past but also to the future: 'The knowledge of the past gives us power over the future', he wrote in the introduction to his *Russian History*. But historians were by no means the only ones interested in shaping the future; there seemed little point in perpetuating history as an academic discipline. Pokrovsky died in 1932; shortly after his death his school fell into disrepute; Stalin began to take a personal interest in the writing of Soviet history. Pokrovsky was accused of having clung to an economic determinism rather than to dialectical materialism. It was all very well, his critics said, to stress the class struggle and the role of merchant capital in Russian history. But Pokrovsky had clearly overdone it; he had belittled, even denied, other influences in history. His books dealt with socio-economic abstractions, human beings hardly figured in them. It is possible that Pokrovsky would have been forgiven for these mistakes, which in any case he had begun to correct towards the end of his life. But politically, his schemes were unsuitable in the thirties, and not only because Stalin did not figure in them. Nationalist trends inside the Soviet Union were one of the consequences of 'Socialism in one Country': Dmitri Donskoi and Ivan Grozny, Peter the Great, Suvorov and Kutuzov once again became heroes of Russian history. Such a patriotic upsurge was clearly incompatible with Pokrovsky's concepts. For him nationalism was a deadly sin; he had nothing but scorn for the national heroes of the past, in so far as they appeared at all in his writings. And so the Pokrovsky school had to disappear because it had done much harm by ignoring the study of the heroic traditions of the Russian people and by not arming its youth with feelings of love for their country and hatred for its enemies.

After Stalin's death Pokrovsky and his school were rescued from oblivion and rehabilitated – though not without reservations. But this is not the place to discuss these later developments, or the various manifestations of the new patriotic historiography before, during, and after the second world war; most of it relates to the writing of pre-revolutionary history. Until well into the thirties there were no new-style textbooks of Russian (or Soviet) history. One of the immediate assignments put to Soviet historians by Stalin in 1934 was to produce a text that could be widely used. A competition was organized but no history of twentieth-century Russia pleased the highly-placed jury. Instead an elementary school textbook prepared by Shestakov was selected for wide adoption. It covered the whole of Russian history from the early stone age to the Stalin constitution in little more than 200 pages. In its introduction it says that the Soviet Union is not only the only socialist country in the world but also the largest and the richest in natural resources:

The working people of the USSR are becoming more prosperous all the time, and their life is becoming better and happier . . . In no other country in the world is there such friendship among the various peoples as in the USSR . . . In the past our country was a backward country; now it has become the most advanced and mighty country in the world. That is why we love our country so much; that is why we are so proud of our USSR – the Land of Socialism . . . We love our country and we must know its wonderful history. Those who know history understand present-day life better, are better able to fight the enemies of our country, and make Socialism stronger.[10]

[10] Quoted from the 1938 English edition, *A Short History of the USSR*, Moscow, 1938, pp. 7–8.

The Stalin period produced this basic textbook on Russian history – to be followed by another, during the war, on Soviet history, but it stifled all other research and publications. The periodicals dealing with party and revolutionary history were discontinued, the association of Old Bolsheviks dissolved, and most of its members arrested. According to present-day Soviet comment, the history of the Soviet period suffered more than any other aspect of history from the impact of the 'Cult of the Individual', not merely because it codified Stalin's *obiter dicta* as the fountain-head of wisdom, but because historical research became physically impossible (transfer of archives to the police, etc.). The *Short Course* had been written not to stimulate historical research but to put an end to it. Perhaps the only works of that period likely to survive are histories of local factories. There was one major project probably inspired by Stalin himself; a five-volume history of the Civil War. The value of the first two volumes that appeared while Stalin was alive is about as great as that of the *Short Course*. Soon after Stalin's death the first attempts were made to release Soviet historiography from some of its most crippling shackles. That the situation under Stalin had been intolerable was now generally admitted. Mikoyan at the twentieth party congress said that 'most of our theoreticians are engaged in the repetition and rehashing in every possible way of old quotations, formulas and postulates'. And specifically about history: 'Research in the field of our party and Soviet society is, perhaps, the most backward sector of our ideological work.'

In the decade thereafter, Soviet historical research and writing greatly expanded. New periodicals were established, new institutions founded for the study of Soviet history. Access to archives again became possible, a great many collections of documents were published, including the protocols of past party congresses. A ten-volume *World History* was published and a five-volume history of the second world war. Other major projects, such as the *Historical Encyclopedia*, were still in progress; some were in an initial stage (the ten-volume history of the USSR, the history of industrialization in the USSR). But it is now possible without undue difficulty to summarize the character of post-Stalin Soviet historiography. After some uncertain probing (in 1956–8), the new official line has been firmly established. It has, broadly speaking, remained static and it is not likely to be basically modified unless there are substantial changes in Soviet domestic politics.

For the period up to 1923 the current official line sticks closely to Lenin. The main differences from the Stalin version are shifts in emphasis – with regard to the role of the Social-Revolutionaries, the Mensheviks, various old Bolsheviks, or such question as the periodization of the early history of Bolshevism. The major revisions concerning the Stalin period have already been indicated: Stalin's handling of the collectivization drive – but not the drive itself – is criticized, so is the persecution of the 'opposition' (and many who did not belong to it) beyond what seemed necessary. There is criticism of Stalin's policy on the eve of the second world war and during its early stages. The excesses of the 'cult of personality' during the last years of his life are condemned. Of Stalin's ambitions to pass as a major ideologist not much remains. But the overall assessment of Stalin, the faithful Leninist and successful organizer of party victories, remains positive, and is likely to remain so unless there are structural changes in the political system that he so largely moulded. History, after all, is not only a party science; it is, as Pokrovsky once wrote, *the most political* of all sciences. The historiography of the USSR is not merely a function of party politics – it *is* party politics. Throughout history there has been a close connection between history and politics, but never so close as in the Soviet Union. Elsewhere this had its compensations; the historians could, if they had such ambitions, make history from time to time. A Soviet Thiers or Guizot is unlikely to have such scope.

The late 1950s witnessed a great advance over the Stalin era, although at first there were illusions about the limits of the new orthodoxy, which were thought to be more elastic than they really are. Contrary to common belief, the post-Stalin period is not simply a return to the more propitious climate of the nineteen-twenties. Before Stalin established absolute power around 1929, historians of various schools both within the Marxist camp and even from outside were reasonably free to do research, to publish, and even to quarrel publicly. When the Society of Marxist Historians was founded in 1925 it had altogether forty members; by 1929 their number did not exceed 350. (In 1962 there were 17,000 historians in the Soviet Union, presumably all Marxist-Leninists.) Of these early Marxist historians the more prominent half was not composed of genuinely orthodox Old Bolsheviks. Of the members of the Socialist Academy, almost half were former Mensheviks (Ryazanov, Steklov, Larin, Veltman, Sukhanov), not to mention Bolshevik deviationists of 1906–9 vintage

153

(Bazarov, Bogdanov). Ryazanov, the greatest Marxologist of the time, and perhaps of all time, and head of the Marx-Engels Institute, declared in 1924 'I am not a Bolshevik, I am not a Menshevik, I am not a Leninist, I am only a Marxist, and as a Marxist, a Communist.'[11] A Soviet observer today notes with some chagrin that the name Lenin hardly appeared before 1924 in the party theoretical journals, and that even Pokrovsky had to admit in 1924 that he was not really familiar with Lenin's writings on history. The general consensus of opinion among Soviet historians (and philosophers and economists) was that Lenin's genius was that of a practical politician, not a theoretician, that he had provided a method, not a doctrine.[12] Leninism as a doctrine appeared only after Lenin had died and Lenin's contemporaries had disappeared. The basic difference between the sixties and the twenties is that a historian needs now not merely to accept Marxism in general, he has to subscribe to a far more specific and narrowly-defined doctrine, developed first in the late twenties, and in particular under Stalin, that has been modified in some, but not in its essential aspects since Stalin's death. This means not only theoretical acceptance but also identification with the current party line, and it implies a far higher degree of unanimity than in the twenties. It precludes any individual approach and opinion. It does not necessarily mean absolute rigidity; reliance on Lenin has its compensations. Lenin was not a historian, and never dealt systematically with historical subjects. In his books there are comments which can be adduced in support of a great many sometimes conflicting interpretations of Russian history in the nineteenth and the early twentieth century. For more recent events the Leninist concepts provide no concrete guidance; Lenin could not, after all, foresee how the second world war would be fought, or how the problems of the kolkhoz in a communist society would be solved. 'Leninism' in the context of Soviet history after Lenin's death means, therefore, no more than a number of general principles than can be applied by different people in different ways in accordance with changing exigencies.

The history of the Communist party of the Soviet Union and of Soviet society is likely to retain its Cinderella status. These disciplines involve so many difficulties and are exposed to so many changes that most historians touch these subjects only with reluctance.

---

[11] *Vestnik Kommunisticheskoi Akademii*, 1924, 8, p. 392.

[12] M. E. Naidenov, 'O Leninskoi Etape v istoricheskoi nauke', in *Voprosy Istorii* 2, 1966, pp. 28–9.

There have been complaints that less and less Soviet history is taught in Soviet schools, that such courses have disappeared altogether from the universities of Marxism–Leninism and the nonhistorical faculties in the universities. It has been noted that the new *Historical Encyclopedia* devotes less than 40 per cent of its space to the history of the Soviet Union, and that a chair for party history in a university can get only a fraction of the financial allocation of other chairs. Nor is the prestige of the contemporary historian very high: of roughly 6,000 teachers of the History of the CPSU at institutes of higher learning, only thirty-two are professors or senior lecturers. These complaints are manifestations of a deeper malaise – the sterility of dogmatism and the Nessus shirt of the almost constantly changing party line. In theory dogmatism has never been a virtue in Soviet eyes. Even under Stalin the creative character of the Marxist–Leninist method was always stressed. The *Short Course* proclaimed that Marxist–Leninist theory must not be regarded as a collection of dogmas, a catechism and a symbol of faith, and the Marxists themselves as pedants and dogmatists; the science of the development of society cannot stand still but develops and perfects itself; some of its propositions and conclusions are bound to be replaced by new conclusions and propositions corresponding to the new historical conditions. The 1959 post-Stalin *History* repeats in the same terms the injunction to develop Marxism creatively, to discard outworn formulas. It mentions some revisions ('Enrichments', 'brilliant discoveries'), such as Lenin's realization that communism could not triumph simultaneously in all capitalist countries but that capitalism could be broken at its weakest link. Other creative developments of Marxism–Leninism noted in this context are the discovery of people's democracy as a new form of the dictatorship of the proletariat, and Khrushchev's report at the twentieth party congress about peaceful coexistence and the possibility of averting wars in our epoch.

Such creative development and enrichment of Marxism–Leninism is, however, the monopoly of those who make history, not of the historians who write it. There may be scope for fruitful research and new discovery in medieval history or in Latin American studies; there is no such scope in the field of party history and the history of Soviet society. In these fields, too, the general line will change, and the changes may come sooner and be more far-reaching than we assume today. In all probability the national element will figure more strongly in future in Soviet and party historiography; there will be

155

new friends and new enemies. But these decisions will not be made by the historians.

Each discipline attracts people with a certain predisposition and for the same reason repels others. However staunchly convinced of the rightness of the communist cause, promising Soviet historians are not likely to be attracted into a field which combines the insecurity of sudden change with the lack of scope for individual creativeness and initiative.

History, or at any rate, histories, have been written for a very long time, whereas modern historiography with its strict rules about evidence and integrity is barely two hundred years old. Over long periods historians were told by their elders and betters how to do their job, beginning perhaps with the Pariscop Villas in the Inca Empire, who, upon the death of an Emperor, were advised of the themes which were to serve as the fabric of their narratives and poems. Writing history was considered until relatively recently a dangerous occupation; Luther once said that whoever wishes to write history must have the heart of a lion. The rise of history in Europe as an independent and critical discipline coincides with the overthrow of absolutist rule. Contemporary history even now remains more than any other historical discipline exposed to outside influences; it can flourish only in a temperate climate.

« 8 »

Interpretations of Soviet History

The news of the French Revolution spread like wildfire and the sun of 1793 continued to warm many a radical heart in France and all over Europe throughout the nineteenth century. The impact of the Russian Revolution was far more gradual; the world war was still on, communications between Russia and the outside world almost non-existent.[1] Unlike France, Russia had never been a centre of European culture; few non-Russians knew the language. When Western radical intellectuals came to accept the cause of the Russian Revolution as their own almost a decade had passed since 1917; the Bolsheviks had lasted far longer than the Jacobins. The French Revolution had remained unfinished, a great promise in the eyes of those who hoped that a subsequent revolution (1830, 1848) would carry on where Robespierre had left off.

In Russia revolutionary ideals had already collided with harsh realities, but there was, and remained, a tremendous residue of enthusiasm for the Russian Revolution in Europe and America. Even if there was not necessarily full support for and identification with any and every turn in Soviet domestic and foreign policies, the assumption was that the Bolsheviks were basically right. Their cause

---

[1] How bad communications were, and why a Western newspaper reader could not possibly understand what was happening, emerges from a perusal of *The Times* during the critical days. This was one of the very few newspapers with a correspondent of its own in Petrograd, yet on 6 and 7 November 1917 it carried no major stories from Russia. On 8 November: RUSSIAN FRONT QUIET. On 9 November: M. KERENSKY AND THE SOVIET. GROWTH OF MAXIMALIST INFLUENCE. LENIN'S VISIT TO BERLIN. And then LATE WAR NEWS: AN ORGANIZED OUTBREAK. M. KERENSKY'S MOVEMENTS. 'So far as can be ascertained, the Soviet movement began on Tuesday evening, with the occupation of certain points, such as the post office . . .' What 'Soviet movement?' Why the post office? readers were bound to ask. Mr Wilton, in his book *Russia's Agony* published in 1918, features a picture of Lenin and Trotsky of which it can be said with absolute certainty that it depicts neither Lenin nor Trotsky. (The man purported to be Lenin bears a certain resemblance to D. H. Lawrence.) Whatever his feelings towards them, a leading Petrograd correspondent ought to have known what the rulers of Russia looked like. Yet this incident was typical of the general level of information.

was going to prevail all over the world and they merited support even if they were sometimes mistaken in their tactics, and even if the revolution elsewhere was bound to take place in different conditions and to assume a different political character. The Bolsheviks, in the eyes of their Western supporters, stood for progress, humanism, and a world without war; the only realistic political alternative to Bolshevism was black reaction. It is impossible to understand Western reactions to the Russian Revolution, Soviet Russia, and subsequent Soviet history without taking account of this great reservoir of goodwill among intellectuals in the nineteen-twenties and thirties. Even those who regretfully parted company with them did not repent (to paraphrase a famous saying) that they once had faith and force enough to cherish generous hopes of Russia's destiny, that they could once think better of Russia than it probably deserved.

Against them was arrayed the camp of those who were unalterably opposed to the Russian Revolution, who thought that it was a purely negative and destructive event that was bound to bring Russia to ruin. Gustav Le Bon wrote in 1920 that Cain had been the first Bolshevik. Merezhkovski saw the hand of the Antichrist in the events that had taken place in Russia; others provided an explanation without reference to the Bible or transcendental forces. But all in this camp agreed that it was a disaster.

There was enthusiastic assent and bitter opposition, but there were also many shades in between. To classify the many and often highly complex views on Russia voiced during that period as friendly and hostile would often have been a gross over-simplification; in later years such a scheme would not have worked at all. Historians were under no pressure to vote for Russia or against; they could afford to make reservations or even suspend judgment. Classification, like generalization, is necessary and useful, given a constant awareness of its limitations; but there will never be a Linnaeus in historiography. As a rule, it is not difficult to establish where the basic sympathies and antipathies of a historian lie, but these are neither permanent nor logically consistent. Recently, Professor Billington made a challenging attempt to summarize opinion on the Russian Revolution; he introduced an intricate division of six groups (including an accidental -pathetic and an ironic school of thought).[2] But even such a sophisticated attempt cannot do justice to the manifold views and schools of

[2] James H. Billington, 'Six Views of the Russian revolution', in *World Politics*, April 1966, pp. 452–73.

thought; it has to lump together in the 'visionary-futuristic' section Marxists such as Trotsky and mystics such as Andrei Bely and Alexander Blok. There are other reasons which make classification almost impossible; human beings have a tendency to revise their views from time to time. Some of the most enthusiastic friends of the Russian Revolution ended up as its bitterest critics; some of the early relentless enemies became its foremost advocates two decades later. For these reasons I have refrained wherever possible from systematic classification. The presentation of individual views may be less orderly as a result, but I hope I have done less injustice to them than would have been involved in an attempt to find common denominators for dissimilar attitudes.

Pitfalls of Academe

Western opinion on Russia in the nineteen twenties and thirties was shaped not only by what happened in the Soviet Union, but also to a growing extent by events at home. Beginning with the early twenties, writing on the Soviet Union became, by and large, better informed. There was a certain retreat from extreme positions; the Bolsheviks' sworn enemies began to realize that Lenin had perhaps not destroyed Russia altogether; the early admirers were disturbed by the struggle for power after Lenin's death, by the steady disappearance of inner-party democracy in Moscow, and by other such developments. Stalin's second revolution, the transformation of Soviet agriculture and, of course, the five-year plans, took on a significance they would never have assumed had it not been for the world economic crisis that overtook the West at the same time. The claim that Russia had no unemployed would never have made the impression it did but for the many millions of unemployed in Central and Western Europe and in the United States. Again, Hitler's rise to power and the third Reich had a tremendous impact on the change in attitude towards the Soviet Union, culminating in the wartime alliance between 1941 and 1945.

Few students of Russia were not profoundly influenced by the purges of the late Stalin period. Publicists often reacted with an all-out attack, and their strictures against Stalin often turned into a condemnation of socialism and even of liberalism. Quite a few academics, on the other hand, leaned far backwards in their endeavour not to be caught up in the general trend. Has the charge that has often been made by Soviet censors against their Western colleagues, that they were unduly influenced by anti-communist hysteria, really been justified? Adam Ulam has commented on some of the strange fruits of Soviet studies in American universities in the nineteen-thirties and forties:

> In his attempt to learn as much as possible about the Soviet Union, X between roughly 1930 and 1950 read nothing but the works of reputable non-Communist authors. He grounded himself on the works of the Webbs and Sir John Maynard. Turning to the American academicians he followed the studies of the Soviet government, law and various aspects of Soviet society which might have come from the pen of a professor at Chicago, Harvard, Columbia or Williams. This serious intellectual fare would be supplemented by the reading of the most objective non-academic experts on Russia, and finally of those few journalists who had no axe to grind, especially the ones who had spent a long time in Russia.
>
> His friend Y had an equal ambition to learn, but his taste ran to the non-scholarly and melodramatic. Indifferent to objectivity, he would seek the key to Soviet politics in the writings of the avowed enemies of the régime like the ex-Mensheviks; he would delight in the fictional accounts à la Koestler and Victor Serge. Sinking lower, Y would pursue trashy or sensational stories of the 'I was a Prisoner of the Red Terror' variety. He would infuriate X by insisting that there were aspects of Soviet politics which are more easily understood by studying the struggle between Al Capone and Dan Torrio than the one between Lenin and Martov, or the dispute about 'socialism in one country'. Which of our fictitious characters would have been in a better position to understand the nature of Soviet politics under Stalin? Of course, this confrontation is not quite fair. There was a number of scholarly works which were quite realistic and dared to call a spade a spade. But in general it remains true that the average Anglo-American academician writing of the Soviet Union during the period under discussion approached categories like the 'police state', 'terror', 'totalitarianism' with the same trepidation and distaste as the Victorian novelist felt when he had to allude to the sexual act . . .[3]

If there was a bias among academic students of Soviet affairs in England and America in that period, it worked more often than not in favour of Stalin's régime. For academics are committed by hallowed tradition to measured comment and moderate opinions. Such an education has great advantages but it is not ideally suited for coping with extreme historical situations and régimes that are not moderate in character. Unable to overcome their habitual pattern of thought,

[3] Adam Ulam, 'U S A: Some critical reflections', in *The State of Soviet Studies*, ed. W. Laqueur, Cambridge, 1965, p. 15.

the academic will be tempted to describe extremist rule as far more moderate, reasonable, and normal than it really is.

That Western attitudes to Russia were influenced by events in the West was inevitable, and it was not necessarily detrimental. For events in the West helped in some ways to promote a better understanding of the significance of the Russian revolution. Distortion set in only when the impact became too overwhelming or when Western students accepted passing political phases or intellectual fashions as permanent and absolute. This is all very obvious in retrospect; at the time, it was admittedly far more difficult to form correct judgments, especially for observers in societies and political régimes so totally different from the Soviet Union of that period.

Early German interpretations

Among the writings on Russia in the nineteen-twenties those in Germany deserve special mention. Germany was, by and large, the country best informed about Russia; this had been traditionally so. The German *Ostforschung* was far in advance of that of other Western countries. But it was also politically easier to form a correct appraisal from a Berlin observation point than from London or New York. True, there were some interesting books by British and French professors and publicists, such as for instance James Mavor's massive study of the Russian Revolution published in 1928. While admitting that Bolshevism had become entrenched, Mavor thought that with Bolshevik methods no economic progress or social advance was possible. Most German writers commenting on Soviet developments in the late twenties would have provided less categorical answers, whether they were friendly disposed towards the Soviet Union or not. They were more aware of what would now be called the ideological challenge of communism; in Germany, after all, there was not only more information available on Russia; it had also – in contrast to England and America at that time – a numerous and vocal left-wing intelligentsia with an intense interest in socialist theory and practice. A serious British or American writer was far more likely to write with contempt about the Soviet lack of discipline and orderliness, and the general inefficiency; a communist ideological threat they could visualize only with reference to countries like India. German observers like Feiler, Gurian, or Arthur Rosenberg, to pick three at random, would comment in a different vein, writing as they did in the uncertain political climate of the Weimar republic.[4] Feiler, an economist by training, thought that the Bolshevik experiment should not be underrated; it was of gigantic size and it was far too early to predict either success or failure. He thought that every revolution was an experiment of terrible grandeur, never entirely good or bad but both good and bad at the same time. Like Fülop-Miller and some other contemporaries, he overrated the desire of Bolshevism to 'collectivize' the individual.

Gurian, a theologian and philosopher by training, was extremely critical of Bolshevism; but he was also far from belittling its potential significance. German writers in the twenties, it has already been noted, were on the whole less inclined than their British, French, or American colleagues to take the existing social and political order of things for granted. Gurian saw Bolshevism as an attempt to catch up with Europe, to modernize the country, and he had a high opinion of the political acumen of the Bolsheviks; Lenin, he wrote, was far from being a fanatic. Bolshevism was both the product of bourgeois society and its most decisive challenge. Gurian was also one of the first to stress the character of Bolshevism as a new religion; Keynes had drawn a similar parallel during a visit to Russia in the twenties and Berdyaev was to develop the theme subsequently. According to Gurian, it meant that Bolshevism could not be combatted with political and social arguments; only another religion, a total absolute *Weltanschauung*, could be dangerous to Bolshevism as a *Heilslehre*, a messianic movement. From the Catholic point of view this was certainly a new and far more sophisticated approach to Bolshevism than the traditional tirades against godless Bolshevism. After the second world war some of these views, notably that only a total world view could successfully compete with communism, gained for a while acceptance in some circles.

If Gurian's vantage point was modern Catholicism, Arthur Rosenberg's ideological basis was Western Marxism. He had been a leading communist, member of the Reichstag fraction, but left the party because he thought Bolshevism a specific Russian phenomenon, inapplicable in other parts of Europe. His appraisal of the revolution

[4] Arthur Feiler, *Das Experiment des Bolschewismus*, Frankfurt, 1929, translated as *The Experiment of Bolshevism*, London, 1930. Waldemar Gurian, *Der Bolschewismus*, Freiburg, 1931, translated as *Bolshevism, Theory and Practice*, London, 1932. Arthur Rosenberg, *Geschichte des Bolschewismus*, Berlin, 1932, translated as *History of Bolshevism*, London, 1934. All three authors eventually went to the United States and became professors.

of 1917 was positive without reservation. Bolshevism had achieved what it set out to do: with the help of the proletariat it had overthrown Tsarism and completed the bourgeois revolution. It had overcome Russia's backwardness and introduced a state-capitalist form of economic organization. But the heroic feats of the Russian workers had made people overlook that while Bolshevism had been a progressive force in Russia it was reactionary when applied in Western and Central Europe, where the bourgeois revolution had been achieved long before. For that reason it was mistaken to assume that the working-class movements outside Russia would follow the Bolshevist lead; even in Asia the Comintern had not made much headway. The international bourgeoisie was right to fear the international proletariat and the world revolution. But Russian Bolshevism was really no menace from their point of view. These ideas, first developed by Rosenberg, gained wide currency especially among the left in Western Europe and America in the thirties: the achievements of Bolshevism and the Soviet government were extolled but the claims of the Comintern to lead the international working-class movement were rejected.

Having left the communists, Rosenberg became an independent socialist. But most socialists would not have agreed with his views on the Russian Revolution. The European continental socialist movement was in its majority anti-Bolshevik with the exception, to be sure, of some groups on the extreme left. A non-Marxist radical like Bertrand Russell took a position much closer to that of Rosa Luxemburg, suggesting that ultimately the stand taken by an outsider depended on his character, his revolutionary enthusiasm, his sympathies or antipathies, rather than on theoretical considerations about the proletarian revolution and its socio-economic prerequisites. Both Luxemburg and Kautsky anticipated the failure of the Russian Revolution; 'of course, they will not be able to maintain themselves,' Luxemburg wrote, but she nevertheless gave the Russian revolution enthusiastic support whereas Kautsky bitterly opposed it.[5]

[5] For Rosa Luxemburg's views on the Russian revolution see: *Die russische Revolution*, Berlin, 1922, English edition, London, 1922, and various other editions; see also the biographies of Rosa Luxemburg by Paul Froelich and J. P. Nettl; K. Kautsky, *Terrorismus und Kommunismus*, Berlin, 1919, English ed., London, 1920; also his later collections, *Bolshevism at a Deadlock*, London, 1931 and *Social Democracy versus Communism*, New York, 1946; Bertrand Russell, *The Practice and Theory of Bolshevism*, London, 1920; Martov's writings were published in *Mysl*, Kharkov, in 1919, in the *Sotsialisticheski Vestnik*, Berlin, in 1921, in *Mirovoi Bolshevism*, Berlin, 1923, and *The State and the Socialist Revolution*, New York, 1938.

The Socialist critics

When the Bolshevik revolution took place Rosa Luxemburg was in a German prison; her famous critique came out eight months later. Her disagreements with Lenin went back many years, and arose partly from the disputes about Marxism and national self-determination; this is, however, of no immediate interest in the present context. But Rosa Luxemburg was also critical of the Bolsheviks' pressing for an immediate peace treaty; Hindenburg and the German nationalists would (she wrote) have the last laugh, for Russia's capitulation would only stiffen the hopes of the German militarists. She also opposed immediate distribution of the land to the peasants; this was not a step in the direction of socialist policy in agriculture and it would also create a new and powerful stratum of enemies of socialism, but she conceded that the mistakes of the Bolsheviks were only partly their fault. They were caught in a cleft stick, in an impossible situation, and all they could do was to choose between two evils. Others were responsible for the fact that the devil was the beneficiary of the Russian Revolution. Social-democracy in the highly developed West consisted of wretched and miserable cowards who would look quietly on and let the Russians bleed to death. The doubts she had about the Russian Revolution had arisen more from the objective circumstances than from the Bolsheviks' subjective actions, it was the fatal logic of the objective situation that every socialist party which came to power in Russia was bound to follow false tactics, so long as the advance guard of the international proletarian army was left in the lurch by the main body.

But there was one aspect of the Russian revolution for which it was difficult, or even impossible, to find mitigating circumstances – the trend towards the concentration of political power in very few hands. Rosa Luxemburg commented on this in a prophetic passage:

. . . with the repression of political life in the land as a whole life in the Soviets must also become more and more crippled. Without general elections, without unrestricted freedom of press and assembly, without a free struggle of opinion, life dies out in every public institution, becomes a mere semblance of life, in which only the bureaucracy remains as the active element. Public life gradually falls asleep, a few dozen party leaders of inexhaustible energy and boundless experience direct and rule. Among them in reality only a dozen outstanding heads do the leading and an *élite* of the working class is invited from time to time to meetings where they are to applaud the speeches of the leaders, and to approve proposed resolutions unanimously: at bottom, then, a clique affair – a dictatorship, to be sure, not the dictatorship of the proletariat, however, but only the dictatorship of a handful of politicians, that is a dictatorship in the bourgeois sense of the rule of the Jacobins . . . Yes, we can go even further; such conditions must inevitably cause a brutalization of public life; attempted assassinations, shooting of hostages, etc. . . .

The Bolsheviks were and still are unhappy that Rosa Luxemburg 'being insufficiently informed' (as they put it), misjudged the tactics of the Bolsheviks. They note that after her release from prison she changed her views. Whether this is so we do not know, for Rosa Luxemburg refrained from commenting on the Russian Revolution during the last few months of her life after her release. This, however, had more to do with the German than with the Russian Revolution; 'Spartacus' had imposed an embargo on any criticism of the Soviet state.

Some of Luxemburg's criticism was tactical in character – that part, for instance, which concerned the agrarian policy of the Bolsheviks. But her views on the future of democracy in Russia are in a different category; they reflect the basic differences between Western and Eastern Marxism. Let us assume that Luxemburg was justified in saying that Russia was the only country where revolutionary ideals still had some value, whereas the Western socialists were 'miserable cowards'. As a good Marxist, should Luxemburg have put so much stress on heroism and cowardice? Were there not good objective reasons why the revolutionary potential was so much greater in the East than in the more developed countries of Europe? What should Lenin have done in the circumstances? Should he have abdicated because the expected support from the Western European proletariat did not come? Luxemburg wrote that any defeat, even the ruin of the Bolsheviks in honest struggle in the teeth of the historical situation, might be preferable to the moral collapse of the Social-Democrats. But the real dilemma of the Russian Revolution was exactly the opposite: it was victory in the teeth of the historical situation, with all its consequences. Whether Rosa Luxemburg's hope that the rising of the European proletariat would not only have saved the Bolsheviks from their immediate isolation but also helped them to overcome the internal dangers – dictatorship and 'brutalization of political life' – is open to question. Can it be said with any certainty that the dangers Rosa Luxemburg predicted

165

were rooted only in Russia's past and in its isolation after 1917? Kautsky had been the keeper of ideological purity in the international socialist movement, the teacher of revisionists and revolutionaries alike. True, there had been a gradual estrangement from the left-wing radicals in the years before the first world war and the rift became wider after 1914. While not a 'defencist', Kautsky refused to go along with Liebknecht's and Lenin's revolutionary defeatism. He was attacked by the critics from the left for adhering to the letter of Marxism while lacking entirely its revolutionary spirit. This may have been a correct appraisal of Kautsky, but did not Kautsky's politics reflect the adjustment of Marxism to a country in which a revolutionary situation did not exist? Was it therefore assailable from the orthodox Marxist point of view? Soon after the October Revolution, Kautsky came out against the Bolsheviks: he admitted that dictatorship as a form of government in Russia now was as understandable as the anarchism of Bakunin. Freedom was a new thing in Russia, it had no roots among the people. But to understand this did not mean to justify it. There were two roads open to Lenin – the united front of all socialists, or the dictatorship of the Bolsheviks over all the rest. As a result of Lenin's policy a new autocracy with its militarist bureaucratic machinery was set up, and since Lenin did not have the confidence of the majority of the working class, it was compelled to employ terror.

The consequences, according to Kautsky, would be that the methods of Soviet Russian communism would achieve exactly the opposite result from the one promised. Socialism without democracy was impossible, and not to have understood this was the cardinal sin of Bolshevism. Dictatorship, like war, Kautsky wrote, was easy to start, but one could not get out of it if and when one wanted.

Kautsky underrated the fanatical dedication of the Bolsheviks and the strength of their organization. For many years after the revolution, he expected Bolshevism to collapse. He thought the Bolsheviks would never advance beyond some form of primitive state capitalism, and make substantial economic progress; whatever their subjective intentions, soon nothing would remain but the naked violence of the dictatorship. Kautsky's expectations with regard to the collapse of Bolshevism were decisively refuted by the subsequent course of events, but five decades of Soviet history have also shown that his fears about the character of a socialist state that dispenses with democracy were only too justified.

The dilemma of another Marxist, Julius Martov, was even more painful. For obvious reasons it was easier for a socialist to criticize the Bolsheviks from outside; what would Kautsky have done in Russia, facing the counter-revolution? Martov was convinced that conditions in his country were not ripe for a socialist revolution. The dictatorship of the working class was impossible there; what could be achieved was, at most, the dictatorship of a number of professional revolutionaries. Sovietism would give way to such a dictatorship and would lead the Bolsheviks along a road they had not really intended to take. Yet at the same time Martov stressed the revolutionary character of the dictatorship; he opposed the economic blockade of Russia, denounced the campaign of vilification against Bolshevism, and called his followers to join the Red Army to defeat Kolchak and Denikin. It was possible, on a philosophical level, to combine a critique of Bolshevism with the defence of the Soviet Union. But how could this be done in politics, and in face of the monolithic character of the Communist party and the Soviet state? It was an impossible situation; Lenin helped to resolve it by exiling Martov and the other leading Mencheviks. Yet the basic dilemma continued to face left-wing socialists throughout the twenties and thirties. In a modified form it has existed to this very day, and we shall have to deal with it further on.

Bertrand Russell (subsequently Earl Russell) visited Russia in early 1920. Following his visit he published a book that has retained more interest than any other document of that early period of the Russian Revolution. More than thirty years later it was reprinted without change. Russell, from the very beginning, enjoyed certain advantages: unlike Kautsky, Martov, or Rosa Luxemburg, he was not a political leader; he was speaking for no one but himself. He did not have to provide practical answers to pressing political questions for his followers, nor did he have to take any decisions. In the absence of such responsibilities, in the sphere of pure thought, in which there is room for half tones, qualified phrases and reservations, the elegant phrase and the detached view, it is no doubt easier to analyse historical processes.

The Russian Revolution, in Russell's view, was an event greater in importance than its French predecessor; Bolshevism deserved the admiration and gratitude of all progressive mankind. The holders of power outside Russia were evil men and their social and political system was doomed. Russell was in full agreement with the ideals of the Bolsheviks; he criticized them only when their methods seemed to depart from their own ideals. He disliked the militant certainty and dogmatic beliefs of Lenin and the other Bolshevik leaders; with all his antipathy to the Western world, he himself shared its sceptical temper, he had been brought up in the tradition of the love of liberty: 'I went to Russia as a Communist; but contact with those who have no doubt has intensified a thousandfold my own doubts, not as to Communism in itself, but as to the wisdom of holding a creed so firmly that for its sake men are willing to inflict widespread misery.' This scepticism raises what is no doubt the most important question for Russell: will the price that will have to be paid be worth it? True, the benefits of communism, once achieved, would be lasting. But would a social system such as the communists envisaged result from the adoption of their methods? Or would not the decades of bitter struggle result in the brutalization of political life? Was it really right to assume that there was no slavery but economic slavery and that there would be perfect liberty once the means of production had been nationalized? Russell's political philosophy is not Marxist; he thought that the materialist conception of history left out very important human instincts and desires. Was it not almost inevitable that the Bolshevik leadership would be loth to relinquish their monopoly of power? He saw no reason whatever 'to expect equality and freedom to result from such a system except reasons derived from a false psychology and a mistaken analysis of the sources of political power'. And so he came in the end to reject Bolshevism because the price for realizing it was too high and because he believed that the result would not be what the Bolsheviks professed to desire. Communism could be achieved only if it was inaugurated in a developed and prosperous country and if the transition were gradual. When Russell wrote about the 'tragic fatality' brooding over Russia and Bolshevism he did not mean that the communists were bound to be defeated by their external enemies:

It may be that Russia needs sternness and discipline more than anything else; it may be that the revival of Peter the Great's methods is essential to progress. From this point of view, much of what is natural to criticize in the Bolsheviks becomes defensible; but this point of view has little affinity to Communism. Bolshevism may be defended possibly as a dire discipline through which a backward nation is to be rapidly industrialized; but as an experiment in Communism it has failed.

Russell's views on Russia, and especially on Soviet foreign policy, continued to change; in the nineteen-forties and fifties they led him on occasion into extreme positions of rejection and admiration. But these latter day comments were connected mainly with the over-riding menace of the nuclear age, which made the preservation of peace an even more urgent task than the struggle for a new social system. On the basic questions of the Russian Revolution he did not comment later on, and, since his early book was published in the fifties without comment, it is doubtful whether Earl Russell has changed his views in any substantial way. *The Practice and Theory of Bolshevism* remains probably the most brilliant essay on the character and prospects of the Russian Revolution ever written; it is a triumph of what Russell called that temper of constructive and fruitful scep-ticism which constitutes the scientific outlook. It shows that political analysis can be undertaken and contemporary history written even at a time of revolutionary change.

The prodigal sons

One of the great difficulties in putting labels on commentators and opinions on the Russian Revolution is the fact that time does not stand still. This tritest of observations needs to be made from time to time. Historians, politicians, and publicists have sometimes changed their opinions in an extreme way as the result of events in Russia and in the world in general. Mention has been made of the fact that some of the most severe critics of the Russian revolution subsequently became sympathizers or even fervent advocates of the Soviet cause. The name of Prince Mirsky has been mentioned; there was the 'Smena Vekh' group in Paris and Prague in the early twenties, which advised its members to return, since Russia needed them. Their Russian patriotism proved to be stronger than the political antag-onism that had made them oppose Lenin in 1917–8. Life in Russia would be hard; they had no illusions on this score. But at least there would be hope instead of the all pervasive despair of the emigration in Europe. Ideological rationalization proceeded on various lines; some, such as Prince Mirsky, were converted to Marxism–Leninism. Others like Ustryalov, predicted a return to 'normalcy' in the Soviet Union, and thought that time would greatly modify the Soviet régime. Lenin and his comrades who had set out to achieve inter-nationalism would make Russia stronger than ever before. Among those who returned were some of the greatest names in contemporary

Russian literature – Alexei Tolstoi, Ilya Ehrenburg, Marina Tsvetaeva, Alexander Kuprin. Few non-communist politicians actually returned, but there was a sizable number of men in each political party, ranging from the far left to the far right who late in life accepted what may broadly be called 'Soviet patriotism'.

Soviet spokesmen have claimed from time to time that much of the misinformation spread about their country was the work of *émigrés* in key positions in the press or in the field of Russian studies. Recently a Russian commentator drew attention to the fact that about 30 per cent of all those engaged in Soviet studies in the United States are of foreign origin, immigrants.[6] There is no denying that, especially during the early years after the revolution, emigrants played a harmful role in disseminating misinformation about events in Russia. Russian *émigrés* brought the 'Protocols of the Elders of Zion' to Germany, Britain, and America. On Russia there was not much expertise in the Western capitals in those years and some of the emigrant publications only added to the general confusion. Yet this is certainly not true for the later periods – quite apart from the fact that the defeated have the same right as the victors to comment on the history of their native country. If the writings of some were so emotionally charged as to be of little value, the accounts of others were almost astonishingly objective considering how directly they had been involved in the events described. Even Soviet historians will hardly dispute the value of Denikin's memoirs or of the *Archives of the Russian Revolution* published in Berlin – to give but two examples. If some *émigrés* continued to take an intransigently hostile line towards the Soviet Union, others, including such prominent men as Dan and other leaders of the Russian emigration, became strongly pro-Soviet towards the end of their lives. Among leading Western exponents of the Marxist line on Russia, from Baran to Deutscher, from Herbert Marcuse to Rudolf Schlesinger, the majority are of eastern or central European origin. Soviet fears about the baneful influence of the *émigrés* seems therefore misplaced. At most they could argue (as Oliver said about the Jews in 'Jean Christophe') that they were both among their greatest friends and bitterest enemies.

The case of a Russian Social Democrat like Theodor Dan is far more complicated than that of the Russian *émigrés*, the 'returners'

---

[6] V. P. Kanevski in *Voprosy Istorii*, 5, 1966, p. 182. The author includes in his statistics emigrants not only from Eastern Europe, but also from Central and Western Europe as well as other parts of the world.

who, first and foremost Russian patriots without any very distinct ideology, decided to throw in their lot with 'Sovietism' in the early twenties. Dan had been one of the leaders of Menshevism in 1917, and after Martov's death became the head of the party in the emigration. He had been one of the sharpest critics of Bolshevism, a régime which he had defined as a terrorist dictatorship that had nothing to do with socialism and democracy.[7] But in the late thirties and especially during the second world war Dan and some of his followers, such as Yugov and Max Werner (Alexander Schifrin), came to accept Stalin's domestic and foreign policy almost without reservation; Bolshevism had now become the bearer of the key idea of the age, a direct child of the revolutionary struggle of Russian social-democracy. The dictatorship of 1917 had been necessary; there was no other way in a country like Russia, but the demo-cratization of the Soviet régime began almost from the very first day; the Stalin constitution had been a further great step forward. Dan and his friends admired the great achievements of Soviet power. Western capitalist democracy, on the other hand, was doomed: the Soviet régime would become ever more democratic and in this way the 'Russian idea' was becoming universal and would prevail all over the world. Dan died soon after the second world war; there is no saying whether he would once more have modified his views had he lived longer.

The profound change in the attitude of men like Dan can be ex-plained without undue difficulty by reference to the rise of fascism. The impact of Hitler in particular was tremendous, even if it did not always induce socialists to change their attitude to Russia so radi-cally as in the case of Dan. But it had a palpable effect on liberal and socialist opinion throughout the Western world. The impact was powerful, in particular, on Marxists; Western Marxists had asserted all along that the Soviet Union was not a socialist country, that it was deviating from pure Marxist doctrine, and that it was bound to stray even further in future. They were also convinced that such a mistaken policy would lead to setbacks on all fronts. But the years passed, the means of production remained nationalized, and it became more and more difficult to argue from orthodox Marxist premises that the Soviet Union was not a socialist country. At the same time there were

[7] See for instance: Martov-Dan, *Die Geschichte der russischen Sozialdemokratie*, Berlin, 1926, pp. 304–5; for his later views, *The Origins of Bolshevism*, London, 1964, Epilogue.

considerable achievements, especially in heavy industry, and there could be no doubts about the growth of Soviet power. In the circumstances there were but two ways open to orthodox Marxists; to admit, like Dan, that they had been wrong and Lenin and Stalin right; or to realize, albeit belatedly (like Hilferding in a famous essay), that the Soviet Union constituted a new phenomenon that could not be measured against the traditional schema of the correlation between state and economy; that the fact that the means of production were nationalized and that a country had a plan did not *per se* provide evidence of the political character of the régime; that, in other words, the economic character of a régime did not necessarily determine its political character. Hilferding concluded his essay by saying that the controversies as to whether the Soviet Union was 'capitalist' or 'socialist' seemed to him pointless: 'It is neither. It represents a totalitarian state economy.'

Ultimately, it again boiled down to the question whether there could be socialism without democracy. Dan and his friends opted for the first alternative, and so did other left-wing socialists throughout Europe in the thirties. Their ideas were expressed most forcefully and systematically by Otto Bauer, the leader and ideologist of the Austrian Social-Democrats. Bauer, too, had been critical of Bolshevism in the early years, but in the twenties he began to advocate co-operation with the Soviet Union in the ranks of the Socialist International. In the thirties, under the impact of fascism, he went even further and declared that the Soviet Union was the leader of the working class everywhere, that the victory of socialism in the USSR was now a fact, the most important fact in world politics, that the social order established there was immensely superior to that of any other country. The cause of the Soviet Union was the cause of socialists everywhere; they were in duty bound to propagate its tremendous achievements all over the globe.[8] True, the Soviet Union was not yet as democratic as Bauer wanted it to be, and he stressed that the international proletariat should not refrain from criticism when measures taken by the Soviet leaders seemed to contradict the 'historical task of progressive democratization of the Soviet régime'. But since Bauer, again on the basis of his own brand of Marxism, thought such democratization inevitable, there could be disagreements, he thought, between him and Stalin only on secondary,

[8] For O. Bauer's views see, in particular, *Zwischen Zwei Weltkriegen*, Bratislava, 1936.

tactical, not on fundamental issues. Bauer died at the time of the purges, a disappointed man; had he lived a few years longer he would no doubt, as Dan did, have drawn fresh inspiration for his concept of Soviet development from the wartime alliance.

Bernard Pares (British School)

Dan, Otto Bauer, and their followers were induced by the iron logic of their Marxist analysis to accept *post factum* not merely the progressive character of the October Revolution but even Stalinism. Professors Pares and Harper, whose names have already been mentioned, were anything but Marxists. They had been great friends of Russia before 1917 and the Bolshevik revolution came to them as a big shock. Pares had been sent by the British government to help the interventionist armies; Harper did what he could in Washington to spread the truth about that new world danger, Bolshevism. Mr Richard Pares has given a moving account of his father's dilemma after 1917:

He was in a certain sense, an exile; cut off from the country whose recent history was his chief interest and his business, and necessarily influenced by other exiles who (as always) underrated the stability and overrated the difficulties of the régime they hated . . .

Pares went up and down the country engaging in debates against communists and fellow-travellers. He condemned the Soviet Government by quoting exclusively from Soviet sources. 'But even thus he was misled, for he continued to believe, down to the advent of Hitler, that the end or at least the total transformation of the Soviet régime was just around the corner.' Yet a few years later 'Moscow admitted a critic' (to quote the title of one of Pares' books). The ice was broken eventually, and not much of the critic's criticism remained; Pares again became a fervent believer and propagandist of the Russian cause in the West. He found excuses for almost everything that Stalin did, including the purges, with the exception perhaps of the Soviet policy of the closed door, as shown in their unwillingness to admit foreign students. This was a cause dear to Pares' heart and the Soviet refusal to co-operate hurt him.

Pares explained his support for Stalin's policies with reference to the changes that had taken place in the Soviet Union. According to his *History of Russia*, the early revolutionary period had been pretty chaotic and ghastly. With the early, original communism of Lenin and Trotsky one could not really do business, but then along came Stalin and things greatly improved: a little knowledge will tell us (Pares wrote) that the

original fantastic experiments of the militant Communism of 1917 were abandoned in 1921, for the simple reason that they did not work and led themselves to a colossal and devastating famine; that the authors of all these wild experiments have all been eliminated by the present holder of power in Russia (p. 615).

Stalin had countered Trotsky's permanent revolution with one of commonsense construction; he wanted peace with the West, not revolution; the product of his rule was a new race of technicians. Stalin's Russia, in other words, was a far more normal country than Lenin's, much more in line with the Russia he had known before 1917. All this was no doubt sincerely believed by Pares and quite a few others; there was, after all, a grain of truth in their arguments. For if the main enemy was revolution rather than tyranny, Stalin's rule was indeed the lesser evil in comparison with the first Soviet decade. But behind these arguments there was yet another assumption, conscious or not: in contradiction to all the prophecies, the Soviet experiment had lasted; if so, it was a working concern. According to one of the golden rules of Anglo-American pragmatism one had to accept it and to make one's peace with it.

Bernard Pares was not alone in rejoicing about the general course of events in Russia after Lenin. There were many, especially outside the socialist camp, who thought with N.S. Timasheff that a 'great retreat' had taken place, in particular since the middle thirties, which would not be followed again by a new revolutionary period. Among some Marxists, too, there was appreciation of the historical role of Stalinism; in the books of R. Schlesinger, for instance, the necessity of the 'revolution from above' was emphasized as distinct from the traditional, left-wing, 'revolution from below'. The virtues of Stalin the realist were extolled *vis-à-vis* Marx and Lenin the semi-utopians.

The very features of Soviet rule that attracted these well-wishers antagonized others, including many early supporters. The gradual disillusionment was reflected in a growing stream of critical writing. Different people have come to sympathize with the Soviet régime or to dislike it for a great number of reasons, sometimes subjective or personal, and it cannot possibly be our endeavour to list all of them. We have mentioned the literature of admiration; a broad analysis of the critical and hostile literature of the Soviet Union over several decades shows, however, three major periods of disillusionment which were reflected in waves of books and pamphlets.

The first such period came after Lenin's death, with the struggle for his succession and the changes that took place in the CPSU and the Comintern. This led to the estrangement of Boris Souvarine, Max Eastman, Victor Serge and others, whose subsequent writings had a considerable impact in the West. A second oppositionist wave was caused by the 'middle Stalin period', in particular the trials and purges of 1935–8, the Soviet-German pact of 1939, and Soviet policies as a whole in the middle and late thirties. The list of names of sympathizers who became critics in these years is too long to be enumerated. The third period of disillusionment began roughly speaking in 1947 and lasted until after Stalin's death. All this is of course well known, but it needs restating from time to time; it is not enough to know about the politics of the historian. Often it is very useful to know when and in what circumstances his works were written. Historians are only human, olympian attitudes among them are found only infrequently, and are mostly not genuine, pose rather than substance. A historian writing on the October Revolution at the time of the battle of Stalingrad or the fall of Berlin in 1945, however detached and objective, would approach his subject differently from his colleague writing at the time of, say, the Bukharin trial or in the winter of 1952–3. The one would be impressed by Soviet strength and look in his research for its sources. The other, more likely than not, would feel that the present plight of Russia should be traced back to an earlier period; he would look for the seeds of Stalinism in Lenin, and perhaps even in Marx. This is not to say, let it be repeated once again, that all truth about Russia is relative; it simply means that in different periods, under the direct impact of current events, different aspects of Soviet history have been emphasized and others neglected.

All historiography has been exposed to such influences, and no irreparable harm has been done, provided these influences are clearly recognized. If Clio had to be silent in unquiet times, not much history of value would have ever been written.

The literature of the fifties

Western studies of Soviet history during the last decade have attained, by and large, a higher degree of objectivity and sophistication than the literature of previous periods. Not that the passions have died down, that historians have mellowed and feel less inclined now than before to take a clear stand. True, the extremes are now less extreme than they used to be; but more important is the fact that students of Soviet affairs are less likely to be shocked, or their enthusiasm is less likely to be evoked by any sudden event or startling new revelation. The Stalin period was the great divide, the period of dramatic and unexpected changes. Historians and political scientists continue to differ about the character of the Soviet régime but the era of surprises seems to be over. With this some of the excitement has gone out of the field and a quieter atmosphere has prevailed; this has made it easier in some ways for the historian to ponder Russia's recent past.

The post-war period has brought a spate of histories of the Soviet Union and of works of a more specialized character. They represent all possible viewpoints – orthodox Stalinism (Andrew Rothstein), Khrushchevism (Aragon), outright rejection from a Menshevik point of view (Abramovich), or a right-of-centre outlook (Georg von Rauch). The unhurried nineteenth century produced multi-volume histories on the French Revolution; few nineteenth-century historians thought they could do justice to such a vast subject in one volume. With the exception of E.H.Carr's writings and a very few other works, there have been no general histories on the grand scale in the more hectic twentieth century. (One of the reasons is, of course, the paucity of sources.) Since these comparatively brief histories limit themselves to a general outline of the most important developments, there is bound to be a great deal of overlapping in the subject matter, though not, of course, in approach. Among the most valuable works of this character are Donald Treadgold's history of Russia in the twentieth century, Leonard Schapiro's history of the Communist Party of the Soviet Union, Robert Daniel's work on the oppositions and Hugh Seton Watson's *The Pattern of Communist Revolution* (*From Lenin to Malenkov* in the United States). Professor Seton Watson's work has widely been accepted as a standard survey of communist history both in the Soviet Union and outside. Its virtues are conciseness and lucidity, the emphasis put on national factors, the relationship of Communist movements to social classes, and on the internal balance of power in each respective country. Professor Seton Watson looks at the Communist movements from outside, not from the inside, the method usually adopted by ex-communists.

These histories tried to confine themselves, to quote Leonard Schapiro's preface, to the unvarnished facts. This does not imply that the authors have no definite viewpoint or that they refrained from value judgments. A history of the Soviet Union – or of any other subject – which abstains from drawing conclusions, would be of scant value. Schapiro's basic point of view is put both in the work already mentioned and in the introduction to his *Origins of the Communist Autocracy*:

> I have a certain predilection for old fashioned principles, respect for human life and dignity, freedom of thought and speech, justice, truth, and peace between man and man . . . I do not pretend to conceal my own predilection for a society based on an established legal order, in which varying and conflicting interests both of individuals and the state are reconciled with the aid of a minimum of government compulsion.

Professor Schapiro views the analysis of history and the messianic prophecies of Marxism with scepticism; nor does he think highly of the attempts to look at Soviet history *sub specie aeternitatis*. For such an approach necessarily makes the assumption at one stage or another that things happened because they were bound to happen in that particular way. Schapiro believes that an industrial revolution may well have taken place in the Soviet Union for a great variety of reasons, 'but I see no valid reason for assuming that it had to take place at the time and in the manner which Stalin determined, other than the reason that Stalin so determined it, and was able to put his determination into effect'. Daniels in his book does not want to assess the virtue or the universal applicability of the proletarian socialist ideal. But he is convinced as a result of his studies that the ideal proved to be unrealizable under the particular Russian conditions in which it was attempted and that the revolution was corroded from within by the methods adopted in pursuit of the goal: 'Therefore the ideal could not be attained, and any claims to the contrary could only mask the establishment of some other kind of social order.'[9]

Professor Schapiro's first book was devoted to the activities of the political opposition in the first phase of the Soviet régime; the choice of the subject may not have been accidental. Unlike some of his

---

[9] Leonard Schapiro, *The Origin of the Communist Autocracy*, paperback edition, New York, 1965, pp. x, xi; *The Communist Party of the Soviet Union*, London, 1960, pp. ix, x; Robert V. Daniels, *The Conscience of the Revolution*, Cambridge, Mass., 1960, pp. 8, 412 .

contemporaries 'upon whom the hand of Hegel, still lies somewhat heavily' (sapienti sat), Schapiro feels no predisposition in favour of the seemingly victorious side in history. 'Who are the victors, after all and who the vanquished? Was Cromwell victor or vanquished? Was Napoleon victor or vanquished?'

These questions touch upon a number of important problems. Some students of the Soviet Union are confident that the question of victory and defeat in twentieth-century Russian history has been settled once and for all. They believe that the verdict of history has already been passed and they have no doubt which it is. Schapiro and others are far less confident on this score. Both sides, however, take it for granted that there exists something in the nature of a verdict. But experience (a third school of thought maintains) shows us that there is not one historical verdict, but several; historical periods (if they are of sufficient importance) are interpreted and reinterpreted by each generation anew. Should a historical figure be judged mainly in the context of his time, or ought one wait for the revisions made later on?[10] These problems were first discussed by a group of French historians in the nineteen-twenties.

Lévy-Bruhl mentions the case of a famous politician who in his own lifetime was thought to be a very great man. Subsequently it appeared that he had been a great failure. Alternatively the case of a usurper could be mentioned who made his contemporaries believe that his rule was legitimate. Lévy-Bruhl and others thought that the judgment of contemporaries should matter more in the eyes of the historian than the verdict of posterity. Even if the greatness of the politician or the legitimacy of the usurper are purely mythical they are still important. The fact that they were widely accepted turned them into historical facts, temporarily at any rate, quite regardless of whether the belief itself was in accordance with the facts. Is not the myth itself, after all, also a historical fact?

We do not have to wait for the judgment of posterity to establish the importance of Lenin or Stalin. The views of their contemporaries matter, and the state of Russia in 1924 and in 1953 respectively may be more relevant for the verdict of history, than any later events. For as time passes it becomes more and more impossible to disentangle historical causation and connections, the might-have-beens and the would-have-happened-anyways. Napoleon was to some

---

[10] Lévy-Bruhl, '*Qu'est ce que le fait historique?*', in *Revue de synthèse historique*, December 1926. See also L. Febvre, *Combats pour l'histoire*, Paris, 1953.

extent responsible for the rise of nineteenth-century European nationalism – and Bismarck for the first world war. But somewhere there has to be a limit to historical responsibility.

Professor Schapiro lets the unvarnished facts speak for themselves; his book is certainly one of the most balanced in existence – the whole tenor is deliberately unemotional. But his reference to the unvarnished facts raises the question: what constitutes an historical fact? For the writing of history is selective; no one could possibly describe and analyse all the facts and trends which in combination constitute a historical situation. A pro-Soviet critic of Schapiro's book would argue no doubt that, while his facts are correct, undue emphasis is put on some, and adequate emphasis denied to others. Schapiro's book deals in great detail with the struggle for power and the various purges. It is far more summary on economic and social developments; apart from a few sentences about the 'astonishing rate of industrial development' in the nineteen-thirties and again after the war, the reader is likely to hear more about the difficulties in agriculture than the achievements in industry. Neither Magnitogorsk nor Komsomolsk is mentioned. It could be argued that a detailed description of Russia's industrial development has its place in an economic rather than a political history, that the purges were a unique and unprecedented historical phenomenon, whereas rapid rates of growth have been achieved in other parts of the world. But was not forced industrialization as much a part of Soviet reality in the thirties as the purges? Did it not play a central role in all the activities of the party? Is it possible to describe the development of Soviet society without constant reference to the paramount importance of industrialization? A communist would argue no doubt that industrialization was the salient fact in Russia's development in the thirties, while the purges were marginal; whereas Professor Schapiro holds that the ravages of over-rapid industrialization offset to a certain extent the achievements made during the period, and that therefore it was not of central historical importance. Historical facts themselves can be adduced to prove almost anything, because there are so many of them. But the choice of the really relevant facts is much more limited. And even if the philosophers regard the very existence of truth in history as an unresolved problem there is a difference between the honest man and the liar, in everyday life as in the writing of history. Stalin's *Short Course* and Schapiro's *History* are not equidistant from historical truth.

THE FATE OF THE REVOLUTION

There are now quite a number of political histories of the Soviet Union but comparatively few on social history, on the ordinary Soviet citizen who was neither a revolutionary hero nor a victim of the purges. Most Western studies have been preoccupied with the 'commanding heights' and the institutions; sympathetic observers such as Messrs Carr and Deutscher have been even more extreme in this respect than the critics. But the history of a country is not only the record of the action of its political leaders. To write the history of the common people is probably impossible and to tackle social history is admittedly difficult, but its total omission is in the long run intolerable. We have become critical of histories of the middle ages exclusively preoccupied with dynastic squabbles. The question of what life was really like for Soviet citizens outside the Kremlin remains to be answered.

Kremlinology

One way of interpreting Soviet history, exclusively concerned with the 'commanding heights', is the classical Kremlinology of the late 1940s and early 1950s. Its leading practitioner was Franz Borkenau (d. 1956), a brilliant if often erratic sociologist of wide-ranging interests. Borkenau, a communist until 1929, had worked for the Comintern; he had come to regard the struggle for power, the Leninist 'who-whom', as the key to an understanding of Soviet politics. Unlike most academic observers of the Soviet scene, of whom he did not think highly (and who did not take him quite seriously), he specialized in predictions. Some of these were borne out by subsequent events, as, for instance, his writings on the character of a future Sino-Soviet split.[11] Others were not, but even the false predictions – and their number was not small – usually offered food for thought, for they were based on close reasoning and much ingenuity; Borkenau's mistakes were frequently more interesting and suggestive than the less erroneous analyses of other writers.

Borkenau defined his method as a species of content-analysis, taking its departure from what was known about the structural peculiarities of the Soviet régime and Soviet society. He interpreted the whole course of Soviet history before, during, and after Stalin as an endless chain of internecine strife. It was the task of the interpreter

[11] F. Borkenau, 'Getting at the facts behind the Soviet Facade', *Commentary*, April 1954, p. 399.

to ascertain the nature of these conflicts, the issues at stake, and their effect on Soviet politics. In this context the institution of patronage (*chefstvo*), the client-relationships in Soviet politics, seemed to him of decisive importance. Every big Soviet boss had a personal, unofficial clientele in addition to his official *apparat*; even more than feudal Europe, the communist world was ruled on the principle of *nul homme sans seigneur*. The obituary announcements in Soviet newspapers, the lists of guests at formal receptions, editorials, reports of speeches, etc., were therefore the most reliable guide to the standing of an important Soviet leader, his clientele, and his policies. Since open debates were infrequent, great attention had to be paid to quotation and citation. Soviet newspapers made boring and depressing reading matter, but at the same time they offered the key which would reveal the realities behind the verbiage. Sometimes a minute alteration in an accepted formula indicated an important policy change, and Borkenau's second golden rule, after the principle of *chefstvo* was: 'Political issues must be interpreted in the light of formulas, political and otherwise, and their history; and such interpretation cannot be safely concluded until the whole history of the given formula has been established from its first enunciation on.'[12]

In January 1953 Borkenau predicted Stalin's imminent demise; one year later he revealed, as an illustration of his method, how he had reached this startling conclusion. It had been based on a resolution by the East German Socialist Unity Party in January 1953 on the 'lessons of the Slansky case':

Malenkov was quoted at inordinate length ... By quoting him in his fashion and by adding his own yelp to the anti-Semitic chorus, Ulbricht, the animator of the resolution, proclaimed himself a Malenkov client. But even more important; while Malenkov was cited at length, Stalin was quoted with a mere half sentence dating from 1910. Such a deliberate affront could have been offered only by people sure of that tyrant's approaching downfall, or else out of the reach of his retribution. Otherwise it was sure suicide. It was primarily on the strength of the evidence found in this resolution that I then predicted, in print, Stalin's imminent death, which, sure enough, came seven weeks later.

Whether Borkenau had just hazarded a lucky guess on the basis of a wild surmise, or whether this was a triumphant confirmation of his method, may be left to the discretion of the reader. To some extent the methods of Kremlinology were practised at the time by all

[12] Ibid., p. 400.

observers of the Soviet scene. *Chefstvo* did indeed exist and provided, within limits, a key to the understanding of current events; so did, admittedly to a lesser extent, the analysis of quotation and citation. The practitioners of the method were often mistaken, because they were looking for rational explanations or causal connections where often there were none. But weak and unsatisfactory as the method was, it was almost the only one available in the absence of other sources of information to explain the political struggle.

The late Stalin era and the first years after his death saw the heyday of Kremlinology; since then this school has been in decline. The absence of a political leader from a state banquet no longer implies that he is in disgrace; an unorthodox statement by a minor political figure is not necessarily inspired by some powerful boss or faction. Other sources of information about Soviet affairs have become available. Kremlinology has been criticized for overrating the role of personality: the more one is concerned with micro-history, Mr Nove has written, the greater the role of the manœuvres of individual politicians. 'Conversely, developments over a longer period tend to have causes of a less personal kind.' Kremlinology has been ably defended by Robert Conquest as the 'Namierism of Soviet studies' and by Professor T. H. Rigby and others. Mr Conquest asserts that it was a great discovery of the twentieth century that political and political-military techniques and organization can be developed to such a degree of power and efficiency that they are able for the first time in history to engage the economic forces head on and thwart and divert them: 'Sociologically the totalitarian state is a lever by which one man, or a small group, can exert the same weight as whole social classes.'[13]

The totalitarian state

Kremlinology has been the centre of one unfinished debate, totalitarianism the main issue of another. Post-war Western studies have all been influenced in some degree by the debate on totalitarianism which raged in the nineteen-fifties, and has not yet quite dried out.

[13] See the contributions by Robert Conquest, Alec Nove, T. H. Rigby, and Arthur E. Adams in *The State of Soviet Studies*, Cambridge, Mass., 1965, ed. W. Laqueur (first published as a special issue of *Survey*, January and April 1964); also R. Conquest's books *Power and Policy in the USSR*, New York, 1961, and *Russia after Khrushchev*, New York, 1965, and Professor Myron Rush's *The Rise of Khrushchev*, Washington, 1958, and *Political Succession in the USSR*, New York, 1965. See also my review of Conquest and Rush in the *New York Review of Books*, 5 August 1965.

The first studies on totalitarianism, its political, social and intellectual origins were connected with the rise of fascism and national socialism. It was widely (though not universally) realized in the nineteen-thirties that Nazi Germany under Hitler represented a departure from the traditional authoritarian régimes and dictatorships of the past. The combined use of terror and propaganda was unprecedented, and, again unlike the traditional conservative or military dictatorships of the past, it aimed at radical change in some respects. Hitler had been in power only six years when he unleashed the second world war, which accelerated the trend towards fully-fledged totalitarianism in certain directions, and retarded it in others. After the defeat of Nazi Germany and in the optimistic climate of the immediate post-war period the totalitarian danger seemed to have waned. But with the hardening of Soviet domestic policies, and the other manifestations of the late Stalin period, the conviction grew among Western students of the Soviet Union that none of the traditional models fitted Stalin's Russia – certainly not the Leninist concept of the withering away of the state. It was generally realized that state controls and pressures on the individual were more comprehensive and more intensive in the Soviet Union than they ever had been anywhere.

The picture of Soviet totalitarianism as it emerged in the early fifties was forbidding; dire predictions were made not only by impressionable students of political philosophy but also by political scientists intimately involved in the study of Soviet affairs.[14] Grim as the existing situation was, some observers drew even more pessimistic conclusions about the future, predicting that the régimes would become even more totalitarian. Professors Friedrich and Brzezinski subsequently (1965, in a second edition of their book) abandoned this idea, but another thesis of the authors has not been disproved so far, namely that a totalitarian dictatorship was unlikely to be overthrown by revolution from below; in modern conditions such a rising was most unlikely to succeed.

This concept of totalitarianism was rejected not only by the Russians who regarded it as a calumny on their country and party, but also by Western Marxists. For them it was politically unacceptable, glossing over the basic differences between communism and

[14] Totalitarianism, New York, 1954, a series of papers given at a conference sponsored by the American Academy of Arts and Sciences; also the first edition of Friedrich and Brzezinski, Totalitarian Dictatorship and Autocracy, New York, 1956.

fascism. They also resented the theoretical implications; they could not concede to political power an independent, let alone a decisive role in the historical process. Various predictions have been made with regard to the future of totalitarianism. According to one school of thought Russia's economic development, industrialization and urbanization work towards a more rational, eventually perhaps even constitutional order. It was argued that the economic reforms of the middle sixties (decentralization, Libermanism) would in the long run have marked political effects; interest groups within the régime would become more vocal and powerful and this would eventually lead towards a general liberalization. Both Western Marxists and some non-Marxists have argued that economic and social development, higher education, etc., will more or less automatically bring about the gradual disintegration of totalitarianism. Against this it has been maintained that while the importance of technicians and managers will increase in an advanced industrial society, and while the requirements of bureaucratic organization may make a less coercive form of régime necessary, these trends could well be contained within the framework of the existing order of things. The régime, in other words, may be streamlined without necessarily becoming more liberal. The Sino-Soviet conflict and other dissensions within the formerly monolithic communist bloc have, on the other hand, introduced an element of uncertainty into the future of totalitarian rule. It has been suggested that with the spread of polycentrism on the global scale, factions may appear (and ultimately be sanctioned) within the communist parties, and that in this way totalitarian rule may be modified from within without any change for a long time to come in the one-party system. That internal transformation is a possibility, few observers would now deny. But few believe that this will come about more or less automatically; it may happen in the foreseeable future in some countries but not in others. And no one has been eager to predict in what specific way such a transformation would take place.

The mechanism of totalitarian rule under Stalin and the changes that have taken place since 1953 have been described in Professor M. Fainsod's *How Russia is Ruled*, one of the standard works in the field of Russian studies (first published 1953, a second edition appeared in 1963). Fainsod described in impressive detail how, after the second world war in particular, the party leadership pursued a campaign to tighten its unremitting grip on every facet of Soviet life, how the bureaucratic model of Stalinism left no room for autonomy. The emergence of Stalinism in the conservative garb of the party of tradition and order induced some people, quite mistakenly, to describe it as the 'Great Retreat'. But Stalin, Professor Fainsod shows, in utilizing traditional pillars of authority such as nationalism, the family, and the church, did not surrender power. He tapped the wellsprings of national sentiment and thus broadened the base of his influence:

The great *tour de force* of Stalinism was the construction of a totalitarian edifice which sought to bestride the revolution and the authoritarian heritage of Leninism, the traditional nationalism of Tsarism, the stabilizing equilibrium of conservative social institutions, the dynamics of rapid industrialization and the terror apparatus of a full-blown police state (p. 116).

Professor Fainsod was not unmindful of the changes that have taken place since the middle fifties and the emergence of a more sophisticated variant of Marxism–Leninism. But this does not mean that the whole structure will be thrown overboard:

The régime is still committed to the doctrines that Communism is the wave of the future, that the party is the true custodian of the interests of the toilers, and that it must remain dominant even after the Communist utopia is realized (p. 596).

Professor Fainsod did not think that improvements in the standard of living will necessarily make Soviet society more conservative or that it is bound to make for a more peaceful foreign policy. He does not deny such a possibility – the Soviet Union seeks to avoid a thermonuclear war which would destroy all that has been built at so heavy a cost since 1917. But there is also no doubt that the Soviet leaders will continue to take risks to speed the victory of Communism in other countries; foreign successes after all can compensate for domestic failures.

The discussion about the future of totalitarian rule is unfinished and there are still wide divergences about its origins and historical role in the past. Professor von Laue among others believes that, given Russia's backwardness and the Bolsheviks' commitment to rapid industrialization, the introduction of totalitarian methods was more or less inevitable – and is likely to be repeated in other countries in similar conditions. Others (with Professor Ulam) regard totalitarianism as a disaster that was not inevitable. Russia was not that backward,

185

Ulam argues; on the contrary, it was a rapidly developing and industrializing society. Stalin destroyed completely and beyond the possibility of early restoration whatever there was in the way of humane and democratic forces in Russian Marxism and in Russian society. Nor was he entirely successful in his totalitarian methods:

> It must be suspected that the concept of human nature towards which totalitarianism strives is as much of a myth as the early liberal ideas; a political man who responds obediently to artificially stimulated hysteria and indoctrination and who seeks only security and rewards, has not been perfected in the Soviet Union.[15]

Among other questions debated by students of Soviet affairs in recent years are the functions and importance of ideology in the Soviet system. Most, if not all observers agree that the importance of doctrine has gradually decreased, but there is no unanimity over the degree. Is traditional Leninist doctrine gradually being replaced by an ideological mixture of some of the tenets of Marxism–Leninism with strong nationalist-populist elements? Is the function of ideology to diminish even further? If so, what will be the function of the party in the Soviet system? Can the Soviet régime exist without a central doctrine providing ideological legitimacy? Such questions will no doubt be debated for a long time to come. The Soviet system is novel and unprecedented; there is nothing in the past of Russia or of any other country to guide the outside observer. There should be no illusions, therefore, about the limits of historical experience in this context. Parallels with authoritarian régimes in the past or with the great world religions may obscure rather than illuminate the issue now at stake.

Convergence

The late Stalin era gave birth to the debate about totalitarianism; the period that followed his death produced the convergence theory. This theory is based on the assumption that industrialization and urbanization create a civilization common to all modern societies, not only similar forms of production but also political institutions that are alike. Industrialization leads to a differentiation of society; interest groups multiply, a pluralistic society emerges. The specialists – not

[15] Th. von Laue in *The Transformation of Soviet Society*, ed. C. R. Black, Cambridge Mass., 1960, p. 209 et seq.; and *Why Lenin, Why Stalin?* London, 1965. Adam B. Ulam, *The New Face of Soviet Totalitarianism*, Cambridge, 1963, pp. 63–4.

only the scientists, but also, for instance, the economists – have to be given a far larger measure of freedom than hitherto to be of any real use to the state and society. It is the role of the state (and of the party) to mediate between these groups.

With the growing prosperity, it is further argued, revolutionary *élan* decreases and the party loses its claim for a monopoly of power, which could have been justified all the time sacrifices and unpopular policies were necessary. In the long run, the party thus loses its *raison d'être*. It was its historical function to industrialize Russia, but the accomplishment of this target is its undoing. For prosperous societies become democratic. Other arguments in favour of converg- ence have been adduced; for instance, that it becomes more and more difficult for the Soviet Union to shut itself off from contacts with the outside world. These contacts are bound to have an impact and produce changes.[16]

The convergence theory in various forms and modifications has been widely accepted; it was implicit in much of Western political thought of the late fifties and sixties. But it also came in for harsh criticism. It has been doubted that there is a direct causal con- nection between the politics of a certain country and its economic stage of development. Brzezinski and Huntington have argued that from an economic-technological point of view there was a great deal of similarity between Essen and Detroit in the nineteen-thirties. But this did not prevent National Socialism from imposing a political system on Essen quite dissimilar to that prevailing in Detroit. The critics of 'convergence' do not dispute that modernization has certain political effects but they attribute greater importance to the social and political character of economic growth. Soviet society was created by the Soviet political system; Soviet economic growth was imposed and directed from above. In America it happened exactly in the opposite way: American politics are a mirror of American society. The critics of convergence believe that electronic brains can be used without major political consequences in a communist society as well as in any other, and they argue that a society with many specialists is not necessarily a pluralist society. The influence of the specialists and the changes they propound can be contained in the

---

[16] The case for convergence has never been put systematically if we except W. Rostow's theory of the stages of industrial development which does not specifically deal with the Soviet Union. The case against is discussed by Peter Wiles in *Encounter*, June 1963, and in Brzezinski and Huntington, *Political Power: USA–USSR*, New York, 1964. It has also been discussed by the economists Jan Tinbergen, Svendson and Prybyla.

present social and political system. Great wealth is admittedly not conducive to revolutionary dynamism. But it will take the Soviet Union a long time to catch up with the present American standard of life. Wealth furthermore does not necessarily lead to democracy. Far-reaching assumptions of this kind are always doubtful: the prophets of the enlightenment for instance, were convinced that democracy and republican régimes could flourish only in a poor, rural milieu. Even if the convergence theory should be correct the equation developed: industrial society = democracy is, at best, an oversimplification. And it is not at all certain that West and East will be more friendly disposed to each other even if they become more similar. The assumption that countries or social systems that are very similar necessarily nurse a feeling of friendship towards each other is not borne out by historical experience.

The convergence theory is bound to stimulate more discussion. It cannot be doubted that modernization, and especially industrial development at an advanced stage, creates problems and ways of solving them that are often strikingly similar. But it is too early to judge to what extent such convergence will be mainly restricted to the modes of production and organization or whether it will influence social life and politics. The arguments adduced by the critics of convergence seem convincing as far as the coming decades are concerned. But it could still be true that in a more distant perspective, in the twenty-first century, convergence will come into its own.

Any interim discussion will have to be concluded at this point with a big question mark. But we have strayed here into a discussion of present and future trends. The assessment of past developments in the Soviet Union despite all the divergencies in approach and opinion has become more realistic; if there are mistakes now they are committed, so to speak, on a higher level of sophistication. In 1917, and for many years after, there was a widespread ignorance. To quote Mr Harold Macmillan's autobiography:

> Russia was then, as it was destined to remain for so long, an unplumbed mystery. At the end of the first world war we knew little about what was happening. All we knew was that Tsarism had fallen and that the Communists had seized power. The civil war and the much disputed intervention were hotly debated, but little real information was available.

In 1917 the general consensus of opinion in Britain, France, and the United States was that Lenin was a hireling of the Kaiser. 'Those whose business it was to instruct and guide the public should have known better', another contemporary observer wrote.[17] But they did not know better. As far as they were concerned Marxism was a secret doctrine and the socialist parties non-existent to the naked eye. To say that Western comment about Russia in the twenties was pre-Marxist would be an understatement. Today there is an impressive body of factual information in the West; Western comment on Soviet history is to a considerable extent post-Marxist in orientation and understands the dynamics of Soviet development as well as anyone inside Russia – which is as much as one can reasonably expect.

[17] E. H. Wilcox, *Russia's Ruin*, London, 1919, p. 246. Wilcox was a former *Daily Telegraph* correspondent in Petrograd.

« 9 »

The Harvest of Two Decades

The end of de-Stalinization

A review of historical writing and how it has changed during the last two decades should begin with the work done inside the Soviet Union, if only because it is the less complicated part of our story. The era of Ilichev, Pospelov, Ponomarev, and Trapeznikov (the leading party ideologists first under Stalin, later under Khrushchev and Brezhnev), witnessed many decrees on the 'improvement of ideological and educational work', which also concerned the writing of history: big projects were announced, better access to archives promised, new institutes opened. A multi-volume *History of the Communist Party of the Soviet Union* (5 parts in 8 vols., 1964–80), appeared under the editorship of Pospelov and, after his death, of Fedoseev. There was also an eleven-volume work on Russian history since the earliest days (1966–80), an eleven-volume history of the second world war (1973–80), an almost equally imposing *History of the Great Patriotic War*, the fifth edition of Lenin's *Collected Works* (1958–65), and a biographical chronicle of Lenin's life in eleven volumes. One of the most ambitious projects was a history of the collectivization of agriculture in the Soviet Union (28 parts in 44 vols.), describing in minute detail the transformation of the Russian village.

Soviet historians devoted much work to the history of the revolutions in 1917 on one hand and the second world war on the other. This was connected, of course, with the various anniversaries that were celebrated. There were many monographs on the composition and growth of the working class, the role of the army, the relations with other parties in 1917–8, and also countless articles and books on minor figures whose paths had crossed that of Lenin at one stage or another. There were many short and long studies attacking foreign ('bourgeois') historians who had falsified and/or denigrated Soviet history.

Very little was published on the Stalin era, excepting only the war years. Some of these new publications were based on new source material, and therefore of some interest also to experts outside Russia. A few daring spirits expressed somewhat unorthodox views, but these refer mostly to the early days of the revolution. By and large the new literature was repetitive, flat, and thoroughly uninteresting, a fact frequently pointed out by Soviet critics. Since there is no reason to assume that Soviet historians are intrinsically less gifted than their Western colleagues, how can this unsatisfactory state of affairs be explained?

The root causes have been mentioned before: Soviet contemporary history has to stick closely to the party line. It is not history in the Western sense but a political guide to action. There may be some room for maneuver and even cautious dissent on subjects such as the origins of feudalism and absolutism in Russia, but there is virtually none for the period after 1917. There still are countless taboos, and if it seemed that de-Stalinization under Khrushchev would make the life of Soviet historians easier and history more truthful, these hopes were soon dashed. Thus for a number of years a more candid picture emerged in the writings about the collectivization of agriculture and about the second world war, but this was followed by a retreat starting in the middle 1960s. Khrushchev had figured prominently in the historical writings as long as he was General Secretary, but his name was systematically eliminated after he was ousted from leadership. But Brezhnev, his successor, fared no better after his death; the average life span of a book on the history of the party became much shorter than it had been under Stalin.

Since the major historical projects of which mention has been made frequently took a decade or longer to organize and write, it happened time and again that the later volumes of a multi-volume enterprise were in stark contrast to the earlier ones, which had to be withdrawn and replaced by others more in accordance with the changed party line. The first volume of the *Historical Encyclopedia* appeared in 1961; when the sixteenth and last was published in 1975–6 a leading authority commented in *Pravda* that because Soviet historical science had 'so much advanced since the early 1960s', the first ten volumes had to be considered faulty in important respects, 'not reflecting the current level of Soviet historical science'. The author suggested that a second revised edition should be published as soon as possible.[1]

The first ten volumes had been written and published under Khrushchev and had been quite critical of Stalin (and generally speaking, somewhat more objective and 'liberal'). Thus they were out of place in a new era. The differences between the various editions of the new one-volume party history (under the editorship of Ponomarev) were equally striking. The second edition (1968) referred in detail to Stalin's shortcomings as a political leader and theoretician, and included five pages on the cult of Stalin. The third edition, which appeared in 1969, had only two pages on the 'cult of the individual' in which criticism was toned down, and this has remained the case since. What negative comments are made appear only in connection with the 20th party congress in 1956 – three years after Stalin's death. His shortcomings were discovered, it would appear, only after he had died.

In theory, books could still have been written mentioning just a bare minimum of names. This would apply, for instance, to economic history; but it was, of course, quite impossible in most other fields. As a result the greatest caution had to be exercised and the results were paradoxical and quite often ridiculous. A few examples might suffice. The fifth volume (part one) of *History of the Communist Party*, a hefty book of more than seven hundred pages, covers the period between 1938 and 1945. Stalin's name is mentioned fewer than thirty times, which is not much considering his crucial role during those years. He is followed in frequency by a few military leaders, such as Zhukov; the civilian leaders most frequently mentioned are Hitler and Churchill, even though they were not members of the CPSU. Beria, one of the most powerful leaders at the time is mentioned only three times; in the preceding volume he is never once mentioned. His predecessor, Ezhov, does not figure in the book at all, nor do the other ministers or deputy ministers of state security. The reader will look in vain for Poskrebyshev, even though Stalin's chief assistant was a man of crucial importance.

The next volume, dealing with the post-war period, was pub-

---

[1] A. Zakharov, *Pravda*, June 28, 1976; see also Kenneth A. Kerst, 'CPSU History Revised', *Problems of Communism*. May–June 1977.

lished in 1980 – it should have appeared thirteen years earlier. This book covers the years between 1945 and 1959, and Stalin, quite rightly, is mentioned more often than any other Soviet leader except, of course, Lenin, who appears three times as often, giving credence to the Soviet slogan: 'Lenin lives'. But Stalin is again followed by two foreigners, Thorez and Togliatti, who score as high as Brezhnev and Khrushchev. (In fact Brezhnev appears more often than Khrushchev, even though his importance was, of course, much less before 1965). Members of the Politburo, such as Frol Kozlov, appear just once or, as in the case of Shelepin or Podgorny, not at all. Kalinin appears eight times, even though he died at the very beginning of the period under review and had played a role of no importance whatsoever. To compensate, all kinds of obscure figures are conjured up, such as M. A. Posmitnii or K. P. Orlovski, who were good and reliable agriculturists but hardly equal in political importance to Malenkov, Molotov, Mikoyan, or Kosygin, to single out only a few, who appear as often as Orlovski and Posmitnii in the pages of party history.

The one-volume *History of the Communist Party* (3rd ed., 1969; 7th ed., 1985), mentions Malenkov once – as having belonged to the anti-party group ousted after Stalin's death. Yet Malenkov at one time had been the heir apparent and, after 1953, Prime Minister. Like most other close collaborators of Stalin, he was deposed by Khrushchev, who became the leading figure and supreme authority for almost a decade. Yet by 1969 Khrushchev too had been overthrown and the same volume of party history, unlike its predecessors, had a great deal to say about his mistakes in agriculture, party organization, and other fields.

At a meeting of the Politburo, not long after the 20th party congress, some of the old-timers such as Molotov and Kaganovitch strongly opposed the writing of a new history to replace the *Kratki Kurs (Short Course)* of 1938. This was in response to Khrushchev and Mikoyan, who had suggested that historians should do their work in the archives rather than on the basis of newspapers. Molotov and Kaganovitch thought that only misfortunes would ensue if archival documents were made available to researchers, and there is no denying that their misgivings were quite justified. Once party history is subjected to critical examination there will be no end to controversy, and it can no longer fulfil its basic educational function; the old certainties disappear and confusion spreads.

This state of affairs has not changed in recent years. One of the most recent textbooks, the *History of the Soviet Union in the Epoch of Socialism* (1985), edited by Y. S. Kukushkin et al., mentions in its chronology the opening of a major south Ural industrial installation in 1953, an event no doubt of major importance for the Soviet economy. But it neither mentions Stalin's death nor the struggle for power thereafter, nor the appointment or deposition of Khrushchev. There is one paragraph on the 'cult of the personality' which, it is said, was of no consequence. True, the appointments of Andropov and Chernenko are listed, as well as that of Gorbachev, but there is no certainty that this might not be considered a mistake ten years hence.

During the two decades after the fiftieth anniversary of the revolution (1967), Soviet historiography had to retreat from the relative openness of the Khrushchev days to a new orthodoxy – not to the *status quo ante*, the 'cult of the personality', for still occasionally mentioned are the 'excesses' of the Stalin era and the 'unjust repression of faithful cadres'. But the fate of these faithful cadres was never spelled out nor was the fact that the Politburo and the Central Committee had virtually ceased to function. According to the party line under Brezhnev and his immediate successors nothing changed with regard to the old assessment of the revolutions of 1917, the civil war, and the events after. The Bolsheviks had been right on all issues of major significance; Lenin's critics inside and outside the party had always been wrong. Most of the major protagonists of the October revolution still remained villains or unpersons, even though some minor figures – junior commanders such as Antonov-Ovseenko or Podvoisky – were rehabilitated. This, to be sure, had also been the case under Khrushchev: communist leaders from Trotsky to Bukharin were still enemies of the party, opportunists, and capitulators. They had tried to prevent the revolution and, after it had prevailed, to sabotage it. True, they were no longer called Gestapo, British, or Japanese agents, but according to the 1976 edition of the *Great Soviet Encyclopedia* Stalin had still been right in carrying out the collectivization of agriculture at a forced pace and enormous sacrifices (and *a fortiori*, industrialization). He had been a close and faithful aide of Lenin, heading the struggle of the party against opposition and deviation in the 1920s. He had led the country to victory in the war. This theme is echoed in countless books. 'Stalinism', as far as the authorities were concerned, was a non-issue; there was no case to answer. As Gorbachev declared in 1986:

'Stalinism' is a concept thought up by the enemies of communism, widely used to discredit the Soviet Union and socialism as a whole.[2]

The general tendency in the Brezhnev era and in the years after was to down play the importance of Stalin, for better or for worse. If mistakes had been committed in the 1930s, life after all had gone on pretty much as usual for most Soviet citizens. If there had been a brilliant victory in 1945, this had been owing to the army and all the people; Stalin had played a notable part in it, but so had many others. If Stalin and other leaders had occasionally made wrong decisions, the party as such had never been wrong. Hence the growing tendency on the part of Soviet historians to refer, not to the sayings of individual leaders, excepting only Lenin, but to the Resolutions of party congresses.

If the overall assessment of Stalin as a historical figure was positive, a leader who had done more good than harm, yet a certain amount of criticism was not ruled out even under Brezhnev and his successors. Thus Mikoyan, who had been a close collaborator, could return to the old theme and criticize Stalin openly and implicitly for not keeping the Soviet armed forces on a high state of alert on the eve of Hitler's attack and for not believing – despite all warnings – in the imminence of the invasion.[3]

In the years since Stalin's death a great many Soviet military leaders have published articles and books about their recollections of the second world war. In fact, it is difficult to think of any major figure among them who has not at least published an article or two. The number of civilian leaders who have published their memoirs, such as the Gosplan chief Zverev, or Vannikov, who had been in charge of machine building, is much smaller.

The approach to the recent past became much less outspoken after 1965. The change is climate appears strikingly in the new edition of books originally published before 1965. Lieutenant General Zhilin, in a book which appeared in 1965, said that it 'might appear with complete justification that had it not been for Stalin's obstinacy, the surprise invasion by Hitler's *Wehrmacht*

[2] *Sovetskaya Rossiya*, February 8, 1986.
[3] *Novaya i noveishaya Istoriia* 6, 1985.

would not have succeeded'.[4] Only one year later this reads as follows: 'It may be claimed with complete justification that, if proper vigilance had been shown at the time, the surprise invasion by Hitler's *Wehrmacht* would not have succeeded'. There are countless similar revisions in the second edition (1970) of the five-volume history of *The Great Patriotic War of the Soviet Union* originally published in 1965. Perhaps the best-known case was that of Alexander Nekrich's study, 'June 22, 1941', which appeared in 1965. He wrote in great detail about the many warnings that Stalin had received but chose to ignore, and the chaos that ensued after the attack. At a meeting at the Moscow Institute of Marxism-Leninism in February 1966 there was much support for Nekrich; many participants in the discussion claimed that the author had not gone far enough. Yet only eighteen months later Nekrich was excluded from the party and his book disappeared. He subsequently emigrated to the West.

Another historical debate that took place in the late 1960s lasted longer and had fewer dramatic consequences for the 'innovators'; they were removed from leading organizational positions but otherwise suffered no harm. This refers to the interpretations of the revolutions of 1917 that appeared in the works of a group of writers, including P. V. Volobuyev, I. F. Gindin, and Gefter. This school emphasized the social and economic backwardness of Russia and its *mnogo-ukladnost* (the side-by-side coexistence of various economic and social structures, such as feudal and capitalist) as the main factor in the revolutions. Because capitalist exploitation was more severe, the Russian proletariat was more ready to support the revolution than workers in more developed capitalist countries. The Bolsheviki had been supported not just by the poor peasants but by the peasantry as a whole, which opposed the feudal landowners. Greater emphasis was put on spontaneity in the February revolution, which is to say that the role of the Bolshevik party was somewhat diminished, and it was implied that the Bolsheviks (and even Lenin) had initially committed certain mistakes. The new historians were accused by the establishment of sensationalism, of trying to be original at any

---

[4] Quoted in James Douglas, 'Stalin in the Second World War', *Survey*, Autumn 1971, pp. 182-3.

cost, and even of revisionism. If the Russian historical development had been *sui generis*, how could one claim that the Russian revolution was of universal validity? True, from a political point of view the new concept also had certain advantages – it made the Russian Revolution a much more plausible model for other backward countries in the third world. However, since the ideological mentors of the party wanted to stress the attraction of the revolution for both developed *and* backward societies, a model which mainly emphasized the third-world character of Russia created major, unwanted problems. It also injured national pride.

The *mnogo-ukladnost* discussion had strong scholastic undertones. It took place within the narrow confines of Marxist-Leninist orthodoxy, with only halfhearted and most cautious attempts to bring in novel ideas. The innovators quoted Lenin as often as the keepers of party orthodoxy. The new views were not remotely dangerous for the legitimacy of the party; hence the fact that the 'discussion' (i.e., the attempt to persuade the perpetrators to admit their mistakes) went on until 1973 and those affected were treated with clemency even though most of them refused to admit that they had been wrong.

These debates concerned events in the distant past, whereas the Stalin issue was still a live one. As far as the 1930s and 1940s were concerned, the issue at stake was not just Stalin's person but the legitimacy of the party and its historiography. Thus it was only natural that continuity in this field has been far more pronounced than the change. In the words of a Western observer:

Stalin created the institutional framework and set the fundamental orientation for party historiography, and these have remained constant under the régimes of both Khrushchev and Brezhnev. Though the spirit of bureaucratic dictation and cynical manipulation that characterized the Stalinist approach has perhaps been moderated somewhat, its basic persistence in the face of immense social change is what seems truly remarkable.[5]

Some Western historians have argued that this continuity reflects the insecurity of leaders never freely elected by a true popular

[5] Sidney I. Ploss, 'Soviet Party History', *Problems of Communism*, July–August 1972, p. 41.

mandate. Others believe that the basic domestic changes that have taken place inside the Soviet Union did not really go as deep as some outside observers had assumed. Yet others maintain that the communist leadership is so deeply entrenched that it could well afford to admit past mistakes, that the conservatism on the ideological front will not last forever, and that sooner or later a more realistic (and honest) approach will eventually prevail in this field as in others. If Stalinism was an aberration from an otherwise healthy system, a real break with the tradition of Leninism, it is only a question of time until the truth will prevail.

The optimists point to the posthumous rehabilitations that have taken place over the last two decades. But so far the limits of rehabilitation, which came to an end in 1965, have been narrow and obvious. Of the thirty-four members of the Politburo who served between 1917 and 1939, fewer than thirty were still alive when the terror got under way. Of these, seventeen were executed or died as the result of their arrest. Of those executed, eight (most of them of lesser importance) were rehabilitated, but nine were not, including all but one (Faisula Khodjaev) of the accused in the Moscow trials. Among those rehabilitated were, above all, the leading marshals and generals from Tukhachevsky downwards. But some were not fully rehabilitated; others were commemorated only in local newspapers. A student of de-Stalinization reached the conclusion that the 'defective rehabilitation of party oppositions causes the historiography of the party to be seriously handicapped'.[6]

It would be more easily understandable if the taboo remained in force with regard to Trotsky and the left-wing communists. There were, after all, considerable ideological and political divergences between them and the rest of the party, and there was a great deal of bad blood, so forgiveness may not come easy.[7] But the taboo

---

[6] Albert P. van Goudever, *The Limits of de-Stalinization in the Soviet Union*, London, p. 161.

[7] As the historian A. Yakovlev has put it: 'The scientific council of the Soviet Academy recently noted a strange phenomenon – a reduction in publications in recent years'. What were the basic reasons? According to Yakovlev 'many works lacked the necessary depth and were written in a boring way. . . . But there had also been an avoidance of sensitive questions which had been exploited by our ideological enemies'. What sensitive questions? 'Let me mention some examples known to me personally. The treacherous activity of Judas Trotsky in specific spheres and in general has not yet been exposed clearly enough. . . .' *Sovetskaya Rossiya* 'Vivid and above all truthful', November 6, 1986.

extended equally to Bukharin, Rykov, Tomski, and other supporters or sympathizers of the 'right-wing deviation', and this
despite the fact that the political differences between them and
Stalin's successors are hardly visible to the naked eye.

An interesting light on the motives that may underlie the rehabilitation is shed by an analysis of changed Soviet attitudes towards
the White emigration. This topic has increasingly preoccupied some
Soviet authors since the 1970s and there have been some notable
shifts in orientation.[8] Among those now occasionally quoted with
favor are not only General Brusilov but even General Denikin,
one of the commanders of the White forces in the civil war (because he advised Russian *émigrés* in France during the war not to
co-operate with Hitler); Maklakov, the anti-socialist *Kadet* leader
(because he headed a delegation congratulating the Soviet ambassador to France at the end of the war); and even Shulgin, a far
right deputy of the Duma (because he returned to the Soviet
Union after the second world war). Readers are now reminded
that no fewer than 250 Tsarist generals fought in the ranks of the
Red Army and that many famous foreign writers, scientists, artists,
and composers are of Russian origin, including Henri Troyat, Peter
Ustinov, George Kistyakovski, Vasily Leontiev, George Balanchine,
Stravinsky, and others. There are major omissions – the attitude
towards the Russian socialist emigration, the Mensheviki, and the
Social Revolutionaries has not changed. No redeeming factors have
been found to soften enmity toward them.

How to explain this? The Mensheviki and Social Revolutionaries
were, after all, even more consistently anti-Nazi than the Russian
right-wingers. Is it because nationalism is more important than
socialism, and Denikin and suchlike figures are now considered
Russian patriots even though ideologically misguided? Or could it
be the fact that the Russian right wing was politically so distant
from the Bolsheviks that it ceased to be a factor of relevance a
long time ago, whereas the ideas of the Russian left are still considered potentially threatening even though their protagonists have
been dead for a long time? There are no obvious answers, only
the curious fact that the name of the first People's Commissar for

---

[8] For instance L.K. Shkarenkov, *Agoniya byeloi emigratsii*, 2nd ed., Moscow,
1986; and A.P. Afanasiev, *Polyn v chuzhikh Polyakh*, Moscow, 1985.

Defense (Trotsky) cannot be mentioned except to brand him as an enemy of the party and of Soviet power, whereas Tsarist generals against whom he fought are dealt with more leniently.

True, compared with the Stalin era, Soviet historiography is no longer monolithic; in one camp one could find the old orthodoxy as expressed, for instance, in Mints' three thousand pages about 1917, in which history regresses to what was known in the earliest age of Greek poetry as 'Praise of the Deeds of Gods and Men' – or, as Horace called it, the *laudator temporis actis*. Though not a man of Homeric talent, Mints is the bard who extols the virtues of the heroes, and denounces the villains.

On the other hand there are the writings of historians such as E. N. Burdzhalov, which, while fully based on *partiinost*, make considerable concessions to historical truth both with regard to the Bolsheviks and their enemies. As Nancy Whittier Heer wrote: 'In the context of the Soviet Union his [Burdzhalov's] treatment [of the February revolution] is breathtaking'. Most of the historical writing has been somewhere in between these two 'extremes'. These nuances come out perhaps most clearly in popular historical writing where the old right-wing allegations about the February revolution as the result of a masonic (and Jewish) plot have reappeared under a slightly different guise.[9]

The struggle against 'bourgeois historiography'

Many dozens of books and countless articles have been written by Soviet authors, individuals and groups, in refutation of 'bourgeois historians' who specialize in Russian and Soviet history. This is a relatively new phenomenon, for only since the late 1950s have Western publications been more or less systematically collected in Soviet institutions of higher learning and become available to the experts. Even now the polemics are selective – Western works on Stalin and Trotsky, on the Gulag or Soviet statistics, to give a few obvious examples, will not be discussed; they would lead Soviet authors onto ground they do not want, or cannot, enter. Most of

[9] I. I. Mints, *Istoria Velikovo Oktyabra*, 3 vols., Moscow, 1967–72; E.N. Burdzhalov, *Vtoraia russkaia revoliutsiia*, Moscow, 1971. The masonic conspiracy appears not only in the national-Bolshevik literature, but also in the writings of mainstream Soviet historians such as V.I. Startsev, *Revoliutsiia i vlast*, Moscow, 1978.

the polemical literature focusses on the revolutions of 1917, the civil war, the immediate post-war period, and the second world war. But there have also been works refuting Western writings on regional history (of the Ukraine, Baltic countries, Central Asia, etc.), on industrialization, and the five-year plans. Virtually all these writings refer to the falsifications and distortions committed by 'bourgeois historians'. This criticism includes the growing literature outside Russia written from a left-wing and even Marxist point of view, which is no more 'bourgeois' than the historical publications in other communist countries not under Soviet control, such as China. The Western 'ultra-leftist' writings, which include Trotskyite, new leftist, and pro-anarchist literature, are subsumed in the 'bourgeois' category on the basis of the argument that since they are critical of the Soviet version, they are closer to the bourgeois historians than to the Soviet studies ('Les extrêmes se touchent'). Therefore, in the final analysis, these writers belong to the 'reactionary camp' which to this day, readers are told, looks for counter-revolutionary alternatives to Bolshevism.[10]

While it is never said in so many words, the underlying assumption of this polemical literature is that it is not really the business of foreigners to dabble in Soviet history; their writings are not Marxist-Leninist – i.e., scientific but ideological in inspiration. Their intention is to distort, to denigrate, and to spread confusion. Western references to objectivity are a mere sham, for a bourgeois historian cannot, by definition, be objective. As for the progressive Western writers – i.e., those who accept Marxism-Leninism in its current Soviet version – there also is no need for contributions on their part, since so much has been published on Soviet history

[10] B. Marushkin et al., *Tri Revoliutsii v Rossii i Burzhuaznaya istoriografia*, Moscow, 1977. Among the many books against foreign historians specializing in Soviet history only a few can be singled out: V.S. Salov, *Kritika burzhuaznoi istoriografii sovetskovo obshestva*, Moscow, 1972; *Protiv burzhuaznikh falsifikatori istorii KPSS i sovetskovo obshestva*, Leningrad, 1974; P.N. Zyryanov and V.V. Shelokhaev on the first Russian revolution in Anglo-American historiography, Moscow, 1976; G.S. Joffe on the treatment of the February revolution of 1917 by British and American historians, Moscow, 1970; B.I. Marushkin, *Istoria i Politika*, Moscow, 1969; N.Y. Naumov on the Great October Revolution in French bourgeois historiography, Moscow, 1975; G.M. Zharkov, *Protiv Burzhuaznoi falsifikatsii istorii Oktyabrya*, Minsk, 1975; G.L. Sobolev on the Soviet revolution and American historiography, Moscow, 1979; and *Burzhuaznaya Istoriografia vtoroi mirovoi voiny*, Moscow, 1985.

inside Russia; their Soviet colleagues have already written definitive, official, and semi-official studies on most subjects.

Even well-meaning foreign writers have had a mixed reception:
Carr and Deutscher have been mentioned on occasion with approval, the former more often, precisely because his positive attitude was based on Sovietophilia rather than on Marxism. But Carr
too has been criticized for, among other things, not being capable
of understanding what a class is, and Deutscher's 'Trotskyism' is
mentioned at virtually every opportunity. Few historians have
done so much to popularize Soviet achievements and to find extenuating circumstances for Soviet failures, but recognition for
these labours has been scant and grudging.

Up to the 1960s Soviet critics tended to see in Western 'bourgeois' historiography one monolithic reactionary bloc, and there
were few, if any, attempts to differentiate among various historians.
This has changed, but even now there is a certain naiveté in much
of the Soviet polemical writings. Since the Soviet critics have little
personal contact with Soviet studies in the West, they find it difficult to decide who are the leading foreign historians, which books
deserve to be discussed in detail, and which are ephemeral and of
little consequence. Important and unimportant works seem of equal
stature from the distance, and the ideological differences between
Western historians are frequently not understood.

However, by and large there has been growing sophistication in
analyzing Western writings on the Soviet Union. The 'Cold War
anti-communist historians' who describe the Soviet Union in their
works as a dictatorship, authoritarian or even totalitarian in character, include (as Soviet critics see it) most leading figures in the
field. However, they have also increasingly acknowledged the existence of a 'realistic' school which, while very chequered in composition, basically regards the Russian revolutions as one specific
form of modernization and believes that in the given historical
circumstances the chances of the Bolsheviks' rivals were virtually
non-existent. The 'realists' reject the totalitarianism model and, by
and large, show more sympathy towards the policy of the Bolsheviks in 1917 and the years after. However, even if some foreign
Soviet experts have been compelled by the logic of history to
recognize that the October revolution was not an accident, not a
conspiracy, but an event of world historical importance; that the
Bolsheviks had mass support, and that Lenin was a leader of

titanic stature, they do not escape without blame. Thus Stephen Cohen and A. Rabinovitch are criticized for describing the Bolshevik party of 1917 as a motley crowd of factions, groups, and trends without much discipline. (Rabinovitch is also upbraided for writing that the Bolsheviks prepared demonstrations and an uprising in July of 1917.) William Rosenberg, the author of a monograph on the *Kadets* is criticized for describing this party as a broadly based movement deriving its support not only from the bourgeoisie but also from other classes. Avrich, the historian of Russian anarchism, is upbraided for not stressing the counter-revolutionary character of the revolt of the *Kronstadt* sailors (1921), which was suppressed by the Soviet rulers. Avrich's book is seen as typical of the most recent trends in bourgeois historiography: the anti-communists are ready to recognize the revolution – not however the real revolution, which brought about the dictatorship of the proletariat – but a democratic, pluralist revolution that would have opened the road to a quick counter-revolution.

Soviet authors note that many bourgeois experts stand for the de-ideologization of the social sciences, trying to give their work a veneer of false objectivity. Others have pointed to a certain defeatism among Western historians, who seem to believe with George Kennan that it is impossible to give an exact answer to many key questions pertaining to the revolution of 1917.

Why should there be so many articles and books, by necessity highly repetitive, against bourgeois historiography? The explanation is by no means clear. The writings of foreign historians are not circulating inside the Soviet Union and there is no danger of ideological infection. Could it be that the polemical writings are an expression of spontaneous indignation rooted in a deep-seated emotional need to defend Soviet historiography against its foreign detractors? Hardly. Books of this kind are not produced in the Soviet Union upon private initiative. Nor does one find among the Soviet polemicists the names of the leading experts, who seem to regard such exercises as a waste of time, to be left to junior people in the field. Do the writers expect that their arguments will persuade Western historians who, as a result, will desist from their evil ways? Or do they perhaps regard this kind of work as an opportunity to familiarize themselves with a foreign literature to which they otherwise might not have access? There is no ready answer to these questions. *Yes there is! It's careerism.*

The literature of dissent and emigration

The Soviet emigration of the 1960s and 1970s has not produced many works comparable to those of the 1920s. Among the emigrants of the 1920s there were not only trained historians of great erudition but many leading political figures, from Milyukov to Kerensky and Trotsky, who were in a position to make substantial contributions simply by publishing their memoirs. Among the *émigrés* of the 1970s there were few historians and no men and women who had been near the levers of power. The ordinary citizen in a closed society has few sources of independent information; he depends as much on the media as the foreign observer. Nevertheless, some of the books of the newcomers had great impact on the general public. Solzhenitsyn is no historian but his writings, above all the two Gulag books, and to a lesser extent *Lenin in Zurich (August 1914)* and the *Red Wheel (October 1916)*, have been more influential than all the books by American academics taken together. The Solzhenitsyn books are not historical studies but, in the author's own words, 'experiments in artistic research'. They do not have the trappings of academic research; prophets do not need footnotes to deliver their message. Solzhenitsyn's message in briefest outline is that the October revolution was an unmitigated disaster for Russia and mankind, that Lenin and Trotsky created the first and greatest totalitarian régime the world has seen, that Bolshevism was flawed from the outset because of the basic belief that human life is determined by external social and material factors, that the old Russia and its leaders were weak but that it was not evil compared with the Soviet régime,[11] and that the answer to the questions concerning Stalin can only in small part be found in Stalin's personality. Stalin was a tyrant, but Stalinism was not a break with the heritage of Lenin and Marx; it was not, in fact, a distinctive phenomenon. Stalin was a faithful Leninist and perhaps even a Marxist, his work the culmination and fulfillment of the ideas of the revolution. True, he differed from Lenin in the way he treated his own party, but with all this the continuity was not broken; he remained a consistent and faith-

---

[11] At the height of Tsarist repression, under Stolypin, 2,200 people were executed; Stalin had almost one million shot in 1937–38.

ful – if also a very untalented – heir to the spirit of Lenin's teachings.[12]

Viewed as works of (academic) history Solzhenitsyn's writings must be seriously faulted and are sometimes worthless. The relationship between Lenin and Parvus (*Lenin in Zurich*) may serve as an example: Parvus, the Russian Jew who became a wealthy businessman and political go-between, is depicted as Lenin's evil genius. It is true that the two did meet on various occasions, but Lenin had an aversion to him and Parvus never served as his guru. Solzhenitsyn was taken to task by Boris Souvarine and others for writing of Lenin's alleged hatred of all things Russian, and for his (Solzhenitsyn's) general tendency to describe Stalin as something of a Lenin *redivivus*, obliterating the important differences between them. Solzhenitsyn would claim that he was striving for a deeper psychological truth; compared with the hagiography with regard to Lenin practised in the Soviet Union, his Lenin is a model of objectivity and restraint. If the Soviet Lenin is all good, Solzhenitsyn's Lenin is by no means all evil. But this is not much of a compliment. Solzhenitsyn's mission is not the search after objective truth; he is not preoccupied with the humanistic intentions of the young Marx and Lenin but with the pernicious political and social system that emerged. He regards it as his main task in demystifying this system to unmask the lies on which it rests. Such a mission may be more important than that of the historian trying to write *sine ira et studio*, and it could well be that Solzhenitsyn, who did as much research in libraries as many history professors, has to offer psychological insights inaccessible to the professional historian sticking to the files in the archives which are always incomplete and usually unsatisfactory. Solzhenitsyn's Stalin and Gulag society seem truer to life than his pictures of a past which he knows only from secondhand accounts. Yet, however valuable Solzhenitsyn's writings, they can never replace professional history, and the argument that much

---

[12] There is a growing literature on Solzhenitsyn's political views, such as Carter, *The Politics of Solzhenitsyn*, New York, 1977; books by S. Allaback and Andrew Kodjack; Solzhenitsyn's exchanges with Richard Pipes and Boris Souvarine; reviews of his books by Leonard Schapiro (*Russian Studies*, London, 1986) and Martin Malia, *Russian Review* 36 (1), as well as Alfred Senn's 'Solzhenitsyn and the Historical Lenin', *Canadian Slavonic Papers*, 1977, 19 (2); the articles by Michel Heller, James Pantuso, and others in *Survey*, Summer 1985, and other publications.

of Western academic history pretending to be objective and detached is also committed to ideological preconceptions has little bearing in this context.

One other work ought to be mentioned: *Utopia in Power*, written by Michael Heller and Alexander Nekrich, two *émigré* historians of the 1970s, is a history of the Soviet Union from the early days to Gorbachev. The authors do not share Solzhenitsyn's religious-nationalist inspiration, but their overall appraisal is not less negative. Their book does not deny that with Stalin's death came the end of the period of an unlimited terroristic dictatorship. But their portrait of the new Soviet man (the most important result of seventy years of Soviet power) is still very sad. They refer to the social contract by means of which the citizens surrender their freedom to the state that in turn guarantees minimal living conditions. The stability of the system rests on a privileged stratum – the party and state bureaucracy, the military brass, the KGB, the corrupt elite of the working class, and an array of dignitaries in science and culture, along with the families and servants of all these people. Those belonging to the Soviet elite enjoy various privileges, but like other Soviet citizens, they have no rights.[13]

To this history of the Soviet Union one could add a fair number of personal recollections, as well as a series of volumes of secret historical documents which in some mysterious ways found their way into *samizdat* (*Pamyat*, 5 vols., 1977–81).

Dissident historical literature written by authors who still live in the Soviet Union is somewhat different in character. Unlike Solzhenitsyn, Roy Medvedev believes that there has been no continuity between Lenin and Stalin. Stalin was a despot who ruled by means of terror and worship of the tyrant. Such rule was not a product of the Soviet social system but an accidental deformation of a basically sound structure. Medvedev's quarrel is not with Leninism, let alone the revolution, but with those refusing to reveal the whole truth about the criminal character of Stalinism, which therefore remains a real threat: 'The defenders of Stalin play into the hands of the Imperialist propagandists'. Medvedev's books, like Antonov-Ovseenko's study of Stalin, contain much interesting material, above all evidence by survivors of the Gulag; but they

---

[13] M. Heller and A. Nekrich, *Utopia in Power*, New York, 1986, pp. 731–2.

do not shed new light on the 'origins and consequences of Stalinism' – which is the subtitle of Medvedev's main work.[14]

There was an inclination in the West in the 1920s and 1930s to discount the historical writings of Russian *émigrés*, because like all *émigrés* they were full of resentment against the régime which forced them to leave. Their accounts were considered, at best, one-sided; they were the losers, the members of classes and political parties which had been defeated. It seemed unrealistic to expect that people of such a background would be able to understand the deeper sources of the events that had taken place in their country. These particular arguments cannot in fairness be made with regard to dissidents and *émigrés* of the 1960s and 1970s. They belong to a generation born after the revolution; they were never members of other political parties or opposition groups within the Communist party. On the contrary, most of them belonged to the party and had been in their younger days fervent believers in the cause of communism.

If they had come to disbelieve the 'official version', it was not the result of foreign inspiration but because the discrepancy between Soviet reality and fiction had become so overpowering that they opted in the end for the thorny road of dissent, or emigration. They would have no doubt been able to lead a quiet life had they chosen to conform like most of their colleagues. The decision to dissent had been their own choice.

Eurocommunism and Soviet history

Under Stalin, and for years after his death, foreign communists did not comment on Soviet history; books such as the famous *Short Course* were widely translated into foreign languages and they served as the standard texts. The very idea that a member of a Communist party would not subscribe to the official Soviet version seemed farfetched. With the spread of various divergent, independent views among West European Communist parties, the Soviet monopoly came to an end and, for almost two decades now,

[14] Roy A. Medvedev, *Let History Judge*, New York, 1971; Roy A. Medvedev, *On Stalin and Stalinism*, London, 1979; Anton Antonov-Ovseenko, *The Time of Stalin: Portrait of a Tyranny*, New York, 1981; Antonov-Ovseenko is the son of one of the heroes of the revolution, and as a child spent many years in the Gulag.

there have been more or less critical studies from what, broadly speaking, may be termed a Western Marxist point of view. The most ambitious such enterprises were the histories of the Soviet Union by Jean Elleinstein, a leading French communist, and Giuseppe Boffa, who had been the representative of *Unità*, the Italian communist daily, in Moscow.[15] Of these two, Elleinstein's work is the less interesting; with certain cuts it could have been published in Moscow in the Khrushchev era. The Stalinist phenomenon, was, as Elleinstein saw it, regrettable; but given the absence of a democratic tradition in Russian history and the outside attacks against the Bolsheviks after the revolution, it might have been inevitable. True, Lenin might have underrated the importance of democratic values, but since socialist legality was reinstated after Stalin's death, this is no longer a major threat to the future of socialism.

Despite the conformist overtones of his work, Elleinstein ran into trouble. After the appearance of the first volume he was told by two French communist leaders, Roland Leroy and Jean Kanapa, that the Soviet party had taken a very dim view of the book. Ponomarev himself had been angry because Elleinstein had quoted Deutscher too often, and there had been too many references to Trotsky.[16] Before the next three volumes were published, they had to be submitted to party censorship, and the result was predictable: basically apologetic books with some concessions to Western taste. After their publication the estrangement between Elleinstein and the French party became deeper, and he eventually left it. In a series of later books his attitude became more outspoken and critical, and in an article in *Le Monde* he called the Soviet Union not a model, but an anti-model, of socialism.

Boffa was (and is) a member of the Italian Communist party and his books were sponsored by it. For Boffa, Stalinism was a typically Russian manifestation of Caesarism, and while he finds much in Lenin to admire he also notes that certain roots of Stalinism must be traced back to the anti-democratic policies of the early years after the revolution. While for Elleinstein almost every-

---

[15] Jean Elleinstein, *Histoire de l'URSS*, 4 vols. Paris, 1973–75; Guiseppe Boffa, *Storia dell'Unione Sovietica*, 2 vols. 1974–7.

[16] Philippe Robrieux, *Histoire du Parti Communiste*, vol. 1. Paris 1982, p. 147; Jean Elleinstein, *Ils vous trompent. camerades*. Paris 1981, p. 28.

thing Stalin did was right (or at least an unpleasant necessity) except only for the purge, Boffa is far more critical. He is committed to the idea that socialism without political democracy is not and cannot be 'real socialism'.

The differences between French and Italian communist historiography fairly accurately reflect, on the one hand, the political differences between these parties, and on the other, the differences between them and current Soviet policies. Neither wants to break with Moscow and neither wants to be identified too closely with official Soviet policies. Italian writers have been, on the whole, more critical. Some have reached the conclusion that it is an open question whether the Soviet régime is socialist; some, such as Vittorio Strada, maintain that it is not.[17] The theoretical center of the Italian Communist party (Istituto Gramsci) held a conference in June 1980 on Bukharin, published a non-hostile appraisal of Trotsky and the struggle of the opposition in the 1920s, sponsored a critical history of the collectivization of agriculture, and even published works by non-communist authors on the origins of Stalinism.[18]

All these signs of a more independent spirit among Western communists may appear as a family quarrel of no great consequence to those who do not subscribe to Marxist–Leninist beliefs, and there certainly was a tendency at one time to exaggerate the 'revolutionary character' of these new trends. But it is also true that even such modest deviations caused considerable aggravation among those in Moscow traditionally accustomed to unquestioning acceptance. They cannot have found it easy to adjust to these new semi-heretic trends in the West, and they have tried to discourage the meddling of well-meaning but confused foreign friends in what they consider their own affairs – and what is (as Kanapa told Elleinstein) in the last resort not an academic problem but an issue of high politics.

[17] Istituto Gramsci, *Momenti e probleme dell' URSS*. Rome 1978; Michael J. Solaro, 'Eurocommunist Views of Soviet History'. *Problems of Communism*, May–June 1980.
[18] Armando Pitassio, 'Su Bucharin e le origine dello stalinismo', in *Pensiero Politico* 41 (2) 1981; Fabbio Bettanin, *La collectivizzazione*, etc., Rome, 1987; Anna di Biagio, 'L'ultima battaglia dell'opposizione', in S. Berlossi et al., *Studio di storia sovietica*, Rome, 1978; M. Reiman, *La nascita dello stalinismo*, Rome, 1980 – originally published in German.

Western orthodox Marxism

No mention has been made of one specific category of writing on Soviet history in the West that has not fared well over the years – books written by orthodox Marxists. More or less ignored by the Russians, who apparently thought them superfluous, they have not attracted much interest in the West either, not because of any conspiracy of silence but simply because they did not contain much that was not said many times before. One of the most ambitious, and within the given limits, also one of the most independent of such works is Tony Cliff's four-volume Lenin biography. The author was for many years the ideological guru of 'International Socialism', one of the more enlightened factions of the Trotskyite movement, which, in contrast to most other Trotskyite groups, maintained that the Soviet Union was not a socialist, but a state capitalist, régime. This implies that something went very wrong somewhere along the line after 1917; was it Stalin's bad character or was the non- (or anti-) democratic character of Soviet communism more deeply rooted? While Cliff is not uncritical of Lenin, he would not go so far as to blame him for what happened after his death.

Neil Harding, who teaches political theory at Swansea in Wales, has composed something akin to a catechism of Lenin's political thought. He tends to believe like the Russians that Lenin was usually right when it mattered; his non-Marxist rivals and Marxist critics were usually wrong. In the light of such certainties, in the absence of dilemmas, alternatives, or new ideas, it is not readily obvious why topics, which have been covered so often and at every level of intellectual sophistication, should be rehashed in great detail even if the books are well written, as in Mr. Harding's case.

Rudolf Schlesinger's *History of the Communist Party of the Soviet Union*, published in 1977, is another example. The author was a learned Austrian Marxist who also lived for some years in the Soviet Union; but he was expelled from the party and left Moscow in 1937, which probably saved his life. Schlesinger has no quarrel with Leninism, and he finds the Stalinist era more or less normal: if there were some excesses by way of repression, they were probably necessary because the revolution faced many dangers at home and abroad. Schlesinger lived to witness the 20th party congress, but he clearly thought Khrushchev's attacks against Stalin (and the cult of Stalin) excessive. His general attitude is not very far from Deutscher's in his Stalin biography. But whereas Deutscher wrote well and gave his theses plausibility, Schlesinger had no such literary gifts, with the result that he could not find a publisher in England or America. His book eventually came out in, of all places, Bombay, India.[19]

Western reappraisals

Western interpretations of Soviet history underwent significant changes during the 1960s and 1970s, but these cannot easily be summarized partly because developments greatly varied from country to country, and also because debates continued inside each country. There was no more unanimity in Soviet studies than in philosophy, psychology, or other fields because of personal predilections, political orientation, and academic interest.

Most of the leading figures in the field of Soviet studies in the early post-war era have passed away – men such as Fainsod, Bertram Wolfe, and Leonard Schapiro. Deutscher died in 1973, Carr in 1983, Hugh Seton Watson in 1985, Souvarine in 1986. Others, such as Adam Ulam, Alec Nove, John Keep, or Robert V. Daniels who had been their students or belonged to a somewhat younger generation, continued their work on the revolutions of 1917, on Lenin and Stalin, and on other subjects in the history of post-revolutionary Russia. Among the new trends, the emergence of a revisionist school ought to be mentioned first and foremost. It questioned the approach of the former generation and by and large took a more benevolent view of Soviet policies past and present. This school was strongest in American universities, much less influential in Britain, and hardly represented in France, where the ideological pendulum was swinging out in the opposite direction.

As the revisionists saw it, Soviet studies had been too much politicized (and had become policy orientated); they had been

---

[19] Tony Cliff, *Lenin*, vol. I, London, 1975; vol. II, London, 1976; vol. III, London, 1978; Neil Harding, *Lenin's Political Thought*, vol. I, London, 1977; vol. II, London, 1981; Rudolf Schlesinger, *History of the Communist Party of the USSR*, Bombay, 1977.

affected by McCarthyism and the climate of the Cold War. Most Western scholars of the previous generation had been committed to an evolutionary democratic political and social system very different from the theories and the practise of the Bolsheviks. They had subscribed to simplified and politically inspired concepts, such as totalitarianism, which had never corresponded with reality and had become altogether misplaced after Stalin's death.[20]

This revolt against the approach of the older generation was not altogether unexpected. Similar reactions have appeared time and again in many countries and in most periods. Politics has always had a strong impact on the writing of history, and those who regretted this have seldom been free of its impact either. Nor has this been necessarily a bad thing. Historians should always be (to quote one of the revisionist critics) as sensitive, fair, and objective to the evidence as possible. But fairness and sensitivity should not necessarily make them more sympathetically inclined towards the subject matter unless there are good reasons for such predilections. Students of Nazism are under no obligation to act as apologists for Hitler, and one could think of many other such instances. The assignment of the historian is not that of a professional moralist, but this does not limit him to a position of equidistance between good and evil. Moshe Lewin, who has done pioneering work in the field of Soviet agriculture, has entered a strong plea for the canons of scholarship against propaganda that 'produce deep-seated hostility, disdain and an emotional need for bad news and horror stories'. And he quotes as a deterrent the anti-Russian vogue sweeping Paris these days: 'Such phobias and fears have more to do with mutations inside the Paris intellectual class' that concerns mostly themselves. That studies of Russia do not fare well in an atmosphere like this is not difficult to show.[21]

Mr Lewin's analysis of the French situation may or may not be correct, but such essays in the sociology of knowledge are danger-ous. For a Frenchman could argue with equal justification that American revisionism reflects American intellectual fads and that

[20] Alexander Dallin, 'Bias and Blunder in American Studies on the USSR', *Slavic Review*, September 1973; Ronald Grigor Suny, 'The Social History of the October Revolution', *American Historical Review*, February 1983; Stephen F. Cohen, 'Scholarly Missions: Sovietology, as a Vocation' in *Rethinking the Soviet Experience*, New York, 1985.
[21] M. Lewin, *The Making of the Soviet System*, New York, 1985, pp. 4–5.

the claims concerning scholarly objectivity are a mere smokescreen to act as a cover for deep-seated political bias.[22]

It is perfectly legitimate to investigate the personal beliefs and values of the historians, but there is also the danger of overdoing it. It is no doubt interesting to know which Sovietologist had at one time belonged to the Communist party, but it is clearly wrong to point to far-reaching conclusions about the disappointment of erstwhile enthusiasts and suchlike explanations. Though Souvarine and Bertrand Wolfe had been prominent members of the Communist party, Leonard Schapiro, Carr, and Hugh Seton Watson never were; Deutscher and Rudolf Schlesinger on the other hand had been communists, and were expelled, which hardly dampened their enthusiasm for things Soviet.

If there were differences between generations of Sovietologists, it is probably more rewarding to point to certain differences in training and life experience. Of the leading figures of the 1940s and 1950s few were academics by profession, and even those who were, spent the war years outside the groves of academe. A few, such as Carr and Schapiro, started to teach relatively late in life, but the training of most of the men of that generation was in fields such as journalism or the law. Not all had academic degrees. Their views on the Soviet Union had been formed well before the end of the second world war; it cannot be seriously maintained that their opinions were influenced by the Cold War. On the other hand they knew more about human affairs and decision making than the subsequent generation who had spent most of their life on university campuses, first as students, later as graduates, assistants, and lastly as teachers. Some had been active on the fringes of student politics, but hardly anyone had been in a position of importance. In brief, they might have a better grasp of the theory of international relations but they lacked, as a group, the exposure to real — that is to say, non-academic — life and a feeling for the realities of politics which books alone cannot convey. True, it could be argued that precisely because they were younger, uninvolved in the disputes of a bygone age, they should have found it easier to preserve

[22] The French Sovietologists could argue furthermore that many of their works have been translated into foreign languages, whereas few of the works of the American revisionists have appeared outside the United States. This is not necessarily proof that their views are correct but it shows that the 'mutations of the intellectual class' are not limited to Paris.

a certain detachment and more objectivity than their predecessors.[23]

Revisionist historiography stressed the need for a concentration of efforts on the social history of the October revolution as distinct from the political (and frequently biassed) history which has prevailed in the past. This meant, in practical terms, labor history – more attention paid to the history of the working class and its organizations (unions, soviets, etc.). While anti-Bolshevik historians had always put the stress on the 'stychic', accidental character of the revolutions of 1917 and the chaos which engulfed the whole country, the revisionists saw one of their main assignments in investigating the role of the Russian proletariat in the revolution, the class struggles, and the growing polarization. They also called for a closer investigation of events outside Petrograd and Moscow. The underlying assumption was that the Bolsheviks were not simply a group of intellectuals who had somehow managed to manipulate sections of the working class (as Maxim Gorky, among others, had written) but were largely a working class party according to their social constitution and the workers had played a leading role in the revolution ('It was, among other things, a soldiers' mutiny, a peasant rebellion, a movement of national minorities. But it was also – and especially – a workers' revolution').[24]

The upsurge of social history coincided with similar tendencies in Britain, West Germany, and France, and it was by no means limited to the study of Russian history. We owe to it a great many monographs on working class organizations in various parts of Russia. Among the topics studied were the composition of the Russian labor force according to origin, sex, race, age, employment, and so on; the changes that had taken place before 1914 and after the outbreak of the war; the migration to the big cities; the militant character of seasonal and migratory workers on one hand and of the workers in the metal industry on the other. The function of factory committees and the movement for workers' control were

[23] The opportunity to visit the Soviet Union created new problems. For there is the danger that publications considered anti-Soviet may result in the closing of doors. It is unlikely that men and women of integrity were influenced by considerations of this kind. It is far more difficult to say whether the danger of the 'closed door' did not perhaps have a more subtle, subconscious impact. This dilemma was, of course, not limited to Soviet experts – it applied to all students of the politics of non-democratic societies.

[24] David Mandel, *The Petrograd Workers and the Seizure of Power*, New York, 1984, p. 418.

the subject of detailed research as were the motives for the strike waves: how class (and politically) conscious were the workers? To what extent was the unrest conditioned by hunger and the fear of losing jobs? How to explain the growing radicalism? Some historians limited their research to factory workers, others included those employed in services, as well as artisans. There have been studies about the revolutionary movement in Baku and Saratov, and to a more limited extent among the peasantry and the army and the newly formed Red Guards.[25]

While much interesting material has come to light, the pattern which emerges is by no means clear and consistent. Some writers see in the movement for workers' control one of the main reasons for the collapse of the Russian economy in 1917–8; others regard it as mainly defensive in character. Some authors stress the deeply rooted democratic character of working class organizations (the 'working class movement was permeated by a commitment to direct democracy' wrote S.A. Smith), whereas others (such as Marc Ferro) detected a movement towards bureaucratization from the very beginning. Some students of the period regarded the actions undertaken by the workers as basically rational, the inevitable consequence of economic decline. Others discern a basically irrational, anarchical element in their activities. Some tend to equate political radicalization with growing class consciousness; others take a divergent point of view. Some consider the revolution and the Bolshevik victory more or less as inevitable, given the growing polarization in the last years before the war and the emergence of a growing discontented and disaffected mass of industrial workers now left largely exposed to the pleas of an embittered revolutionary minority.[26] Writing twenty years later on the basis of a case study of Saratov, another student of the period reaches the conclusion

[25] S.A. Smith, *Red Petrograd, Revolution in the Factories 1917–18*, Cambridge, Mass., 1986; David Mandel, *The Petrograd Workers and the Soviet Seizure of Power*, New York, 1984; Diane Koenker, *Moscow Workers and the 1917 Revolution*, Princeton, N.J., 1981; T. Hasegawa, *The February Revolution*, Seattle, Wash., 1981; Marc Ferro, *October 1917*, London, 1980; R.C. Elwood, ed., *Reconsideration of the Russian Revolution*, Cambridge, Mass., 1976; Robert Service, *Lenin*, vol. I, Bloomington, Ill., 1985; and other books. Ferro's study as well as his book (1972) on the February revolution cannot fairly be included in revisionist literature. In addition there has been a sizeable number of hitherto unpublished dissertations.

[26] L. Haimson, 'The Problem of Social Stability in Urban Russia 1905–1917', *Slavic Review* 23, 1964, p. 639.

that, with all the polarization that had taken place, it is difficult to imagine the Bolsheviks coming to power and creating essentially a one-party government if Russia somehow had withdrawn from the war or had avoided it altogether.[27]

Some of the social history written in the 1970s was orthodox Marxist in inspiration, much was semi-Marxist, some was not Marxist at all. Those trying to apply orthodox Marxist class analysis found themselves facing insurmountable difficulties; Marxist theory, after all, had not developed as the result of an analysis of Russian economy and society, and the revolution occurred as the result of the military and political defeat of the ruling class.

Social history has produced some fascinating footnotes to the events of 1917 but no synthesis or serious alternative interpretation. All other problems apart, it faced enormous difficulties with regard to sources. Social history cannot be written unless there is access to a wide variety of sources. But it is more than doubtful whether enough sources exist for 1917, whereas for later periods they simply are not accessible to Western scholars in sufficient quantities. Heroic efforts have been made to put together a reasonably full picture on the basis of local newspapers, personal collections, or resolutions by factory committees. But it is frequently uncertain how representative these sources are. Some Western historians have been permitted to use a few local archives, but these were, no doubt, carefully screened. Others were not even permitted to visit the cities about which they were writing. It is quite true (as Professor Alexander Rabinowitz has pointed out) that much new material has come to light since W.H. Chamberlin wrote his history of the Russian Revolution in the early 1930s. But how important is this material and how selective?

Tsuyoshi Hasegawa, who has written a valuable study of the February revolution, notes that 'it would be a mistake to characterize the February revolution [as Chamberlin does] as one of the most leaderless, spontaneous, anonymous revolutions of all time', drawing attention to the fact that the Bolsheviks had three thousand members at the time. But Mr Hasegawa was born in 1941, and what can he know that Chamberlin did not know, who talked to countless participants in the events he described? The fact that there were three thousand members (if it is true) cannot have been

---

[27] Donald J. Raleigh, *Revolution on the Volga*, Ithaca, N.Y., 1986, p. 235.

unknown to Alexander Shlyapnikov, who was not only an eye-witness (and wrote several books about 1917) but also the head of the Russian buro of the party. Like most other eyewitnesses, Shlyapnikov called the revolution spontaneous, not organized by the Bolsheviks. Mr Hasegawa may still be right and the eyewitnesses wrong, but more will be needed to disavow the contemporaries than some carefully selected documents dredged up by Soviet historians under Stalin or Brezhnev.

It may well be true, as many revisionist authors maintain, that the workers were no mere pawns in the struggle for power but played an independent, active role. Perhaps the Bolshevik party was (as they maintain) internally relatively democratic, open, tolerant, and decentralized, and had a mass character. But it does not necessarily follow (as Rabinowitz has argued) that the 'phenomenal Bolshevik success can be attributed in no small measure to these specific features of the nature of the party'. If democracy, tolerance, and decentralization would have been the decisive criteria for *phenomenal success*, the Mensheviki would have emerged as the victors in 1917, closely followed by the Social Revolutionaries.

The clarion call in favor of writing social history was sounded by R. G. Suny, who has also written that the picture of a highly disciplined, conspiratorial party seizing power by force and then imposing its will on a reluctant population by terror bears little resemblance to what actually happened on the Apsheron Peninsula.[28] But Mr Suny, alas, wrote about a city in which the Bolsheviks were initially defeated, and after 349 pages of social history (much of it, admittedly, dealing with the conflicts between the local nationalities), he tells his readers that 'there was no Lenin in Baku. . . .' – a correct statement, but one beyond the realm of social history.

This raises the crucial question of the relevance of studies of this kind. Social history and labor history are interesting *per se*, but the idea that minute investigations into what is believed to be the 'social basis' of the revolution offer clues to the question of why the Bolsheviks won in October and why they kept power is a *non sequitur*. That the Bolsheviks had a mass basis in 1917 goes without saying, but so had their rivals. Objective conditions were

[28] R.G. Suny, *The Baku Commune*, 1917–8, Princeton, N.J., 1972.

217

favourable for a violent overthrow of the régime. The soldiers were war-weary, the economic situation was catastrophical, there was virtually no central power. In these circumstances the most radical party – which also had a better sense for power and greater organizational capability – was bound to prevail, especially since it also had fewer democratic scruples than its competitors. As John Keep has shown in some detail in his study of the Russian Revolution, no clear lead came from the moderate socialist parties; their stand was ambiguous and contradictory.[29]

All parties tried to gain influence but the Bolsheviks had a more determined leadership. It was an elemental popular movement inspired by the most libertarian and egalitarian ideals. But it is also true that it was led by a small elite and the masses were caught up in great events over which they had no control. And this revolutionary movement, with its libertarian inspiration, early on become independent of social pressures and established the first experiment in totalitarian rule. The other parties were eliminated or integrated by the Bolsheviks after a few months. The old bureaucracy, members of other parties, joined in, including even generals of the Tsarist army. A mere four months after the revolution in March 1918 the *Gleichschaltung* was almost complete; the workers became disaffected, but this had little effect on Bolshevik policy.

Not a few historians have argued that the dictatorship was inevitable given the military attacks against Soviet rule in 1918–9. But even after the civil war had ended in 1921 there was no move back to a freer political system. The last remnants of the other political forces were suppressed; later on inner-party dissent was stamped out and, as Rosa Luxemburg and others had predicted, it all ended in the rule of a dictator. It can be endlessly discussed whether this development was inevitable; only firm believers in historical inevitability will argue that there were never any realistic alternatives. But most students of Russian history tend to believe that once the Bolsheviks had seized power the prospects for democratic rule were not good; given the Bolsheviks' low opinion of all other parties – including those on the left – the idea of sharing power must have appeared to them as something akin to betrayal.

If one were to summarize fifteen years of revisionist studies pre-

---

[29] John L.H. Keep, *The Russian Revolution, a study in mass mobilization.* London, 1976, pp. 468–71.

occupied, not with the political elites, but with the 'people in the streets', what major new insights have emerged? That the economic situation was bad and rapidly deteriorating, that the struggle between the upper and the lower classes became more acute, that the Bolsheviks had genuine support among sections of the workers not only in Petrograd but also in Moscow and other places, that on top of the instinctive rebelliousness of part of the Russian workers (many of them recent arrivals from the countryside) there was support for the Bolsheviks on the part of skilled urban cadres. Some have gone further and claimed that the revolutionary unity of March 1917 fell apart along 'class lines', and that the October revolution was a confrontation of 'class against class', with the Bolsheviks offering the most realistic, consistent analysis of the situation and the most determined leadership.

Revisionist historiography found more or less what it expected, and hoped, to find. Some of the conclusions seem perfectly correct, but they were not startlingly novel. Others were not altogether untrue but exaggerated, the inevitable result of the attempt to superimpose ideological preconceptions over a reality that was very complex. It is perfectly correct, as the revisionists have argued, that the key to the questions of why the Bolsheviks succeeded in seizing power and maintaining it cannot be found *only* in politics and ideology. But this has been largely a fight against windmills, for no serious student of the Russian Revolution, apart perhaps from a few inveterate believers in the conspiracy theory of history, has ever denied that after three years of unsuccessful war, after economic breakdown, and more important yet, after the disintegration, largely from within, of the old régime, there was an 'objective revolutionary situation'.

As all students of revolutions know, such 'objective situations' frequently occur without a revolution taking place. On the other hand, there have been successful revolutions – such as in Cuba or Iran – without specific 'objective reason'. Most great revolutions of our time have occurred, not because metal workers became more class-conscious and went on strike or because factory committees passed resolutions concerning higher wages or shorter working hours, but because of some major catastrophic events such as wars, foreign occupation, and other misfortunes. The general situation worsened because the incumbents lost self-confidence, were gradually isolated, and eventually forced to resign.

In these circumstances truly popular movements developed; if there was a capable leadership it wrested power from the incumbents. While the analysis of revolution can never be based on politics alone, the political factors are the decisive ones; attempts to downplay or even ignore them are bound to lead to misleading conclusions. Revisionism may add to our knowledge about the living and working conditions of Russian workers during the war in 1917 and after. But it has shed no new light on the motives and circumstances of the revolutions.

The problem for which Marxist scholars have not found a satisfactory answer is the fact that the revolution was, in the final analysis, the work of one man. Without him the revolution would not have happened, and there is no Soviet history book which has not stressed this many times over. The Russian government would somehow have gotten out of the war (or the war would have ended), some of the demands of the peasants would have been met, the workers would have been disarmed. The fleeting moment would have passed, since no other Bolshevik leader with the exception of Trotsky was in favor of an armed rising. But Trotsky was a newcomer and had no power base inside the party. It can be said about Lenin, as about Hitler, that the fate of the world depended on one man. Without Hitler's relentless drive the Nazis might not have come to power, and if they had, Nazi foreign policy under a Goering or a Hess would almost certainly not have led to a second world war with all its political consequences. For this reason the attempt to look for social explanations and class analyses is not very helpful. It can show us whether the preconditions for a revolution existed, but not why it took place. This reasoning has never been put more succinctly than by George Lichtheim in a short article in the 1960s.[30]

But the story does not end here. What if the October revolution had not taken place? The prospects for democracy in Russia were not good; the old elite would still have been discredited, the left still disunited. After a short period of chaos a military dictatorship might have emerged. No one can say for certain what would have happened from this point on – the country might have fallen apart, with the emergence of an independent Ukraine, a sovereign

---

[30] *New York Review of Books*, December 17, 1964, reprinted in G. Lichtheim, *Thoughts Among the Ruins*, New Brunswick, N.J., 1987, pp. 309–312.

Georgia, Central Asia, and so on. But this is probably the least likely possibility, for the centrifugal forces inside the Caucasus, in Central Asia, and Siberia were at least as strong as the wish to secede from Russia. It is more likely that an old-fashioned dictatorship of the generals and landowners would have seized power, but how long would it have lasted? The left was still revolutionary and the peasants dissatisfied. But (to follow Lichtheim) it would not have been a Bolshevik left. After a while the old dream of agrarian socialism would have faded and the bourgeoisie would at last have taken over, 'and would its leaders have looked and sounded so very different from technocrats like Brezhnev and Kosygin'? Millions of people have perished but communism such as Lenin envisaged has not come into being.

There were other possibilities: what if some Russian version of national socialism, not Stalinism, would have triumphed? It would have crushed the labor movement; dragooned the peasants; set up concentration camps; militarized the country; persecuted minorities, Jews, and intellectuals. 'It would have done, in short, what Stalin did, though probably less effectively. Industrialization might have been pushed a little less rapidly, and there would have been no Kolchoz. But heavy industry would have been nationalized, war with Germany would have come and also the invasion of Eastern Europe. The ideology would have been different; there would have been no Marxism, just plain national socialism'. Writing in 1964 Lichtheim thought that 'this might still happen anyhow'. Which is to say that in the end even Lenin made no difference.

This argument could be challenged for underrating the importance of Leninism. Lichtheim admits that changing Soviet ideology would not be an easy job, but it may not even be necessary:

On the whole they are better off with Leninism, on condition that they do not take it too seriously. For Leninism is no longer relevant to Russia anymore. . . . Yet the creed also serves the régime by providing it with a doctrine, a good conscience, even the semblance of an universal idea. The political elite is *not yet* an ordinary ruling class; sheltering behind slogans it has ceased to believe. . . . It will probably get there in the end (and then we shall see the start of true political warfare, perhaps even a two-party system). But for the time being the illusion still holds'.[31]

---

[31] Lichtheim, loc. cit., p. 312.

Revisionism and the Leninist heritage

Revisionist studies on the whole have centered on the very early days of Soviet rule and the most recent period, with very little in between. This has largely to do with the lack of sources for the time after 1920 – with some notable exceptions, on which more below. Not much new can be said on Lenin and Leninism; few stones have been left unturned in this particular field of study. If there have been new attempts to revaluate Leninism, they have mainly come from the other side of the political spectrum. Alain Besancon sees the intellectual roots of Leninism in the congenital weakness of civil society in Russia of the nineteenth century. Lenin appears as a descendant of the Russian radicals of the mid-nineteenth century, totally preoccupied with the struggle against Tsarist autocracy. His ideology is based on a kind of gnostic-chiliastic salvation. Leninism has nothing to do with either Russian tradition (on this, as on other points, Besancon fully agrees with Solzhenitsyn) or with science, though it is a child of the age of the optimistic belief in science and uses pseudo-scientific arguments. Seen in this light the October revolution was the seizure of power by the radical intelligentsia. Its continued hold rests not on ideology but on power, and for this reason it is doomed to immobilism.[32]

There have been biographical studies of Lenin (and the Lenin cult after his death) as well as of some of his contemporaries, such as Bukharin, and also of Trotsky and his political thought. These works have contributed to our knowledge, but they have not given rise to major controversies.[33] Views still differ acutely with regard to events of the late 1920s – above all those concerning the collectivization of agriculture and, more generally, Stalin's great jump forward. The late 1920s was the period of forced, rapid (and uneven) industrialization, and a major war scare, and they gave birth to Stalinism and the destruction of the opposition.

The horrors of collectivization have been frequently described but seldom more eloquently than by Robert Conquest.[34] The econ-

---

[32] Alain Besancon, *The Rise of the Gulag: Intellectual Origins of Leninism*, New York, 1981.

[33] For instance, by Stephen Cohen, Baruch Kneipaz, Harold Shukhman, and others.

[34] *Harvest of Sorrow*, New York, 1986; see also Moshe Levin, *Russian Peasants and Soviet Power*, London, 1968, and his later books.

omists, however, were less interested in how it happened; almost everyone agreed that it was 'a most dreadful thing' (A. Nove) and that Stalin was showing the face of an 'Oriental despot'. But was there perhaps an objective necessity (or the belief in such a necessity)? Professor James Millar is firmly convinced that the official version – that collectivization was necessary to pay for industrialization – is wrong from beginning to end. Even Soviet historians have shown of late that Soviet agriculture did not contribute in any significant measure to industrialization in the first five-year plan. There was no shortage of labor as far as industry was concerned, nor was there any danger that the peasants would 'withdraw from the market', i.e., refuse to deliver grain to the city. In other words, collectivization was not only disastrous in its effects, it did not rest on rational assumptions. Alec Nove is less convinced: given the logic of the one-party state and the desire to change society from above, Stalin may have thought that the survival of the régime depended on these measures and that the 'military-feudal exploitation of the peasants' (Bukharin's words) were the only source of accumulation.

The Western debate rested largely on the reinterpretation of facts which for the most part had been known for a long time, but also, to a certain, limited degree, on materials which have become known only in recent years. This refers both to Soviet sources and to the writings of some younger German scholars, who discovered internal, apparently authentic, Soviet documents in German diplomatic archives. But these new accounts only help to deepen the mystery. Both collectivization and the first five-year plan were explained at the time with reference to the allegedly growing danger of war. But there was no danger of war in 1927–8, nor did Stalin believe there was; had he done so, the immediate emphasis in industrial development would have been on the production of armaments, which it was not.[35] In fact, Stalin took various steps likely to aggravate relations with the outside world. The Shakhty trial is one example; the aggressive policy of the Comintern,

[35] Manfred von Boetticher, *Industrialisierungspolitik und Verteidigungskonzeption der UDSSR 1926–30. Herausbildung des Stalinismus und aeussere Bedrohung*, Duesseldorf, 1979; Michael Reimann, *Die Geburt des Stalinismus. Die UDSSR am Vorabend der zweiten Revolution*, Frankfurt, 1979; this book was scheduled for publication in the U.S. in 1987.

THE FATE OF THE REVOLUTION

adopted by its 6th congress (1928), another. Had Stalin really
believed in the imminent danger of war, he would have favored
a 'popular front' policy and reconciliation with the Western powers,
as he did in the mid-thirties.

Nor is it likely that Stalin should have hoped that as a result of
these measures the advent of 'socialism' in the Soviet Union would
be hastened. It is virtually certain that the Soviet economy, both
agricultural and industrial, would have made more progress if
something akin to the 'New Economic Policy' had been pursued;
nor would the hold of the leadership have been in danger. The
most likely explanation is that Stalin had no clear idea concerning
either the economy or the international situation, and decided in
favor of a 'jump forward', his revolution from above, because he
felt he could not go back. But there is no certainty as far as these
assumptions are concerned and there may not be for a long time
to come.

Communists and non-communists do not agree on Lenin and
Leninism, and probably never will. The battle lines were drawn a
long time ago and it is difficult to think of any new aspects or
arguments which have been adduced and which could rekindle the
debate – except perhaps the question of to what extent Stalinism
was rooted in Lenin, a debate to which reference has already been
made. The discussion about Stalin and Stalinism on the other hand
has continued unabated.

Again, there is an interesting parallel with revisionist tendencies
in German historiography of the Nazi era. Professor Ernst Nolte
suggested in 1985 that the Nazi period should not be taken out of
isolation, no longer be demonized, but be seen as part of human
history. After all, Nolte argued, nothing in history is completely
good or bad, light or dark. Nazism has been one response to the
industrial revolution, and so, revisionist historians argue, was
Stalinism.[36]

If Trotsky (who was one of the inventors of the term) has
called Stalinism the syphilis of the working class movement, if
Djilas called Stalin the greatest criminal of all times, the revisionists
stood for what they thought was a more objective and detached

[36] E. Nolte, "Between Myth and Revolution" in H.W. Koch, ed., Aspects of the
Third Reich, London, 1985.

approach. Following E. H. Carr's lead, some have strongly admonished their colleagues not to be unduly preoccupied with moral judgment. True, a high price had to be paid for Stalin's revolutionary transformation of Russia, but in the final analysis we are given to understand that the game was worth the candle: 'If a revolution survives and assumes permanent form, the presumption must be that it has satisfied some social demands and honored at least some of the revolution's promises'.[37] Another author says that the picture of a "terrorised and atomized society' under Stalin has been far from the truth. Stalin carried out a major cultural revolution, he provided upward mobility for many millions, and this, given the resistance and outward pressures, could of course have been done only by a strong leader. Seen in this light, Stalin was a little authoritarian from the beginning and became more so in the course of time.[38] The revisionists believe that the totalitarian model is misleading and should be unreservedly rejected.[39]

Going one step further we find the argument that Stalin was not a strong leader, but a rather weak one, constantly under pressure from within and without: his control over party and state was far from complete. Basically a peaceful man, he was forever challenged by the marshals and the top economic managers at home, as well as by deviating party bosses and by foreign communist leaders who disagreed with his advice.[40] Thus this lonely man, perhaps a democrat at heart, was driven by cruel circumstances and fierce opponents into a role which cannot have been to his liking.

Lastly, the purges: Mr Hough says that the number of victims has been vastly exaggerated; similar claims have been made with regard to Hitler's victims. Mrs Fitzgerald and others compare them to the struggle between Ivan the Terrible and the Boyars, who had to be destroyed in order to build a modern state. Mr Arch Getty goes yet one step further; with him one is no longer quite certain whether the great purges did in fact take place. His book on the

---

[37] Sheila Fitzgerald, *The Russian Revolution 1917–1932*, New York, 1982, p. 161.

[38] Jerry Hough in Sheila Fitzgerald, ed., *Cultural Revolution in Russia 1928–31*, Bloomington, Ill., 1984, pp. 247 et seq.

[39] The revisionists would probably prefer to abolish the very term but this has become difficult, for even in the Soviet Union the word has been adopted – even by Gorbachev. (Report to the Central Committee February 1986.)

[40] William O. McCagg, *Stalin Embattled 1943–48*, Detroit, Mich., 1978.

subject does not deal with the trials, which is like a new edition of Hamlet without the Prince of Denmark. As he sees it, Western commentators were as wrong as the official Stalinist version. He does not trust available sources – some were too close to the events, others too remote. As he sees it, there was high-level confusion all along; Stalin was not a strong leader but made his decisions tentatively, belatedly trying to arbitrate between various warring factions. It was a struggle of the center against local bosses, a fight over high-level disputes about development and modernization plans. The *Ezhovzhina* was not an initiative to stamp out dissent but a radical, even hysterical, *reaction* to curb the bureaucracy. In fairness, it should be added that the author expresses on occasion doubts about his own wisdom ('Some will feel that this study had taken a naive view of Stalin's role as planner and perpetrator').[41] The fact that Soviet authors began to write more freely about the harmful consequences of Stalin's rule following Gorbachev's rise to power and in particular about the extent and the brutality of the purges further undermined the credibility of Western revisionist writings.

A more moderate revisionist version of the purges has been given by Professor Robert Thurston. He believes that the number of victims provided by Conquest, Dallin-Nikolajewski, and others was considerably exaggerated. He claims to have found 'indications' that the Soviet Union in a goodish year like 1935 was not a very repressive dictatorship. But he also makes a number of sensible points – that there were certain high-risk categories in the population, but that for some people life went on more or less as usual, that he does not have much confidence in any method of calculation as far as the number of victims is concerned, and so on. But he does believe that a 'monstrous terror' existed in the 1930s, that there were 'mass arrests of innocents', and so on. The number of the victims will not be known for a long time, if ever, but the issue is less important than Thurston seems to believe. The number of those purged on top (party, government, army, secret police) was very high, far higher than in Nazi Germany or Fascist Italy. Whether ten million or one million died in the Soviet Union makes a great difference as far as the dimension of the human tragedy is concerned. From a political point of view and as far as the

[41] J. Arch Getty, *Origins of the Great Purges*, Cambridge, Mass., 1985, p. 203.

assessment of the character of the régime is concerned, it is of little importance. The number of anti-fascists executed during the twenty years Mussolini was in power was less than one hundred.[42]

Revisionism in German and Soviet historiography

Revisionists in the field of Soviet studies have looked with envy at the progress made by their colleagues in recent German history and vice versa. Thus H.W. Koch, who teaches modern history at the University of York in England, has asked: 'Why do historians find it so difficult to give credit to Hitler which many of them are willing to extend to Stalin'?

If we look at the treatment of Stalin by historical biographers in the West, his mass murders, which exceed those of Hitler many times over, are deplored, on occasion even only peripherally mentioned, but on the whole he is credited with having pulled Russia firmly into the twentieth century, built up a highly industrialized society, and so forth. In other words, whatever else he did, he nevertheless brought about progress. The excesses may be deplorable . . . but in the end they are relativized, so that when the balance sheet of Stalin's rule is studied, a plus emerges.[43]

If this is so, asks Koch, why not give Hitler his due? After all, he also provided upward mobility and established something like a classless society. The number of working-class children in Germany who gained access to institutions of higher learning was higher in 1945 than in 1933. And the generals of Germany's armed services in 1944 were on the average much younger and of much more socially diverse origins than the generals of 1936. These examples may not be ideally chosen, for Germany would not have stood still in 1932, Hitler or no Hitler. For all one knows, more children of lower-class origin would have received a higher education in any case fifteen years later. As for the generals, it was of course inevitable that with the great expansion of the officer corps during the war the oligopoly of the aristocracy would

---

[42] Robert W. Thurston, 'Fear and Belief in the USSR's Great Terror', *Slavic Review*, Summer 1986, pp. 219–234. Thurston is, of course, perfectly correct, arguing that the period of the purges was not a grim one for the Soviet people as a whole. Some, no doubt, were very happy to see the departure of the hated commissars. But this idea has occurred to others before Thurston.

[43] H.W. Koch, ed., *Aspects of the Third Reich*, London, 1985, pp. 483–4.

be broken. But the overall idea of treating Hitler more 'objectively', following the example of Stalin and with similar arguments, clearly emerges from writings of this kind.

Such similarities with revisionist trends in the historiography of the Nazi era recur time and again. This refers to the thesis that Hitler was, in the final analysis, a weak dictator, that there was a great deal of chaos on top of the Third Reich all along, that the traditional bureaucracy was deeply entrenched and very strong, and frequently the dictator reacted to events rather than taking the initiative. Mrs Fitzgerald's assertion that Stalin provided upward mobility is not, of course, entirely without foundation. In a slightly different form similar assertions had been voiced by the late G. Barraclough with regard to Nazism – which uprooted the Junkers and modernized Germany. Since then some revisionist historians of Nazi Germany have returned to the upward mobility concept to explain Nazism – its motive force, its social base – as one in a long tradition of levelling efforts in European societies.[44]

What is one to make of reassessments of this kind? If a sufficiently large number of people in high positions are killed in a certain country, opportunities open for the rise of a new class. The 'purged' generals and marshals have to be replaced by majors and colonels who have every reason to be grateful to the dictator to whom they owe their promotion. It is equally true that it was physically quite impossible for Hitler, as well as Stalin, to be responsible for every decision taken in their societies. But they had to know and to approve of every important decision and this, of course, is the only thing that matters.

These reappraisals of Stalin and Stalinism have not produced convincing new arguments, and it is doubtful whether they ever will. Stalin is not promising material for Marxist analysis. The wish to de-demonize Stalin was part of the general protest against 'Cold War' historiography, psychologically quite intelligible. Perhaps the revisionists were puzzled by the paradox that a despot of this kind happened to be quite popular; perhaps they thought that such a man could not have been all bad. But Hitler was even more popular. A comparison with the vicissitudes of Nazi studies might have saved some of the revisionists from various embarrassments.

---

[44] See, for instance, William Janner, Jr., 'National Socialists and Social Mobility', *Journal of Social History* 9, 1976.

Revisionism, to be fair, is by no means a monolithic bloc, and not all of its adherents have been convinced that the (partial) rehabilitation of Stalin was the commandment of the hour. If Sheila Fitzgerald and Jerry Hough believe in a strong continuity between Leninism and Stalinism (an assumption they share with bitter opponents of both), Stephen F. Cohen rejects decisively this thesis: Stalinism was not full-blown Bolshevism, not a function and extension of 1917.[45]

The basic tenets of the revisionist school can be traced back two or even three decades and have been defined as the 'dictates of modernization'. Reviewing in 1983 certain ideas first articulated by himself in the 1960s, Theodor von Laue still expressed the belief that Stalin should be seen as one of the most remarkable products of the 'world revolution of Westernization'. He lived in an age of final solutions; Russia had to be industrialized to survive; the result was bound to be repulsive yet inevitable. In the absence of any prior experience Stalin had to proceed by trial and error. Whatever his faults, he remained dedicated, even in his senility, to enhancing his country's security.[46]

But the 'inevitability thesis' has still not been found very persuasive by most historians, for at most critical junctures in Soviet history there were alternatives. Alec Nove, who at times reveals sympathy for this concept ('Where was industrialization ever carried out with consensus? Who else could have saved the country in 1941'?), hesitates to accept unequivocally the ideas proposed by von Laue. Having made the case in favor of Stalin, Nove notes that precisely from the communist point of view a strong case can be made against a leader who 'perverted the original ideology of the revolution and destroyed the party that Lenin knew and who created a society which is essentially characterized by an anti-socialist way of life, and thus did immeasurable harm to the socialist ideals'.[47]

Revisionists both radical and moderate share one important article of belief: whatever Stalin's shortcomings (or crimes), they were not irreparable. Their effect is not bound to be lasting, provided a determined effort is made to eradicate them. The road back to the erstwhile ideals of the revolution has not been barred for-

---

[45] S. Cohen, loc. cit., p. 62.
[46] Theodore H. von Laue, 'Stalin in Focus', *Slavic Review*, Fall 1983, pp. 387–8.
[47] Alec Nove, *Stalinism and After*, London, 1975, p. 110.

ever. While de-Stalinization came to an halt after a promising beginning, chances are that the forces of reform and progress will ultimately prevail. Stephen Cohen writing in 1985 does not share the 1953 enthusiasm of Deutscher, who thought that freedom in Russia was just around the corner, but he feels quite certain that it will come in the not-too-distant future.

Post-revisionism

Revisionism seems more or less to have run its course. Did it have a major impact? Institutionally, its influence has been considerable, inasmuch as many of its proponents were appointed to important positions in the academic world in the 1970s. But in the annals of intellectual history it will hardly figure as a long and weighty chapter. As far as the early period in Soviet history is concerned, its influence was limited and short-lived. Outside the academic world it has been largely ignored; in the new Stalin biographies which appeared in recent years there is hardly a trace of revisionist influence. The revisionists may argue that this is the result of intellectual laziness and/or political bias. But such arguments are unconvincing. If a strong, plausible case had been made in favor of revisionism it would have been impossible to ignore it.[48]

Should revisionism perhaps be regarded as the 'antithesis' of the views of many of the earlier generation of students of Soviet affairs? If so, has the time not come for a synthesis, in which the opinions of the revisionists should serve as a corrective to the excesses of the 'Cold War historians'?

Revisionism has given an impetus to the study of social and institutional history, whereas earlier on there was sometimes exclusive preoccupation with the elite and ideology. To this extent revisionism has fulfilled a useful function. Yet seen in retrospect the elite and the ideology were of decisive importance, even if the 'specific weight' of communist ideology in the general equation has considerably declined since the early days. Revisionism has com-

---

[48] This refers to the new edition of Boris Souvarine's *Stalin*, Paris, 1977; Ronald Hingley, *Joseph Stalin, Man and Legend*, London, 1974; Alex de Jonge, *Stalin and the Shaping of the Soviet Union*, London, 1986; Adam Ulam, *Stalin the Man and His Era*, New York, 1973, as well as other books; Robert C. Tucker, *Stalin as Revolutionary 1879-1929*, New York, 1973, takes in some respects a position *sui generis*, but it certainly cannot be included in the mainline revisionist literature.

pelled students of Soviet history to rethink certain tacit assumptions. But this is not to say that their propositions had to be accepted. Intellectual history is not a series of dialectical processes in which every thesis and every antithesis is of equal (or almost equal) validity. True, leading experts of the 1940s and 1950s were deeply involved in the political struggles of that period, a fact which sometimes beclouded their historical judgment. Some of them failed to see future alternatives to Stalinism. But this involvement helped to sharpen their understanding of the phenomenon which they were facing. For the revisionists the excesses of the Stalinist régime belong to the past; the fights between Stalin and his rivals, the purges and trials, are no longer live issues. But this leads to a point already made: the detachment of the 'sons' (in contradistinction to the prejudices of the 'fathers') did not go that deep on closer scrutiny. They lacked the international background of their predecessors, were more parochial in their approach, more vulnerable to 'mirror imaging'. Many of them lacked the political instinct that develops out of experience and leads to deeper understanding.

The debate on Stalin and Stalinism continued throughout the 1970s but the contribution of the proponents of social and labor history was relatively small. It concerned among other things the old issue of continuity and discontinuity between Tsarist Russia and the Soviet Union. While Stalin has been dead for many years, the topic still has strong political overtones. For if successive Soviet rulers refused to face the Stalin heritage, if they argued that the very problem did not exist, this gave rise to fears that a re-Stalinization of sorts could not be ruled out and, at the very least, strong Stalinist elements continue to exist in Soviet society and influence Soviet politics.

This debate cut across the traditional right-left dividing lines. If for Solzhenitsyn Bolshevism was an 'alien corn' in Russia, for Stephen Cohen only Stalinism was an alien corn not rooted in the Russian revolutionary tradition, a perversion of early Bolshevism. ('But it must have come from somewhere', a participant at a conference interjected. 'It did not develop out of Buddhism'.)

On the other hand Richard Pipes saw close (too close, his critics thought) links between Muscovite autocracy and Bolshevik dictatorship. Moshe Lewin argued from the left that Stalinism was a hybrid of Marxism and Tsarism: 'The Stalinist system was less a product of Bolshevik programs or planning than of desperate attempts to cope with social pandemonium and crises which it had created'. Leonard Schapiro saw in Stalinism a reversion to Muscovite serfdom, but also noted that all elements of Stalin's system had been present at least in an embryonic form in Leninist political practise. But old Russia had been more than a backward police state, and it was equally true that there were substantial differences between Lenin and Stalin, not only because far fewer people were killed under Lenin.

How important was Stalin's personality? Here again the views sharply differ. The emphasis on the greyness of Stalin appears not only in the writings of Trotsky, who could never understand how he had been defeated by a mediocrity of this kind; it also emerges from the pages of Carr, Deutscher (his almost 'impersonal personality'), and the latter-day revisionists. But Solzhenitsyn's conclusions are not that dissimilar: Stalin was not only Stalin but expressed the views and desires of a great many people inside the Soviet Union. It was not just that this society had not prevented Stalin's rise to power. Stalin found, probably to his own amazement, that mass terror and the hysteria of the 1930s brought him genuine popular support and made it easy for him to rule. Without the help of hundred of thousands – not all of whom were terrorized into collaboration – the system would not have functioned. As Milovan Djilas put it: Stalin satisfied a need. And in contrast to defeated Nazi Germany, the murderers were never brought to trial.

But if Stalin had a great deal of help, he was still a highly unusual person and some of his actions have remained a mystery to most observers to this day. References to Russian backwardness, to outside pressure, to the need to combat barbarism with barbarism, may contain a grain of truth – sometimes a very small one. But there still remains a profound irrationality, and the attempt to use psychoanalysis and various comparative cultural approaches seems not to have helped greatly to provide satisfactory explanations. What would a Marxist class analysis have shown? That socio-economic factors were not the decisive driving force in this system which was largely independent of social classes.

Whatever Stalin's motives, there still remained the question of the consequences. According to Djilas a different course of action could have been taken after 1924. But given Lenin's revision of Marxism and the traditional contempt for democracy in Russia, the cards were heavily stacked against it. The road was open to bureaucratic despotism; a new *millet* system, as practised in the Ottoman empire; industrial feudalism; and the rise of a new class.[49] If, in Djilas' view, Stalinism is alien to the strong spiritual components in Russian culture, it is also true that it has taken root in Russia and is nourished by the missionary despotic and imperialist element in Russian history. Leszek Kolakowski, the leading Polish philosopher, also sees the new man produced by the régime as perfectly willing to live with the official slogans. For him Stalinism is the necessary and unavoidable product of (Soviet) Marxism, not merely a latter-day incarnation of certain traditional traits in Russian culture. The difference with Nazism was that the Nazis stated openly the intention to exterminate some nations, whereas Stalinism had to hide behind a false facade. It had to pay lip service to the old socialist tradition; it had to talk about internationalism, social justice, freedom, and equality, mixing communist with nationalist slogans – effectively killing, by the way, the communist idea: 'That skull will never smile again'.

If some historians were trying to 'relativize' Stalin and Stalinism, others still have very strong feelings about the subject even three decades after the death of the dictator. They saw Stalinism as a key to the development of the Soviet Union and they believed that concepts like upward mobility or even modernization were inadequate, if not altogether ludicrous, to explain the specific character of the phenomenon and its political consequences.

There is no consensus and the basic problems continue to be debated. But it is also true that distance in time at least helps better to understand what the crucial issues were; it has also become easier to divide the chaff from the wheat. How have the major works on the Soviet Union stood the test of time?

There is the tragi-comic story of Fainsod's *How Russia Is Ruled*, a standard text which was revised by Jerry Hough, who had been Fainsod's student at Harvard. However, Hough had reached conclusions about how Russia was ruled (institutional pluralism) that were almost diametrically opposed to those of his teacher. Such a revision was certainly a novel idea; with equal right one could

---

[49] The two most interesting volumes on Stalinism are G. Urban, ed., *Stalinism*, London, 1982; and Robert C. Tucker, ed., *Stalinism. Essays in Historical Interpretation*, New York, 1977.

have asked von Hayek to prepare a new edition of *Das Kapital*. As Leonard Schapiro noted, 'It is regrettable that reputable publishers should have allowed a work which is little related to Fainsod's outlook or in merit to share the lustre of his name'.[50] But this was by no means a typical case. B. Souvarine's *Stalin*, perhaps the most uncompromising anti-Stalin work and also a study of enormous scholarship, was triumphantly re-issued in 1977 after forty years of neglect and deliberate suppression, an event which attracted much attention, not only in his native France. On the other hand history had not dealt too kindly with the late Isaac Deutscher. His *Stalin* is still read as a work of literature, but the fact that so many of Deutscher's prognostications have not come true has caused closer scrutiny of his historical work. True, he still has his sympathizers who loyally defend him, but even a leading revisionist such as Stephen Cohen has noted with the benefit of hindsight that Deutscher, with all his merits, has produced near-apologetics for Stalinism.

A critical study of Deutscher and his work, which began to appear during Deutscher's lifetime, had to be discontinued following a threat to sue the author. Its publication was completed only many years after Deutscher's death. Leopold Labedz's harsh assessment stresses in a few sentences the clue to the essential problem:

> If Deutscher's book aroused so much passionate resentment and hostility (as he notes in his 1960 introduction) this had to do not so much with what he said; after all there were far more emphatic apologies for Stalin published at the time, but none tried to pass as an objective study by a detached scholar.[51]

Nor has E. H. Carr fared as well as many expected. In a little book published shortly before his death that summarized his views on Soviet history Carr went as far as calling Stalin a 'ruthless despot', an assessment for which one would look in vain in the fourteen volumes of his *History of the Soviet Union*.[52] It is also true that the sheer magnitude of his enterprise continues to evoke admiration even among his critics. Thus John Keep: 'A towering

[50] L. Schapiro, *Soviet Studies*, London, 1986.

[51] L. Labedz, 'Deutscher as Historian and Prophet', *Survey*, Summer 1977–8, p. 155.

[52] E.H. Carr, *The Russian Revolution. From Lenin to Stalin*, New York, 1979, p. 172.

scholarly monument, in its shadow the rest of us are but pygmies'. But Carr has also come in for heavy criticism. Labedz noted that Carr's adulation of power basically flawed his enterprise; being satisfied with appearances, whether of Hitler or of Stalin, he perpetuated myth in the name of realism.[53]

Norman Stone in a severe indictment of Carr both as a man and a historian, says that Carr never quite said what he meant, that he covered his tracks, never drew recognizable conclusions, and for this reason his work is difficult to review.

'Much of the book concerns economics, a subject on which Carr was hardly an expert. The lack of definitive point in the book . . . makes it dull and unrevealing. Like Carr himself it peters out'. True, Stone has some better things to say about Carr's section on foreign policy, a subject closer to Carr's heart. Yet his overall assessment could not be more negative:

> Carr's *History* is not a history of the Soviet Union, but effectively of the Communist Party of the Soviet Union. Even then, much of it is the kind of unreconstructed Stalinist version that could not now see the light of day in Russia itself. . . . I am nearly tempted to exclaim that no more useless set of volumes has ever masqueraded as a classic. Carr's real talent lay in mathematics. . . . From the mathematical spirit he took a quality not so much of abstraction as of autism, which was carried over into his historical work. The result is a trail of devastation.[54]

This assessment has been criticized for appearing so soon after Carr's death: *De mortuis nil nisi bunkum.* Perhaps a later date of publication would have been more appropriate. But does this affect Stone's basic arguments?

With his apparent reticence Carr's book was deeply partisan and in the final analysis unreliable – not so much because of what he wrote but what he left out. Carr, the author of *Bakunin, Dostoyevski*, and the *Romantic Exiles*, will be remembered and read; his *History of the Soviet Union* will probably share the fate of the

---

[53] 'He tended to confine himself to the penumbra of official formulations and of ideological formulas which always concealed, rather than revealed, real Soviet life', L. Labedz, *Times Literary Supplement*, June 10, 1983. In an interview with the *New Left Review* in 1978 Carr said Stalin had 'no moral authority whatsoever', and he censured 'the long blindness of the left intellectuals in the West to the repressive character of the régime'. Carr, not a man of the left, fully shared this attitude.

[54] Norman Stone, 'Grim Eminence', *London Review of Books*, February 2, 1983.

seven volumes of Treitschke's history of Germany in the nineteenth century, also a work on a grand scale, now mainly remembered as an exhibit, a manifestation of the *Zeitgeist*. By the time Treitschke's works finally appeared, towards the end of World War One, the Germany Treitschke had known and admired had disappeared, his adulation had been overtaken by events. The break in the Soviet Union has been much less dramatic, but Carr's uncritical approach seems now almost equally out of date.

Any attempt to summarize the main lines of development in the study of Soviet history is bound to be incomplete, mainly with regard to the good, solid work that has not been mentioned. Much of what has been said in the preceding pages does not apply to the study of Soviet economics, or to give another example, to Soviet literature. There have been violent controversies in these fields, as in others, but also a great deal more consensus than in political history, the main subject of our review. Our preoccupation was with the Soviet past, and this also explains why hardly any reference has been made to various social science models concerning current Soviet politics which, at one time or another, have been widely discussed and were regarded by some as very promising.

It is my impression that the enthusiasm about these models has waned in recent years. But even if my appraisal should be wrong, it would be of only marginal importance in the present context. It could be said with greater justification that too much attention has been paid in this review to certain trends in historical studies that were quite prominent at one time, but whose real importance, in retrospect, was less than it seemed – to the detriment of the unspectacular work, which, it now appears, has had a more lasting influence. This is a perennial problem and if I have not found an answer, I am not aware that others have a prescription.

« 10 »

The End of Totalitarianism?

No idea in our time has provoked more impassioned debate than the idea of totalitarianism. Used indiscriminately by some as a synonym for fascism, or communism, or both, it is abhorred and denounced by others as a source of deliberate confusion and a propaganda weapon. The debate has concerned not only the past and present political character of the Soviet Union but also, in retrospect, the political character of Nazi Germany. Unlike some other current controversies, the debate over totalitarianism has not been a purely academic enterprise. In part it is about words, categories, and definitions; above all, however, it concerns political realities, and it is therefore of considerable practical importance.

Although it is widely believed that totalitarianism as a concept was invented in the 1940s and 1950s by Western cold warriors trying to prove there was nothing to choose between Hitler and Stalin, in actual fact the term goes back to the early 1920s when it was first used by Italian anti-fascists and later picked up with some gusto by Mussolini, who wrote a famous article on the subject. (While the Italians 'invented' totalitarianism as a theoretical concept, however, their practical contribution to the form was quite modest; of all the great dictatorships of our time, Italian fascism was the least totalitarian.) The concept was then taken up and elaborated by social scientists, mostly *émigrés* from Nazi Germany. It was also used on many occasions by left-wing writers like Victor Serge, and by Marxists like Trotsky, Otto Bauer, and Rudolf Hilferding. It is now used by Gorbachev.

All these writers claimed – correctly, in my judgment – that while dictatorships and tyrannies were as old as the hills, there was a qualitative difference between all previous despotisms and the dictatorships which emerged after World War One. To put the difference negatively, old-fashioned, traditional dictatorship had not used propaganda and other means of social control (including terror) to anything like the same extent as did the modern ones. They had not tried to mobilize the masses. Ideology played a far lesser role in their self-conception. There was no monopolistic state-party. And while, in a 'traditional' dictatorship, the legal order was always affected to some degree, it was never disregarded as completely as it was in a totalitarian régime.

Finally, if one wished to be crude about it, one could argue that any régime attracting 99 percent of the votes in an election was by definition totalitarian. For an old-fashioned dictatorship would not have been able to induce virtually everyone to vote, or to bring about a result like this by either fraud or pressure; for that matter, it would not have felt the need in the first place to gain such pseudo-legitimacy. This definition of totalitarianism may be regarded as simplistic, but it is probably as good as, if not better than, the more complicated ones developed in more recent decades.

Two works which appeared soon after World War Two helped to popularize the idea of totalitarianism: Hannah Arendt's *The Origins of Totalitarianism* (1951) and, more influential in the academic community, Carl Friedrich's and Zbigniew Brzezinski's *Totalitarian Dictatorship and Autocracy* (1957). Both drew attention to the correspondence between Nazi Germany and Communist Russia, Arendt stating that they were two 'essentially identical' systems. Friedrich and Brzezinski that they were 'basically alike'.

But both also put forth theses which were not borne out by later events, in particular that totalitarianism is an end in itself, that a totalitarian system is bound to become more totalitarian all the time, and that an omnipotent leader is a precondition for totalitarian rule. When Stalin died, and changes took place in the Soviet Union culminating in the famous attacks at the 20th party congress of the CPSU on the 'cult of personality', Arendt quickly retreated from some of these positions. Friedrich and Brzezinski also modified their views, conceding ten years after the first edition of their book that Hitler and Stalin represented not the norm but extreme instances of totalitarianism, and that too much significance had been attributed to certain personal (and therefore transient) features of their régimes which were not necessarily intrinsic elements of totalitarian rule.

* * *

It was in part because of flaws like these that some dismissed the totalitarian concept altogether, or at least grew reluctant to use it in describing the régime in the Soviet Union. But only in part; there were reasons of a political or ideological nature behind this reluctance as well. Thus, according to one school of thought, the concept wrongly concentrated on techniques common to Nazi and communist rule – propaganda, terror, the one-party system – while missing the essence of the régimes as revealed in their professed aims. How could one compare the goals of Marxism-Leninism, such as freedom and social justice, with those of fascism and Nazism? Besides, one could point to certain social and economic achievements of the Soviet régime; if actual performance fell woefully short of the claims that had been made for that society, these might be just temporary distortions bound to disappear in the course of time. Fascism, by contrast, was intrinsically evil, immune to change for the better either through evolution or through reform. In this reading, then, totalitarianism, if useful at all in understanding dictatorial régimes, might be applied to Nazism but not to communism.

In the 1960s the totalitarianism concept as applied to communism fell into further disrepute. In the Soviet Union Stalinism had been replaced by something more difficult to analyze and define, the mass purges had ceased, and the population of the Gulag greatly decreased. In addition, the worldwide communist monolith was splitting apart. These and other developments seemed to show that communist totalitarianism as described by Arendt and Friedrich-Brzezinski had either passed from this world, or had perhaps never existed. And so burial rites were held. One critic wrote that the so-called totalitarian state had been neither total nor a state. The author of the entry 'Totalitarianism' in the second edition of the *Encyclopedia of Social Sciences*, predicted that just as there had been no such article in the first edition, there would be none in the third.

But if the concept of totalitarianism was buried, communist régimes continued to exist. How to define them? According to the new consensus, the Soviet and other communist systems were authoritarian.

Unfortunately, 'authoritarian' is one of those terms that can mean a great many different things. A political régime completely devoid of authority is unthinkable, at least for any length of time.

Every dictatorship or semi-dictatorship is *a priori* authoritarian, be it a monarchy (Saudi Arabia, Jordan under Hussein, Morocco under Hassan) or such disparate régimes as Pakistan, Vietnam, and Indonesia, not to mention all African and most Latin American countries. Even the German government under Adenauer, France under de Gaulle, and Israel under Ben-Gurion were to some extent authoritarian. Of what use is a category which can be applied to nine-tenths if not more of the member states of the United Nations? If we say that the Soviet Union or Bulgaria is 'authoritarian', what new light have we shed on their specific character? And if the totalitarianism concept is to be dismissed as inapplicable in view of the differences between the Soviet Union and Nazi Germany, what is the point of replacing it with a label covering political systems which have nothing in common whatsoever?

Aware of this dilemma, scholars over the years have introduced new terms to define communist régimes, ranging from the obvious but unhelpful to the irrelevant or even ludicrous; neo-feudalism, welfare-state authoritarianism, failed totalitarianism, institutional pluralism, limited pluralism. Others have relied on the concept of modernization, but this too has been of little assistance, for the term totalitarianism refers to the structure of power in a society whereas modernization involves an altogether different set of social processes. Yet another approach – the study of Western management and the way Western corporations are run – proved similarly unenlightening when it came to understanding the specific character of communist societies; ditto with bureaucracy and interest groups.

By the early 1980s even the more enthusiastic advocates of the various 'pluralist' models of communist society had to admit that the announcement of the demise of their rival concept had been premature. Stephen F. Cohen of Princeton has observed with regret in his new book, *Rethinking the Soviet Experience*,[1] that the main impact of his school of thought was felt in the middle 1970s, and that it did not succeed in putting an end to the totalitarianism thesis.

The reason, actually, is quite simple, and has to do with political reality. The revisionists would have easily carried the day if de-Stalinization in the Soviet Union had brought about a radical and complete break with the past: if détente had prevailed in interna-

---

[1] Oxford University Press, New York, 1985.

240

tional relations; if there had been unmistakable signs of the emergence of democratic institutions – or at least of true pluralism – inside the Soviet Union. In the face of such incontrovertible evidence, even the staunchest believers in the concept of totalitarianism would have been unable to keep it alive much longer. But facts, as Lenin liked to say, are stubborn things, and the facts dictated otherwise: de-Stalinization, after a promising start, was halted and later even reversed. Soviet political institutions did not fundamentally change.

In short, if no one today denies that in its early form the totalitarianism model was inadequate and in part misleading, the attempt to replace it with something radically new has failed. I suspect that even the most committed revisionists know this, though they are reluctant to admit it in public.

Where then does all this leave us? If the same term cannot be used for the Soviet Union in the late Stalin era and under Gorbachev, for China under Mao and under its present rulers, for Poland and Hungary in the 1950s and today, is there perhaps a whole spectrum of totalitarianisms?

Leading students of totalitarianism have devoted much thought to this question but there is no unanimity among them. The German scholar Karl Dietrich Bracher, who perhaps has contributed more than anyone else to our understanding of the rise of the Nazi movement and Hitler's takeover, sees no reason to discontinue using the term both for Nazism and for communism. His four criteria are: an official and exclusive ideology; a centralized and hierarchically organized mass movement; control of mass communications for the purpose of indoctrination; and control of the economy and social relations.[2]

Even more important are two basic points which Bracher has emphasized time and again, and which have caused much offense.

---

[2] These bear comparison with the basic features of totalitarian dictatorship listed by Carl Friedrich in the 1950s: an ideology; a single party typically led by one man; a terroristic police; a communications monopoly; a weapons monopoly; and a centrally directed economy. This scheme was criticized, not without justice, for a variety of reasons: the economy under Nazism and fascism was never under full state control; history seems to show that while fascism needs a single leader, Communism can also do with a collective leadership headed by a *primus inter pares*; etc. Bracher's list is shorter and simpler.

Totalitarianism, he says, is not a typical and exclusive product of the interwar period that came to an end in 1945; on the contrary, recent technologies offer modern dictatorships even greater possibilities for the mobilization and indoctrination of the masses and the imposition of strict controls over society. Second, the fundamental dividing line in recent history is not between left and right, and not between capitalism and socialism (despite all the differences between them), but between dictatorship and democracy, despotism and freedom.

A great deal of blindness is needed to doubt or deny the opposition of democracy and dictatorship – yet it has scandalized some for whom the main ideological issue of our time is not political freedom but economic organization. For them, a dictatorship may still be progressive whereas a democracy, so long as it is capitalist, is still pre-fascist or 'potentially fascist'. And since all democracies which have ever existed (except perhaps in Iceland or early modern Switzerland) have been either capitalist or based on a mixed economy, they are all regarded as suspect. Bracher's scheme neatly exposes the political bias behind such a contention.

Bracher also sees a dividing line between totalitarianism and authoritarianism, as does Juan Linz, a leading Yale political sociologist. Linz draws the distinction around three main points. An authoritarian régime can tolerate limited political pluralism, whereas totalitarian rule cannot. In an authoritarian régime ideology is not a central issue; a general perspective usually suffices. Nor does an authoritarian régime need mass political participation directed from above.

This seems to be about the best available key to an understanding of the differences between the two systems. It is not a magic wand for, as Linz has pointed out, there always will be a degree of uncertainty, a gray zone, with regard to the specific character of authoritarian régimes and the direction they are likely to take in the future. Yet the soundness of Linz's approach has been borne out by, for instance, events in Spain during the last decade. Franco's rule was not totalitarian, despite what many claimed at the time; there was no central ideology and no political mass party, only an old-fashioned if altogether unattractive military dictatorship. For this reason, after Franco's death the transition to a democratic régime proceeded without great difficulty. By contrast, no totalitarian régime has ever transformed itself peacefully in a democratic direction; this has happened only following total military defeat.

Bracher and Linz were influenced in their work on the totalitarian state above all by the fascist experience. In the thought of the German political philosopher Richard Löwenthal, it is the impact of developments in the communist world that is central. Like Bracher and Linz, Löwenthal similarly accepts the line between tyranny and freedom, but he believes that the Soviet Union and other communist régimes have definitively moved beyond totalitarianism, toward a stage he calls 'post-totalitarian authoritarianism' or 'authoritarian bureaucratic oligarchy'. There may still be a clearly recognizable leader, but his powers are not markedly greater than those of a Western prime minister over the members of his cabinet. The people still have no means to remove the leadership, but the revolution from above (the most prominent feature of totalitarianism, according to Löwenthal) has run out of steam.

Lowenthal does not argue that the new equilibrium in an erstwhile totalitarian régime offers the prospect of some kind of gradual liberalization; radical opposition to the values and institutions of Western democracy will continue. But in the communist countries he expects a stabilizing of the post-revolutionary institutions of one-party rule, rather than a revival of totalitarianism *per se*: 'Those countries have not gone from tyranny to freedom, but from massive terror to a rule of meanness, ensuring stability at the risk of stagnation'.[3]

Löwenthal's (relative) optimism has been criticized by experts on the Soviet Union and China who have noted that while there have been thaws in both countries, the totalitarian iceberg has not melted.[4] Besides, can it really be taken for granted that the experience of Stalin and Mao has immunized these régimes forever against the grosser forms of despotism? Or could it be, as some believe, that they are fated for a long time to come to alternate between cycles of relative relaxation and strong oppression, with the single-party dictatorship and the old structures and institutions remaining intact?

[3] "Beyond Totalitarianism," in *1984 Revisited*, edited by Irving Howe (1984).
[4] See, for example, A. Schifrin in *Totalitarian Democracy and After*. International Colloquium in Honor of Y. Taimon (Jerusalem, 1984).

Like Löwenthal, Pierre Hassner, the author of a recent masterly review of the subject,[5] recognizes that far-reaching changes have taken place in the Soviet bloc, but they have not in his view gone beyond the point of no return. The new régime is not authoritarian in the traditional sense, but rather represents a form of totalitarianism in decline. Seen in this perspective, 'post-totalitarian authoritarianism' is only a totalitarianism which has lost some of its dynamism, and its capacity to control a society which has become more complex and/or more resistant. In the Soviet Union such a development has resulted in fewer purges and less mass terror and perhaps a greater degree of *Realpolitik* in foreign affairs – though in this last respect the difference with Stalinism is not that great. But it has not resulted in a significantly more liberal régime, and not even in a massive strengthening of interest groups – unless one regards the interpenetration of party, KGB, army, and the commanding positions in the economy as a form of pluralism.

Nor, as Hassner sees it, has there been any fundamental change in Soviet foreign policy. The question of whether the Soviet leaders truly believe in world revolution is irrelevant; perhaps they never did. But:

In the absence of traditional or democratic legitimation, the régime keeps the country in a state of permanent insecurity. In order to maintain their power, the leaders must keep control over their empire and society. In order to achieve this they have to be armed against all outside influences, which means the need for an ideology involving hostility vis-à-vis the outside world, and power which makes it possible to defeat, potentially at least, every outside threat. And these defensive and conservative considerations may push them toward expansion and conflict as surely as any crusading messianism.

If one were to summarize the debate at this stage, then, it seems undeniable that the totalitarianism concept in its original form is in need of modification. But the attempt to substitute the authoritarian label has proved altogether misleading, and the other terms suggested are no better. Among those other terms I myself would include still another that has been suggested, 'failed totalitarianism' (Michael Walzer). In fact, it could be argued that if there has been a certain relaxation of domestic pressure in the Eastern bloc, this is

---

[5] "*Le totalitarianisme vu de l'Ouest,*" in *Totalitarianismes,* edited by Guy Hermet (Paris, 1984).

a consequence of the triumph rather than the failure of totalitarianism; the opposition has been crushed, large parts of the population have been successfully indoctrinated, and in these circumstances there is no need for more drastic measures such as mass purges and executions. Still less is it clear why the Soviet Union and China should be regarded as failures.

If one wishes to stick to the totalitarian label, it ought to be stressed that present-day totalitarianism is mature, advanced, perhaps even rational in contrast to the frenzied or sultanistic (Max Weber) totalitarianism of an earlier period – paranoiac in Stalin's case, hyperaggressive in Hitler's. Those who prefer another term are obliged to point out that they are referring by it not to old-style autocratic régimes like absolute monarchies or military dictatorships, but to a modern-type dictatorship, based on a full-control system run by the leadership of a political party using high-technology means of repression and indoctrination.

As the totalitarianism debate among students of the Soviet Union and communist affairs has more or less come full circle in the last thirty years, so a somewhat similar course has been run with regard to national socialism. That debate began in the 1960s, when a number of historians and political scientists, mainly German, whose anti-Nazi credentials were above suspicion, began to claim that the earlier interpretations of Nazism had been mistaken.[6]

Nazi policy, these scholars asserted, far from being monolithic and centralized, was frequently incoherent. Nor was it true that all power was concentrated in Hitler's hands; the old social structures continued to exist and to be active under the surface. Nazi ideology, too, was less important than had commonly been thought; policy evolved as the result of an interaction between doctrine (ideology) and improvisation, the latter being triggered by all kinds of objective pressures and factors over which the Nazis had little or no control.

In short, if, according to adherents of the totalitarianism model (as in Nazi mythology itself), everything in the country was done in a purposeful way, the machine ran smoothly, Hitler's power was unlimited, and there were no serious conflicts among the Nazi

[6] One of the first American protagonists was Edward N. Petersen, *The Limits of Hitler's Power* (1969).

leaders; according to the revised view Nazi Germany was ruled in a casual way, the machine ran anything but smoothly, Hitler's power was quite limited, and underlings maintained their private empires virtually up to the very end. Some revisionists went so far as to describe the political structure of the Third Reich as 'polycratic chaos'; others used less extreme formulations. But the general trend of the critique was unmistakable: like Stalin, Hitler had been a mere 'authoritarian'.

Even the history of the Holocaust came in for radical reinterpretation. It was not denied that millions of Jews were actually killed, but it was argued that there was no straight line leading from Nazi ideology to the Holocaust (the so-called 'linear thesis'), that there was no coordination and planned Nazi policy toward the Jews, and that the mass murder was not an aim that Hitler had set *a priori*. Rather, the Holocaust was a *Flucht nach vorn*, an endeavour to find a way out of a blind alley into which the Nazi leaders had maneuvered themselves. These leaders did not so much plan the Final Solution as more or less stumble into it: because many Jews had already been taken away, the others also had to be deported; since there was no place to resettle them, they had to be exterminated. And so one thing led to another, in considerable part by mere accident, and there was a cumulative radicalization of policy during the war which Hitler had neither foreseen nor planned.

The controversy between 'intentionalists' (those stressing the impact of Nazi ideology on Nazi policies) and 'functionalists' (or revisionists) has been part of a larger debate over the character of Nazi rule, and it is by no means over. Some of the points made by the revisionists are irrefutable, although they concern allegations never advanced by serious scholars. Thus, as the revisionists say, it is indeed physically impossible for one man, even the most efficient and hard-working leader, to control every aspect of life in a big country. No more than decisions concerning the organization of schools in Uzbekistan were made by Stalin personally did Hitler, who had no interest in economics in the first place, set the norms of production for the Upper Silesian coal industry. Although Nazi mythology, like communist mythology, described the leader as omnipresent and omniscient, that was even less true in Germany than in the Soviet Union, if only because Hitler had only six years from the seizure of power to the outbreak of war to establish his control mechanisms, not enough time for a major endeavour of this kind. Once war broke out, everything was subordinated to the military effort, and tinkering with political and social institutions was discouraged.

Nevertheless, it is crucial for the understanding of totalitarian régimes to recognize that while not all decisions are actually made in and by the center, *no* truly important decision is made without the knowledge, let alone against the wish, of the leader. It is equally important to realize that while not all decisions are made by the supreme leader, all *could* in principle have been made by him.

Private empires and divergent interests existed in the Third Reich; people quarrel and try to expand their power wherever they work together. But without the good will of the leader, satraps lose their power base from one day to the next. Recent purges and reshuffles in the Kremlin show that nothing has changed in this respect. There is no justification for calling a society pluralistic simply because some of its leaders may disagree – or even try to kill each other.

'Functionalist' historians claim that 'intentionalists' have taken at face value Hitler's speeches, Nazi editorials, and *Mein Kampf*. In actual fact, they argue, Nazi ideology was never that important – and in any case, the Nazi régime like all others was subject to 'routinization', the iron law according to which revolutions lose their impetus through the passing of time, human nature, and the need to make concessions for various reasons. (Similar views have been expressed by revisionist writers in the Soviet field.) But this 'law' hardly applied in Nazi Germany; as already noted, Hitler had only six years to make domestic changes, and in this period the trend was certainly toward radicalization rather than toward moderation. What would have happened if Germany had won the war is another question altogether, but in any case the 'law' of routinization disregards some of the basic features of totalitarianism, in particular the fact that the power concentrated in a few hands is so great that it can be defeated only from the outside.

Functionalism puts excessive emphasis on 'objective' social factors. It largely ignores ideology, it trivializes the crimes of dictators and makes them appear almost harmless. In the functionalist perspective, indeed, there seems little to choose between life in a dictatorship and a democracy; there as here people are born, go to school, work, and eventually die. Hitler in this view turns into a near-figurehead, a modern Hamlet unable to make up his mind and only half-aware of what is going on around him. So many other historical culprits, individuals as well as 'structures', have been found by the functionalists in their searches that any competent lawyer acting for Hitler and Nazism in the court of history could without great difficulty obtain a verdict of diminished responsibility by reason of extenuating circumstances. This kind of interpretation is a travesty of what really occurred.

Yet as in the field of Soviet studies, the functionalists, though they have enjoyed a vogue, have finally failed to displace the older understanding of the nature of Nazism. Stephen F. Cohen (in *Rethinking the Soviet Experience*) has invoked a parallel between the totalitarianism debate in Soviet and in Nazi studies:

> Uncharitably, we might contrast the post-revisionist situation in Sovietology to that in Nazi studies, where a totalitarianism school also once prevailed. A major scholar in that field tells us: 'Each new detailed study of the realities of life in Nazi Germany shows how inadequate the concept of totalitarianism is'.

But in actual fact the debate over Nazism does not provide any comfort to revisionists in the Soviet field. Despite the anti-totalitarianism trend in recent German historiography, it would be difficult to think of a single major figure in the field willing to abandon the concept, and this applies even to those who for a variety of reasons find it not wholly satisfactory. The anti-totalitarianism upsurge has had less to do with the shortcomings of the concept than with the fact that it was politically inconvenient to a new generation of scholars and writers anxious to absolve the German past of its unique character and to see Nazism as just another variant of a general modern disease.

But intellectual fashions tend to change; a better gauge of opinion is to be found in the leading German scholarly review, *Neue Politische Literatur* ('New Political Literature') which every few years features massive review articles on specific topics. In 1975 the review article on totalitarianism noted that the concept was on its last legs, in a 'state of agony'. The 1983 article was entitled: 'Renaissance of the Totalitarianism Concept'? There is reason to believe that by the next review, the question mark will have been dropped.

* * *

The debate over the character of Nazism is now mainly of historical interest. By contrast, the question of whether totalitarianism survives in the contemporary world and has a future remains one of the key issues of our time. Most proponents of the various 'pluralistic' models, after all, have been driven (some openly) less by scholarly consideration than by a desire to prove that the Soviet Union is neither as evil nor as dangerous as the totalitarianism model suggests; others have been intent on finding a rationale for supporting or coopting Marxist revolutions in the third world.

In other words, the crucial problem is not whether the Soviet Union or China or some third world country can be made to fit into a concept, old or new, simple or elaborate, for purposes of classification. Definitions are never absolutely perfect, and classification, of great value in botany or zoology, is far more problematical in international politics. All democracies (like Tolstoy's happy families) are alike, while tyrannies (like unhappy families) are tyrannies in different ways. The basic task is not to find ingenious formulas but to reach a deeper understanding of the essention character of certain political régimes, and the direction in which they are likely to develop.

This much we can say after thirty-five years of analysis and discussion: in the Soviet Union no dissent will be tolerated which will endanger the perpetuation of the régime and the hold of the leadership. Despite much talk about *perestroika* (restructuring), basic political reform (or revolution), which is possible in an authoritarian set-up, has not so far taken place under the Soviet system. In this sense, the Soviet régime is still totalitarian, but that does not mean, as the exiled Soviet philosopher Alexander Zinoviev has asserted, that it will last forever. Everything is subject to the law of change, and in circumstances which no one can foresee today the Soviet Union might one day begin to transform itself. Even in the shorter run there will be some economic reforms, overdue in any case, and the resistance to some harmless Western fashions, intellectual or sartorial, has already ceased.

But there are no cogent grounds for believing that either economic reform or the introduction of rock music will give major impetus to a real democratization of Soviet politics. If the 'cult of personality', the permanent mass purges, and some other specific features of the Stalinist régime have been abolished, or at least greatly reduced in scope, the reason is that these measures not only proved unnecessary to perpetuating the role of the party hierarchy, they actually threatened it. The party leadership has not forgotten that Stalin, after all, liquidated proportionately many more communists than other Soviet citizens; no communist in his right mind wants a recurrence of this.

Tsarist Russia was not a particularly effective régime; it was run by a mere few hundred thousand officials and other pillars of society. But it still took three years of war in which the country suffered one defeat after another to overthrow Tsarist rule. The Communist party has many more cadres, and in modern conditions social and political control of the masses has become much easier – provided always that there is no split in the ruling stratum. This is the one mortal danger facing such a system, but there are millions of people in the Soviet Union who have a vested interest in the survival of the present order, and who would go to great lengths to prevent its break-up. Nor should one assume that the Soviet people are themselves seething with discontent. They may complain and grumble, but the majority cannot envisage a truly different régime.

What are the prospects of the third world? Most of these countries are dictatorships, but except, precisely, for the communist régimes in China, Cuba, Vietnam, and perhaps a few others, they have not yet reached a stage of social, cultural, and technical development in which totalitarianism can be successfully imposed; there is no political party or ideology to provide control and cohesion. True, a few non-communist régimes have moved in a totalitarian direction – Egypt under Nasser, Syria under Assad, and Iraq under Sadam Hussein. The hold of the leaders in these régimes is quite strong, owing to the great effectiveness of the political police and tight control over the officer corps. But political police and army alone do not make for totalitarian rule: these régimes usually stand and fall with the person of the leader, and once he disappears anything can happen. Seen in this light, such régimes are authoritarian; the changes that have taken place in a totalitarian direction are not irreversible, not even in the short run.

As for that other contemporary phenomenon, radical nationalism combined with fanatical religious belief à la Khomeini, its resemblance to traditional despotism – which was often quite durable and lasted for long periods – would still appear much greater than to modern totalitarianism. Thus, in a long-term perspective there may be reason for cautious optimism so far as those countries are concerned – though this is far from predicting a trend toward freedom there.

In Eastern Europe, and in China, there is also the chance of an evolution, however slow, toward some modern version of bureaucratic autocracy. At least such a development is conceivable there. Is it conceivable in the foreseeable future in the Soviet Union? In principle, yes, but the retarding factors are very strong. The totalitarianism of the communist type (to quote Richard Löwenthal) could not create and preserve its unique character without a profoundly utopian faith. This faith was bound to founder eventually 'as it conflicted with, and eventually succumbed to, the necessity for economic modernization'. The loss of utopian faith has ended recurrent attempts at ever new 'revolutions from above', the horror of periodic measures of mass annihilation of entire social or national categories as distinct from the persecution of individual dissenters. For Löwenthal the end of the utopian faith is the end of totalitarianism, the present communist régimes are post-totalitarian even if they are not the least bit 'liberalized'. They are post-totalitarian single-party régimes. A return to their totalitarian origin is excluded – 'that particular secular religion is dead – at least in those countries that have tried it out'.[7]

All this may well be true, there certainly has been a great decline in both faith and indiscriminate violence, and it is probably also correct that the 'excesses' of Stalinism, such as the purges, had an immunizing effect. But this raises several questions for which there are no obvious answers. Are utopianism and terror the two decisive features of totalitarianism? Are there no others? There have been no significant changes in the monopoly of political power in the Soviet Union, in the pervasiveness of propaganda, and in other respects. Nor is it certain that if the holders of political power were challenged, they would not resort to violent means to defend their positions.

The loss of the utopian faith syndrome is not of much use for the understanding of events in Germany between 1933 and 1945. It helps, perhaps, to understand the decline of Stalinism but not why totalitarianism developed in the first place. Was it perhaps 'objectively necessary' to carry out the revolution from above, as

---

[7] Richard Löwenthal, *Commentary*, January 1986.

a precondition for certain social and economic changes? But totalitarianism, ('mature Stalinism') came into being only after the collectivization of agriculture had been carried out and after the five-year-plans had been launched. Such an interpretation tends to belittle the political aspects of totalitarianism; could it not be argued equally persuasively that, to keep in power, effective dictatorships in developed countries in the modern world *have* to use means quite different from those which were sufficient to sustain an absolutist régime in the eighteenth century – or even Tsarism before 1917? The ruling elite in a post – totalitarian régime stands for a rational policy, no major social upheavals, no mass terror. But equally it wants to hold on to its privileges and to power; millions of people have a vested interest in the perpetuation of the political régime.

There are a great many one-party authoritarian régimes in the third world, but they are quite different from those ruled by communist parties; they may kill many more people but they are still not totalitarian. The character of a political régime is not measured only by the number of its victims.

The communist régimes in their present form will not last forever; they will undergo further transformation. If Stalinism is taken as *the* model, they are no longer totalitarian. But for the time being it is the issue of irreversibility which constitutes the dividing line between authoritarian régimes and between dictatorships of a different, more deeply rooted, more lasting kind, whatever label we chose to attach to them.

« 11 »

Lessons of Seven Decades

The highways and byways of contemporary history are strewn with pitfalls and dead-end streets; within this general field there is probably no more dangerous ground than that devoted to the study of the Soviet Union. For here, all the problems and difficulties facing the contemporary historian are bound to come up sooner or later, usually with a vengeance. The lone wanderer in this uncharted and forbidding landscape knows, in theory at least, that there will be no short cuts on the long road ahead. He is charmed against the various temptations that will come his way, against self-confident dogmatism and despairing scepticism. He has learned from his own painful experience and from that of his predecessors; it may be useful to recapitulate at this stage some of these lessons.

Admirers and critics of the Soviet Union have drawn certain conclusions from their study of seven decades; occasionally they even concur about them. Most of them agree that there was a revolutionary situation in Russia in 1917, but that this chance would in all probability have passed if Lenin had not been at the head of the Bolshevik party. There is fairly general agreement among students of history that, at least in their early phases, there are considerable similarities between revolutions; few would dispute that the periods of thaw since Stalin's death have been cyclical in character, or, to give an even more commonplace example, that the concentration of absolute power in the hands of one leader is, at best, a very risky venture. No one is likely to deny that the Soviet system has shown more achievements in heavy industry than in agriculture, and not only because for many years there was a decision to give priority to heavy industry. One could easily point to further lessons that can be drawn from the Soviet experience; some of these conclusions are specific to Russian conditions and therefore inapplicable to any other country or period, others seem to have a more general validity. There are few if any cut-and-dried lessons, but there is a vast body of experience which no one can ignore. That this experience is anything but foolproof, that most of these 'lessons' may be negative (don'ts rather than do's) hardly matters.

If some disregard history, which they think is an ingenious form of idleness, there is the opposite danger of too much history, of failing to understand what is essentially novel in a new situation, of misapplying historical experience, of false analogies. Most professional historians of Russia failed to understand the significance of 1917 because their outlook had been shaped exclusively by the elements of continuity in Russian history: Tsarism, its institutions, the whole social and political order which, with all its weaknesses, seemed unshakable. For that reason most of them were quite incapable of recognizing and assessing correctly the elements of change. True, some, like Hoetzsch and Pares or Sir John Maynard, later on came to accept the new order, but they thought it essentially the old, traditional, holy Russia in a new disguise; they over-emphasized the elements of tradition, they had no feeling for the depth and importance of the revolutionary changes that had taken place. Again, during the second world war, there was a spate of works stressing the 'big retreat', 'eternal Russia', and in general over-emphasizing the importance of the elements of tradition.

To take a more recent example: the role of Marxism-Leninism has traditionally been ignored in England and America for doctrine has never counted for much in the politics of these countries. But in the late nineteen-forties, and in particular in the fifties, there was a reaction; the Essential Marx, Lenin, and Stalin now found readers among ministers, generals, and other high officials in the West. This in itself was perhaps an encouraging phenomenon but it often had unfortunate results. The lessons came too late, and they were often studied out of context. Those who were then first making the acquaintance of proletarian revolution, dialectical materialism and the like, regarded these tenets as unchangeable components of Soviet policy. The diligent study of Lenin and Stalin (it was thought) would provide the key to the understanding of Soviet behaviour. Reality, alas, was not that simple; decades had passed since these doctrines had been formulated. The formulas *per se* had not been superseded (which only helped to compound the confusion) but the 'specific weight' of ideology as a motive in Soviet policy both at home and abroad had decreased. New problems and developments made new policies necessary, often irrespective of doctrinal tenets. This inability to appraise new trends correctly was reflected, to give yet another illustration, in an extreme way in the unwillingness of some circles not so long ago to accept the possibility of a rift between Moscow and Peking. The recent converts to the importance of Marxist–Leninist theory argued that there could not possibly be a quarrel between Russia and China since both systems were Marxist–Leninist in persuasion and thus subscribed to proletarian internationalism. One school of psychological thought (Harry Stack Sullivan) has called this *parataxic distortion* – the compulsion to meet current situations exclusively in terms of earlier ones, the inability to grasp what is new in each situation. But it was not really a revolutionary discovery of modern psychological thought: Mark Twain had given warning in *'Puddn'head' Wilson* . . . 'lest we be like the cat that sits down on a hot stove lid. She will never sit down on a hot stove lid again – and that is well. But also she will never sit down on a cold one anymore'.

It may be possible now for a student of modern history to take a position *au dessus de la melée* towards the French Revolution, to do justice at one and the same time to Jacobins, Girondists, and the forces of the *ancien régime*. Polemics about the French Revolution still abound but such an attitude is at least conceivable. The Russian Revolution, being of far more recent date, has had a more lasting impact (not only in Russia) and has stirred up even deeper and more violent passions. In these circumstances one must be deeply distrustful of those who claim to deal with the Russian Revolution or Soviet history from a standpoint of strict impartiality. On closer inspection either this impartial attitude turns out not to be genuine, or the authors' competence doubtful. Can one really know about Russia without becoming involved? For this reason, Soviet history is probably the most difficult terrain within the wider field of contemporary history. But being conscious of one's own views and attitudes, and of the impossibility of divesting oneself of one's intellectual equipment, does not mean that free rein can be given to all subjective judgment.

For quite a few of those who have written about Russia, Thierry's candid remark applies, namely, that he began to look into the works of history for proofs and arguments which would support his political beliefs. Or, as Anatole France said about one reader of history books: *il ne cherche jamais dans un histoire que les sottises qu'il sait déjà.* The majority of books on the Soviet Union published during the last seventy years are either indictments or apologias, polemics or hagiography. This is only natural and there is nothing wrong with political pamphleteering; the best of these books will no doubt survive. But there is also the danger that polemical writing goes on too long; if it is to be of any value, a book on the Russian Revolution written now ought to be different in approach from one written by contemporary observers. A biographer of Lenin writing in the 1980s ought to approach his subject differently from one who wrote while the founder of the Soviet state was alive. Objectivity does not imply that the later historian has to be a mediator between extreme positions; he may be as extreme in his condemnation or as ardent in his admiration as any contemporary. But he can no longer be public prosecutor or counsel for the defence; he is obliged to look at his subject from a higher vantage point, to take into consideration all factors and possibilities, however inconvenient and unpalatable. Thirty years after Stalin's death he may still reach the conclusion that Stalin was a great hero or a disaster for Russia, but regurgitating old polemics or panegyrics will be pointless. More than his colleagues in less disputed fields, the contemporary historian is obliged to make a determined effort to lower the temperature, to pursue his studies in a cool, sceptical, and self-searching manner.

Extreme manifestations of subjectivism have provoked some writers, not unnaturally perhaps, to stray too far in the opposite direction. Their proposed treatment has sometimes been worse than the disease they set out to cure. Shocked by virulent partisan spirit and lack of objectivity, by the palpable influence of the Cold War on the writing of history, they have proclaimed that the only duty of the historian is to understand, not to pass judgment, preaching a modernized version of Rankean historicism. But just as Ranke took certain self-evident truths for granted (as, for instance, the superiority of Prussia), these disciples also have their predilections and prejudices while claiming for themselves, and only for themselves, scientific objectivity. They have charged most of their colleagues with writing the history of Russia 'with an eye to shape the future rather than to illuminate the past', as was once said of Charles Beard. The rejoinder has usually been on the lines of Lord Acton's warning against those who merely want 'to understand': that the plea in extenuation of guilt and mitigation of punishment is perpetual in their writing; at every step one is met by arguments designed to excuse, to palliate, to confound right and wrong, and to reduce the just man to the level of the reprobate. Morality is ambulatory, moral notions fluid, a common code does not exist, 'you must consider the times, the class from which men sprang, the surrounding influences, the masters in their pulpits, the movements they obscurely obeyed, and so on, until responsibility is merged in numbers, and not a culprit is left for execution'. 'What execution?' Mr Carr has asked. Is the historian really a hanging judge, and aren't we all against capital punishment now? To which Sir Isaiah Berlin has replied that if all standards are relative one can neither defend nor condemn bias or moralism in history, for in the absence of a super standard all attitudes are morally neutral and nothing can be said on the matter at all.

If excessive moral indignation may blind the historian, the absence of moral judgment leads him into absurd and indefensible positions. That moral standards have varied in time and place has been known for a long time, but it does not follow that the conclusions of the Marquis de Sade are necessarily the correct ones. A historian who refrains from moral judgment could not have opposed Hitler's extermination of 'racially inferior minorities' for any other than aesthetic reasons. The case of this school of thought usually breaks down when pursued to its extreme logical conclusions, or at any rate is modified in practise; the crimes of reactionary movements are more harshly judged than the aberrations and scandals of socially progressive régimes. But if we accept that there are no universal standards, 'progressive' and 'reactionary' lose much, if not all, of their meaning, and a contemporary observer will be unable to decide which is which. Whether our final judgment of a historical movement or figure should depend (as Acton said) on the worst action, or whether, as Mr Carr has argued, it is pointless to condemn historical figures, will continue to be argued. There is no doubt, however, that the school of thought claiming that one ought to discard moral judgment altogether came into being as a reaction against too much moral indignation, and will disappear with the cause that provoked it.

The study of Soviet history has not been able to add much to yet another unfinished discussion of the philosophers – on causation in history, on historical laws, on the role of contingency and inevitability; in fact, it has taught little apart from the ever present need to be wary of sweeping generalizations, and this, too, was known before. We have already said that the 'revolutionary situation' in Petrograd and Moscow in 1917 would not have come to a head without the 'subjective factor', the presence of Lenin at the head of the Bolsheviks. There have been hundreds of revolutionary situations before and since, from Persia to Latin America; in a few the revolutionary party prevailed, in most the opportunity passed unused. In all these cases the presence of one man, or at most of a handful of people, has proved decisive. A revolution has hardly ever come as a bolt from the blue; it would be foolish to reject causality altogether. Even less can one ignore the role of the unforeseen. History shows that there are certain tendencies and trends in what we may call macro-history. One cannot really judge whether the moral standards of mankind have improved over the last two hundred years, and it is doubtful whether the literature and arts of the twentieth century are superior to those of earlier ages; not even an admirer would argue that Sholokhov is a greater writer than Tolstoy. But no one disputes that mankind has grown in numbers, that it is on the whole better educated, that production of most goods has increased, and that in the absence of a nuclear catastrophe all these trends are likely to continue in the developed countries. It is also true that these demographic and economic developments have brought about changes in social organization and that this, too, will continue. These truisms need restating from time to time in the face of extreme relativism and scepticism. But most historians are concerned with what happened in a particular country at a certain time. And in this respect 'historical laws' are only of limited help. If there has been a continuous development in the advanced countries towards higher living standards and, *grosso modo*, greater social justice, these countries have reached this stage (it would be too much to call it convergence) along various ways and byways, under various political systems. There was a predisposition towards a certain development, but there was never an Iron Law. In Soviet history (as in the history of other countries) there has been no inevitability, but there has been something in the nature of a theory of probability. Again, the situation has varied at different times; at certain moments the choice was wide open and the outcome altogether unpredictable. At others, in the nineteenthirties and forties for instance, the choice of possibilities was far more limited, and the course of events seemed predestined. There seems to be freedom of choice at major historical turning points;

but once a pattern has been set, B often seems to follow from A, and C from B, until after a number of years, or decades, the pattern disintegrates and a new turning point is reached. This seems to be one of the few lessons that can safely be drawn from Soviet history. There are not many left who believe in causation in history in the way Bossuet did with his Almighty who *tient du plus haut des cieux les rênes des tous les royaumes.* A believer in historical materialism, taught by much experience, will only profess his belief in the eventual victory of communism; he will try not to be tied down to predictions as to when, where, and how. In Marxist–Leninist theory and practice, the voluntarist element, the supremacy of politics over economic trends and social conditions, has gained steadily in importance from Lenin through Mao to Castro; recently it has even been argued that social development, and even the mass support of the proletariat or the peasants, is not really necessary so long as there are a handful of resolute professional revolutionaries willing and able to cut historical corners. In this sense the victory or defeat of Marxist–Leninist movements are neither proof nor refutation of historical materialism; by its intervention into history its theoretical prognosis becomes self-fulfilling (or self-stultifying). One can talk, therefore, about possibilities and probabilities in Soviet history, which at different times have assumed varying importance; now bordering on the inevitable, now being so vague or conflicting in character as to make the prospect of success or failure a highly hazardous affair. Some historical events are less accidental, and therefore more predictable, than others; most historians will no doubt agree that the second world war was less of an accident than the first. And yet had an attempt on Hitler's life succeeded in 1938, is it really certain that a war would still have been inevitable?

The Bolshevik revolution prevailed because, according to Lenin, Russia was the weakest link in the chain of imperialist powers. But did it happen only, or mainly, because it was the weakest link economically? It would be fairly safe to predict that, had the Revolution not happened, economic development in Russia would have proceeded at a fairly fast rate of growth in the twenties, thirties, and forties. All the same, the prospects for political democracy would not have been good; for reasons broadly similar to those that explain the failure of the Weimar Republic, a democratic government would hardly have stood the economic, social, and political strains of the post-war period. From this point on there would have been a wide number of choices – fascism, communism, military dictatorship, and so on.

The choices at the end of the second world war were limited; given the character of Stalin's régime, or Russia's traditional interests and its duties towards the world communist movement, given equally the interest of the Western allies, the wartime alliance was bound to break apart, once the common danger disappeared that had forged it. It is impossible to see how the cold war could have been prevented unless either side, or both, had not merely undergone a radical change of heart but had disregarded their basic interests. After Stalin's death the number of possibilities was considerably greater: a sudden return of Russia to political democracy was unlikely, as was a continuation of the old régime. But there were a great many possibilities in between.

Accidents, it has been said, matter only in the short range, whereas in a longer perspective the socio-economic trends assert themselves, and only they are decisive. Forecasting the distant future is admittedly less risky than predicting events in the next few months and years. But the socio-economic developments do not take place in a vacuum, they are in constant interplay with political factors. Would a second Lenin have led a victorious communist revolution at the time of the world economic crisis (assuming the revolution in 1917 had failed)? Was a new Hitler bound to arise and to involve his country in a second world war – had Hitler been killed at the time of the march on the *Feldherrenhalle* in 1923? To realize this does not involve a return to Carlyle. But the human factor remains elusive and unpredictable, and no aspect of history can be written ignoring it. Hitler or Stalin may be insignificant interludes *sub specie aeternitatis*; however from such insights philosophers are likely to benefit more than historians.

The task of the historian is not an enviable one. He has to bring order into an essentially disorderly world; he has to do so without doing violence to the multiplicity of facts, to generalize without suppressing evidence, to simplify complicated issues without becoming a terrible *simplificateur*. These seemingly insurmountable difficulties have induced more than one to jettison causality altogether, and to deny the possibility of generalizing about history. If history is intrinsically chaotic, if it is likely to remain so, if, lastly, everything depends on accidents, what is the point of charting certain probabilities and trends on a map most of which will remain *terra incognita* anyhow? Is it really possible to interpret the role of contingency in the framework of the elements of order, as has been advocated? It may seem an impossible task, and yet it is probably the only course of action he can profitably follow. The historian, it has been aptly said, can never be a thoroughgoing positivist; but once he has realized this he must still try to behave up to a point as though he were. For the only alternative is to give up history altogether.

It is not surprising that in the running battle between Marxist and non-Marxist historians the front line suddenly changes when the role of historical law and contingency is discussed against the background of recent Soviet history. Historical materialism charges other schools of historical thought with inability and unwillingness to acknowledge objective laws of social and historical development, with being content to describe the particular, refusing to generalize, subordinating economic to political and cultural history, in the last resort reducing historical development to chance, accident, or at best psychological motives. But the positions change once it is asked whether Stalin (and the whole Stalin era) was an accident or whether it was politically and socially conditioned, whether it was rooted both in Russia's past and in the sort of régime established in Russia after the revolution, whether, in other words, the Stalin era was an inevitable product of the laws of social development or a mere accident. At this point, some Western historians, normally writing empiricist history, adopt the Marxist approach and discover laws and necessities, whereas Soviet historians are forced to give an un-Marxist emphasis to personal and accidental factors. Soviet historians have not yet begun to write the history of this period, let alone to generalize.

Other questions arise from an occupation with Soviet history: Soviet historians regard political and cultural history as epiphenomena and have been severely critical of the schools of thought which have refused to see the decisive role of economic and social history. But what are the driving forces in Soviet history? Can the primacy of the economic and social factors over politics in the Soviet Union still be argued; can Lenin's and Stalin's policies be explained on this basis? Or was the 'jump from the realm of necessity into the realm of freedom' made in the Soviet Union in 1917, in the sense that man now shapes his own destiny, that political decisions are taken in cognizance of objective economic and social laws? Can the political history of the Soviet Union really be explained in these terms?

The Western historian of the Soviet Union has been under great and growing popular pressure not merely to describe the course of events in the last seventy years but to find certain patterns and regularities and to explain their meaning; and this, if possible, not only in terms of the past but also with reference to the present and the future. Those who expected clear-cut answers to topical problems have not been satisfied with the results. The conclusions were too often vague and tentative, if there were conclusions at all. For many historians continue to believe that their task is to deal with particular, unique events on which one cannot really generalize. But even those historians who took a wider and more ambitious view of the significance of history had to conclude all too often as a famous natural scientist once did, saying: *Ignoramus, ignorabimus.*

Where the limitations of history became obvious, sociology, political science, social psychology and other disciplines have stepped in and have tried to formulate explanations of recent Soviet history. While geopoliticians have referred to the undoubted fact that Russia has traditionally been a great landmass power and that, consequently, its foreign policy is dictated by the long-range interest and aspirations deriving from this fact, others emphasize the Slavic character is shaped by traditional Slavic institutions growing slowly through the centuries. Anthropologists of the 'culture and personality' school have explained the norms of Soviet behaviour with reference to national character.

Students of psycho-analysis have argued that character determines politics; they have engaged in character analysis from a distance, drawing attention, for instance, to latent homosexuality in the Russian national character and to Lenin as a 'primal father'. Sociologists, social psychologists, and political philosophers have produced a great number of theories, models and ideal types to explain Soviet operating characteristics, the strengths and weaknesses of the Soviet social system and thus, incidentally, the history of the Soviet Union. Quantification has been brought in and content analysis. Much of this has been abstract theorizing unrelated to the facts of history. What Christopher Dawson said about a certain kind of sociology applies to many of these schools – that they have tended to manufacture a history of their own which will be the obedient servant of any theory it happens to propound. They are often based on historical 'facts' that are unknown to the historians and they offer dogmatic solutions of historical problems which the historians themselves approach with the utmost diffidence. Kremlinologists have explained the course of events in terms of power struggle between individual leaders and interest groups. Western Marxists have offered a half dozen explanations, from the discussion about bureaucratic collectivism (Trotsky, Burnham, Bruno Rizzi, Peter Meyer) to the more recent writings of Isaac Deutscher.[1]

These various theories had their heyday in the nineteen-fifties; they were discussed and have been largely discarded, at least in so far as the more sweeping claims to universal validity were concerned. New theories are like new drugs which, when they appear on the market, are promoted by the pharmaceutical industry as wonder drugs. After a while most are discarded. As for the few that are retained their real spectrum of validity is usually much narrower than was originally thought. Some of the theories of the fifties have already been almost forgotten, for instance the concept of unchanging totalitarianism which arose under the impact of the late Stalin period. Events since have disproved it, even if few observers will dare to predict in what way totalitarian rule will ultimately be transformed. Other discussions have gradually been discontinued because it was realized that they were irrelevant, such as, for instance, whether the Soviet Union was state capitalist or bureaucratic collectivist or still basically socialist. Kremlinology, still a useful tool on occasion, has suffered an eclipse not because the struggle for power has ceased but because it has begun to matter much less who emerges on top. This is not the place to discuss whether the methodology or the various sociological, anthropological and psycho-analytical explanations were sound; the question of immediate interest is whether they have produced new insights. The answer is, by and large, negative. The analysis of a single individual is a very complicated process; to apply analysis to nations one does not know intimately, and great masses of people with whom there is no contact, is a hazardous enterprise. The teaching and insight of psycho-analysis (and of social psychology and cultural anthropology) have been common property for decades and have con-

---

[1] For a fuller discussion see Daniel Bell, 'Ten Theories in Search of Reality', in *The End of Ideology*, New York, 1960.

tributed to a better understanding of certain historical processes. But the specialized techniques developed by these disciplines have been of little help to the contemporary historian; inasmuch as the Soviet Union is concerned they have on the whole been inapplicable. Nor have the sociologists and anthropologists offered much more than a number of commonsense statements. If at present there is too much abstract theorizing in sociology this science is bound to play an important role in providing a general systematic analysis of the Soviet state and society and the Communist party. But to achieve this, sociology needs not only a method, but also facts. So far, almost all of its facts are second-hand, and they cover only certain parts of Soviet life. Conditions being as they are, it may be a long time before Western sociologists can have direct access to facts relevant to their studies.

What then remains in the 1980s of the various approaches propagated only a decade earlier? Little, apart from such commonsense notions that economics and geography matter, that national character is also important and that a study of a Soviet Middletown would, no doubt, be quite revealing. No revolutionary approach has emerged that sheds new light and gives dramatic insights into laws that 'lay hid in night'. Neither sociology nor political science nor social psychology is likely to supersede historical methods in the study of Soviet history. True, the historian will have to be more aware of developments in these disciplines, and be willing to borrow from them whenever necessary without false pride. The debates about methodology have helped the historian to understand better how many factors are involved in the historical process. The old factographic approach is on the way out and it is generally realized that there is not much point in writing political history in isolation from other aspects of life.

The attempt to make the study of Soviet history scientific by basing it on sociological or psychological methods that can be verified experimentally – through the use of statistics, for instance – was bound to fail. But it does not follow that the field is now wide open to all kinds of guesswork. It does not mean that all descriptions and explanations of Soviet history are equally valid. Every man is definitely not his own Sovietologist. There are certain basic rules about evidence, intellectual integrity and truthfulness. Only historians who adhere to these rules are, to quote Walsh, in a position to attain truth and objectivity as far as they are attained in history.

As time passes and as more events and patterns appear in clearer perspective the outlook for a more objective study improves. Our ideal historian of the Soviet Union will be steeped in epistemology and armed against excessive relativism. He will not reveal absolute laws and certainties, but provide a better understanding of probabilities. He will have accumulated considerable knowledge and experience and will exemplify the disciplined approach of the trained mind. He will of course write as well as Gibbon. His motto will be that of Fustel de Coulanges – not the impassioned speaker who told his students that history was speaking through him, but the other Fustel who wrote 'Quaero' – I am seeking.

A historian such as we have been attempting to describe, would indeed be an intellectual prodigy. In his mind powers scarcely compatible with each other must be tempered into an exquisite harmony. We shall sooner see another Shakespeare or another Homer. The highest excellence to which any single faculty can be brought would be less surprising than such a happy and delicate combination of qualities. Yet the contemplation of imaginary models is not an unpleasent or useless employment of the mind. It cannot, indeed, produce perfection, but it produces improvement . . . (Macaulay).

Bibliography

Some books in this selective list have been marked with an asterisk. They have either been discussed in some detail in the text, or are likely to be of most help to the non-expert in the first stages of his studies.

1 Russia and the West

AARON, D., *Writers on the Left*. New York, 1961.

BRASOL, B., *The World at the Crossroads*. New York, 1922.

CARROLL, E. MALCOLM, *Soviet Communism and Western Opinion 1919–1921*. Chapel Hill, 1965.

CAUTE, D., *Communism and the French Intellectuals*. London, 1964.

* *A Collection of Reports on Bolshevism in Russia*. Abridged Edition of *Parliamentary Papers, Russia No. 1* (1919). London, 1919.

* *The German–Bolshevik Conspiracy*. War Information Series No. 20. October, 1918. (Committee on Public Information).

GRAUBARD, S., *British Labour and the Russian Revolution 1917–1924*. London, 1956.

GWYNNE, H. A. (introd.), *The Cause of World Unrest*. London, 1920.

* KENNAN, G. F., *Russia Leaves the War*. Princeton, 1956.

LAQUEUR, W., *Russia and Germany*. London. 1965.

LASCH, C., *The American Liberals and the Russian Revolution*. New York, 1962.

LIPPMANN, W., and MERZ, C., *A Test of the News*. Supplement to *New Republic*, 4 August 1920.

PITT RIVERS, G., *The World Significance of the Russian Revolution*. Oxford, 1920.

PONCINS, VICOMTE L. DE, *The Secret Powers behind Revolution: Freemasonry and Judaism*. London, 1929.

Report of the Committee to collect information on Russia, 1921. Cmd. 1240 (Emmott Report).

ROSS, E. A., *The Russian Soviet Republic.* London, 1923.

SAROLEA, C., *Impressions of Soviet Russia.* London, 1924.

SISSON, E. G., *One hundred Red Days.* New Haven, 1931.

STRAKHOVSKY, L., *American Opinion about Russia, 1917–1920.* Toronto, 1961.

2   The Growth of Soviet Studies

FISHER, HAROLD H., ed., *American Research on Russia.* Bloomington, 1959.

HACKER, J., *Osteuropa Forschung in der Bundesrepublik*, supplement to *Das Parlament.* 14 September 1960.

LAQUEUR, WALTER, ed., *The State of Soviet Studies.* Cambridge, Mass., 1965.

UNIVERSITY GRANTS COMMITTEE: *Report of the Sub-Committee on Oriental, Slavonic and African Studies.* (Hayter Report). H.M.S.O. London, 1961.

3   1917

ABRAMOVITCH, R., *The Soviet Revolution 1917–39.* New York, 1962.

ADAMS, A., ed., *The Russian Revolution and Bolshevik Victory.* Boston, 1960.

ANTONOV-OVSEENKO, VL. ALEKS., *V Revoliutsii*, Moscow, 1957.

ASTROW, W., ed., *Illustrierte Geschichte der russischen Revolution.* Berlin, 1928.

BERDYAEV, N., *The Origin of Russian Communism.* New York, 1937.

BERKMAN, A., *The Bolshevik Myth.* London, 1923.

* BUCHANAN, G., *My Mission to Russia and other Diplomatic Memories.* 2 vols. London, 1923.

BUNYAN, J., FISHER, H. H., editors, *The Bolshevik Revolution 1917–18.* Stanford, 1934.

* CHAMBERLIN, W. H., *The Russian Revolution.* 2 vols. New York, 1935.

CHERNOV, V. M., *The Great Russian Revolution.* New Haven, 1936.

COMTE, G., ed., *La revolution russe par ses temoins.* Paris, 1963.

COQUIN, X., *La Revolution Russe (1917–1918).* Paris, 1962.

BIBLIOGRAPHY

* DENIKIN, A., *Ocherki russkoi smuty*. 5 vols. Berlin, 1921–6.

FLORINSKY, M. T., *The End of the Russian Empire*. New Haven, 1931.

FRANCIS, D. R., *Russia from the American Embassy, April 1916– November 1918*. New York, 1921.

HURWICZ, E., *Geschichte des russischen Buergerkrieges*. Berlin, 1927.

KENNAN, G. F., *Russia Leaves the War*. Princeton, 1956.

KERENSKY, A., *The Prelude to Bolshevism: The Kornilov Rebellion*. London, 1919.

* — *The Catastrophe*. London, 1927.

— *Russia and History's Turning Point*. New York, 1965.

LUXEMBURG, R., *Die russische Revolution*. Berlin, 1922.

MCNEAL, R. H., ed., *The Russian Revolution: Why did the Bolsheviks win?* New York, 1959.

* MELGUNOV, S. P., *Kak Bolsheviki zakhvatili vlast*. Paris, 1953.

* MILYUKOV, P. N., *Istoriia vtoroi russkoi revoliutsii*, 3 vols. Sofia, 1921–4.

MOOREHEAD, A., *The Russian Revolution*. New York, 1958.

NOULENS, J., *Mon Ambassade en Russie sovietique 1917–19*. 2 vols. Paris, 1932.

* *Padenie tsarskogo rezhima* (ed. P. E. Shchegolev and others). 7 vols. Moscow, 1924–7.

* PALEOLOGUE, M., *An Ambassador's Memoirs*. 3 vols. London, 1923–5.

PARES, B., *The Fall of the Russian Monarchy*. London, 1939.

PODVOISKII, N. P., *God 1917*. Moscow, 1917.

* POKROVSKII, M. N., *Oktyabrskaya Revolutsiia. Sbornik Statei 1917–27*. Moscow, 1929.

PRICE, M. P., *My Reminiscences of the Russian Revolution*. London, 1921.

RADKEY, O. H., *The Agrarian Foes of Bolshevism*. New York, 1958.

— *The Hammer under the Sickle*. New York, 1963.

RANSOME, A., *Six Weeks in Russia in 1919*. London, 1919.

* REED, J., *Ten Days that Shook the World*. New York, 1935.

RODZIANKO, M. Y., *The Reign of Rasputin: An Empire's Collapse*. London, 1927.

ROLLIN, H., *La revolution russe, Ses origines, ses resultats*. 3 vols. Paris, 1931.

SADOUL, J., *Notes sur la revolution bolchevique*. Moscow, 1918.

* SCHAPIRO, L., *The Origin of the Communist Autocracy*. London, 1955.

SETON WATSON, H., *The Decline of Imperial Russia*. London, 1952.

SHLYAPNIKOV, A., *Semnadtsatii God*. 4 vols. Moscow, 1925–31.

SHULGIN, V. V., *Dni (Vospominaniia)*. Leningrad, 1927.

SOROKIN, P., *Leaves from a Russian Diary*. London, 1925.

STALIN, I. V., *Na putyakh v oktyabru*. Moscow, 1925.

* SUKHANOV, N. N., *The Russian Revolution 1917*. New York, 1955. English abridged translation of *Zapiski o revoliutsii*. 7 vols. Berlin, 1922–3.

* TROTSKY, L., *The Russian Revolution*. New York, 1936.

ULLMAN, R. H., *Intervention and the War*. London, 1961.

Velikaia Oktiabrskaia Revoliutsiia. Dokumenty i Materialy. 6 vols. Moscow, 1957–62.

WARTH, R. D., *The Allies and the Russian Revolution*. Durham, N.C., 1954.

WILLIAMS, A. R., *Through the Russian Revolution*. New York, 1921.

WILTON, R., *Russia's Agony*. London, 1918.

4 Lenin

FISCHER, LOUIS, *The Life of Lenin*. New York, 1964.

FOX, R., *Lenin. A Biography*. London, 1933.

FÜLOP-MILLER, R., *Lenin and Gandhi*. London, 1927.

GOURFINKEL, N., *Lenine*. Paris, 1959.

GUILBEAUX, H., *Le portrait authentique de Lenine*. Paris, 1924.

HILL, C., *Lenin and the Russian Revolution*. London, 1947.

KERZHENTSEV, P., *Life of Lenin*. Moscow, 1937.

KRUPSKAYA, N. K., *Memories of Lenin*. London, 1930.

LANDAU-ALDANOV, M. A., *Lenin und der Bolschewismus*. Berlin, 1920.

LENIN, V. I., *Sochineniia*. First edition, vols. 1–20. Moscow, 1920–6.

— *Polnoe sobraniie sochineniia*. 5th edition. vols. 1–55. Moscow, 1958–65.

MARCU, V., *Lenin*. London, 1928.

MAXTON, J., *Lenin*. London, 1932.

MIRSKY, D. S., *Lenin*. London, 1931.

POSPELOV, P., *Lenin*. Moscow, 1960.

POSSONY, S., *Lenin. The Compulsive Revolutionary*. New York, 1965.

BIBLIOGRAPHY

RAUCH, G. VON, *Lenin. Die Grundlegung des Sowjetsystems.* Göttingen, 1962.
SHUB, DAVID, *Lenin.* New York, 1948.
SORLIN, PIERRE and IRENE, *Lenine, Trotsky et Staline 1921–1927.* Paris, 1961.
TREADGOLD, D. W., *Lenin and his rivals.* London, 1955.
TROTSKY, L., *Lenin.* London, 1925.
* ULAM, ADAM, *The Bolsheviks.* New York, 1965.
VEALE, F. J. P., *The Man from the Volga.* London, 1932.
VERNADSKY, G., *Lenin, Red Dictator.* New Haven, 1931.
WALTER, G., *Lenine.* Paris, 1950.
WEIDENFELD, K., *Lenin und sein Werk.* Munich, 1923.
* WOLFE, B., *Three who made a Revolution.* New York, 1948.

5 *Stalin*

BAJANOV, BORIS, *Stalin der rote Diktator.* Berlin, 1931.
* BARBUSSE, H., *Stalin, A New World Seen through one Man.* London, 1935.
BASSECHES, N., *Stalin.* New York, 1952.
* DEUTSCHER, ISAAC, *Stalin. A Political Biography.* London, 1949.
— *Stalin.* Revised Edition. London, 1966.
— *Russia after Stalin.* London, 1953.
'ESSAD BEY', *Stalin. The Career of a Fanatic.* London, 1932.
FISCHER, L., *The Life and Death of Stalin.* New York, 1952.
GRAHAM, S., *Stalin. An Impartial Study of the Life and Work of Joseph Stalin.* London, 1931.
HILGER, G., *Stalin. Aufstieg der UdSSR zur Weltmacht.* Göttingen, 1959.
JUST, A., *Stalin und seine Epoche.* Munich, 1953.
* LEVINE, I. D., *Stalin. A Biography.* London, 1931.
LUDWIG, E., *Leaders of Europe.* London, 1934.
— *Stalin.* New York, 1942.
LYONS, E., *Stalin. Czar of all the Russians.* London, 1940.
MURPHY, J., *Stalin 1879–1944.* London, 1945.
NOVE, A., *Economic Rationality and Soviet Politics; or Was Stalin really Necessary?* New York, 1964.
RIGBY, T. H., ed., *Stalin.* London, 1966.
* SOUVARINE, BORIS, *Stalin: A Critical Survey of Bolshevism.* London, 1939.
* STALIN, JOSEPH, *A Short Biography.* (Translated from the Russian.) London, 1940.

STALIN, I. V., *Sochineniia.* vols. 1–13 (no more published). Moscow, 1946–51.

TROTSKY, L., *Stalin. An Appraisal of the Man and his Influence.* New York, 1941.

YAROSLAVSKY, E., *Landmarks in the Life of Stalin.* London, 1942.

6   E. H. Carr

CARR, E. H., *Karl Marx, a Study in Fanaticism.* London, 1934.
— *The Twenty Years Crisis.* London, 1939.
— *The Soviet Impact on the Western World.* London, 1946.
— *Conditions of Peace.* London, 1942.
* — *A History of Soviet Russia:*
— *The Bolshevik Revolution.* 3 vols. London, 1950–3.
— *The Interregnum 1923–4.* London, 1954.
— *Socialism in One Country.* 3 vols. London, 1958–64.
— *Studies in Revolution.* London, 1950.
* — *What is History?* London, 1961.

7   Soviet Historiography

BLACK, C. E., ed., *Rewriting Russian History.* New York, 1956.
BUBNOV, A. S., *VKPb.* vol. XI of the *Great Soviet Encyclopedia.* Moscow, 1930.
DATSIUK, B. D., ed., *Istoriia SSSR.* Moscow, 1963.
Istoriia grazhdanskoi voini v SSSR 1917–1922. 5 vols. Moscow, 1936–60.
* *Istoriia KPSS.* One vol. 2nd edition. Moscow, 1962.
* *Istoriia KPSS.* In five vols. vol. I. Moscow, 1964.
Istoriia velikoi otechestvennoi voiny sovetskovo soyuza. 5 vols. Moscow, 1960–3.
* KEEP, JOHN, ed., *Contemporary History in the Soviet Mirror.* London, 1964.
KNORIN, V. G., ed., *Kratkaia Istoriya VKPb.*
* *Kratkii Kurs Istorii VKPb.* Moscow, 1938.
LYADOV, M. N., *25 let RKPb.* N. Novgorod, 1923.
MARKO, K., *Sowjethistoriker zwischen Ideologie und Wirklichkeit.* Cologne, 1964.
MAZOUR, A. G., *An Outline of Modern Russian Historiography.* 2nd edition. Princeton, 1958.
NEVSKII, V. I., *Istoriya RKPb.* Leningrad, 1926.

BIBLIOGRAPHY

PANKRATOVA, A. M., ed., *Istoriya SSSR*. 3 parts. 15th ed. Moscow, 1956.

POKROVSKII, M. N., *Istoricheskaia Nauka i borba Klassov*. Moscow, 1933.

— *Russkaia istoricheskaia literatura v klassovom osveshshenii*. 2 vols. Moscow, 1927–30.

POPOV, N., *Ocherk Istorii RKPb*. Moscow, 1926.

* SHESTAKOV, A. V., *Kratkii Kurs Istorii SSSR*. Moscow, 1937.

SHTEPPA, K. F., *Russian Historians and the Soviet State*. New Brunswick, 1962.

YAROSLAVSKII, E., *Kratkie Ocherki po istorii RKPb*. Moscow, 1926.

* — ed. *Istoriya VKPb*. 4 vols. Moscow, 1926–50.

* ZHUKOV, E. M., ed., *Sovetskaia Istoricheskaia Entsiklopediia*, in 12 vols. vol. I. Moscow, 1961.

8 *Interpretations of Soviet History*

ARENDT, H., *The Origins of Totalitarianism*. New York, 1951.

ARMSTRONG, J., *The Politics of Totalitarianism*. New York, 1961.

BAUER, O., *Bolschewismus oder Sozialdemokratie?* Vienna, 1921.

— *Zwischen zwei Weltkriegen*. Bratislava, 1936.

BERDYAEV, N., *The Origins of Russian Communism*. London, 1937.

— *The Russian Revolution*. London, 1931.

BRZEZINSKI, Z. K., *Ideology and Power in Soviet Politics*. London, 1962.

— and HUNTINGTON, S. P., *Political Power USA–USSR*. New York, 1964.

CLIFF, T., *Russia. A Marxist Analysis*. London, n.d.

CONQUEST, R., *Power and Policy in the USSR*. New York, 1961.

— *Russia after Khrushchev*. New York, 1965.

DAN, TH., *Sowjet Russland wie es wirklich ist*. Berlin, n.d.

— *The Origins of Bolshevism*. London, 1964.

DANIELS, R. V., *The Conscience of the Revolution. Communist Opposition in Russia*. Cambridge, Mass., 1960.

DAVIES, J. E., *Mission to Moscow*. London, 1942.

DEUTSCHER, I., *Russia What Next?* London, 1953.

DURANTY, W., *I Write as I Please*. London, 1935, 2nd ed. 1937.

* FAINSOD, M., *How Russia is Ruled*. 2nd ed. Cambridge, Mass., 1963.

FEILER, A., *The Experiment of Bolshevism*. London, 1930.

FEUCHTWANGER, L., *Moscow 1937*. London, 1937.

FRIEDRICH, C., and BRZEZINSKI, Z., *Totalitarian Dictatorship and Autocracy*. New York, 1956.

GURIAN, W., *Bolshevism Theory and Practice*. London, 1932.

GIDE, A., *Back from the USSR*. London, 1937.

HINDUS, M., *Humanity Uprooted*. London, 1931.

KAUTSKY, K., *Terrorism and Communism*. London, 1920.

— *Bolshevism at a Deadlock*. London, 1931.

LAUE, TH. VON, *Why Lenin, Why Stalin?* London, 1965.

LOWENTHAL, R., *World Communism. The Disintegration of a Secular Faith*. London, 1964.

* LUXEMBURG, R., *The Russian Revolution*. London, 1922.

LYONS, E., *Assignment in Utopia*. New York, 1937.

PARES, B., *Russia*. London, 1940 and subsequent editions.

— *Russia and the Peace*. London, 1944.

ROSENBERG, ALFRED, *Pest in Russland*. Munich, 1922.

ROSENBERG, ARTHUR, *History of Bolshevism*. London, 1934.

ROSTOW, W. W., *The Dynamics of Soviet Society*. New York, 1953.

RUSH, M., *Political Succession in the USSR*. New York, 1965.

* RUSSELL, B., *The Practice and Theory of Bolshevism*. London, 1920.

* SCHAPIRO, L., *The Communist Party of the Soviet Union*. London, 1960.

SCHUMAN, F. L., *Night over Europe*. London, New York, 1941.

SETON WATSON, H., *From Lenin to Khrushchev*. New York, 1960.

SHACHTMAN, M., *The Bureaucratic Revolution*. New York, 1962.

* STEINBERG, J., *Verdict of Three Decades*. New York, 1950.

TIMASHEFF, N., *The Great Retreat; the Growth and Decline of Communism in Russia*. New York, 1946.

TREADGOLD, D. W., *Twentieth Century Russia*. Chicago, 1959.

TROTSKY, L., *The Revolution Betrayed*. London, 1937.

ULAM, A., *The New Face of Soviet Totalitarianism*. Cambridge, Mass., 1963.

* WEBB, S. and B., *Soviet Communism: a New Civilization*. London, 1935.

WOLFE, B. D., *Communist Totalitarianism; Keys to the Soviet System*. Boston, 1961.

BIBLIOGRAPHY

Some notable books 1966–87

AVRICH, PAUL, *The Russian Anarchists*. Princeton, N.J., 1967.
— *Kronstadt 1921*. New York, 1974.
CARR, E. H., *Twilight of the Comintern*. London, 1982.
— *A History of the Soviet Union*. 14 vols. London, 1950–1978.
— *The Russian Revolution, from Lenin to Stalin*. New York, 1979.
D'ENCAUSSE, H. CARRÈRE, *Stalin: Order Through Terror*. New York, 1982.
COHEN, STEPHEN, *Bukharin and the Bolshevik Revolution*. New York, 1973.
— *Rethinking the Soviet Experience*. New York, 1985.
CONQUEST, R., *The Great Terror*. New York, 1971.
— *Harvest of Sorrow*. New York, 1986.
DANIELS, ROBERT V., *Red October*. New York, 1967.
DAVIES, R. W., *The Socialist Offensive*. Cambridge, Mass., 1980.
DUNLOP, JOHN, *The Faces of Contemporary Russian Nationalism*. Princeton, N.J., 1983.
ERICSON, JOHN, *The Road to Stalingrad*. New York, 1975.
— *The Road to Berlin*. New York, 1983.
FERRO, MARC, *The Russian Revolution of February 1917*. London, 1972.
— *October 1917*. Boston, 1980.
FITZPATRICK, SHEILA, *The Russian Revolution 1917–32*. New York, 1982.
GETTY, J. ARCH, *Origins of the Great Purges*. Cambridge, Mass., 1985.
GILL, GRAEM J., *Peasants and Government in the Russian Revolution*. New York, 1979.
HAIMSON, L., ed., *The Mensheviks*. Chicago, 1974.
HASEGAWA, T., *The February Revolution: Petrograd 1917*. Seattle, Wash., 1981.
HELLER, M. and NEKRICH, A., *Utopia in Power*. New York, 1986.
HINGLEY, RONALD, *Joseph Stalin, Man and Legend*. New York, 1974.
HOSKING, G., *The First Socialist Society: A History of the Soviet Union from Within*. Cambridge, Mass., 1985.
HOUGH, JERRY F., *The Soviet Union and Social Science Theory*. Cambridge, Mass., 1977.
KATKOV, G., *Russia, 1917: The February Revolution*. New York, 1967.

KEEP, JOHN, *The Russian Revolution*. New York, 1976.

KNEI-PAZ, BARUCH, *The Political Thought of Leon Trotsky*. Oxford, Eng., 1978.

KOENKER, DIANE, *Moscow Workers and the 1917 Revolution*. Princeton, N.J., 1981.

KENEZ, PETER, *The Birth of the Propaganda State*. Cambridge, Mass., 1985.

LEWIN, MOSHE, *The Making of the Soviet System*. New York, 1985.

— *Russian Peasants and Soviet Power*. London, 1968.

MANDEL, DAVID, *The Petrograd Workers and the Soviet Seizure of Power*. New York, 1984.

MATTHEWS, M., *Class and Society in the Soviet Union*. London, 1972.

MEDVEDEV, ROY, *Let History Judge*. New York, 1971.

MELGUNOV, S., *The Bolshevik Seizure of Power*. Santa Barbara, Cal., 1972.

NOVE, ALEC, *Stalinism and After*. London, 1975.

PETHYBRIDGE, R., *The Social Prelude to Stalinism*. New York, 1974.

RABINOWITZ, A., *Prelude to Revolution*. Bloomington, Ill., 1968.

— *The Bolsheviks Come to Power*. New York, 1976.

RALEIGH, DONALD J., *Revolution on the Volga*. Ithaca, N.Y., 1986.

RIGBY, T. H., *Lenin's Government*. Cambridge, Mass., 1979.

ROSENBERG, W., *Liberals in the Russian Revolution*. Princeton, N.J., 1974.

ROSENFELDT, NIELS E., *Knowledge and Power*. Copenhagen, 1978.

SAUL, NORMAN E., *Soldiers in Revolt*. Lawrence, Kans., 1978.

SCAMMELL, MICHAEL, *Solzhenitsyn*. London, 1984.

SCHAPIRO, LEONARD, *Totalitarianism*. London, 1972.

— *Soviet Studies*. London, 1986.

SEATON, ALBERT, *Stalin as Warlord*. London, 1975.

SERVICE, ROBERT, *Lenin, a Political Life*, vol. 1. London, 1985.

SHUKHMAN, HAROLD, *Lenin and the Russian Revolution*. New York, 1966.

SMITH, S. A., *Red Petrograd*. Cambridge, Mass., 1983.

SOLZHENITSYN, A., *The Gulag Archipelago*. New York, 1973.

SUNY, RONALD G., *The Baku Commune 1917–18*. Princeton, N.J., 1977.

THOMPSON, JOHN M., *Revolutionary Russia, 1917*. New York, 1981.

BIBLIOGRAPHY

TUCKER, R. C., ed., *Stalinism.* New York, 1977.
— *Stalin as Revolutionary.* New York, 1974.
ULAM, ADAM, *Stalin.* New York, 1973.
— *Expansion and Coexistence: The History of Soviet Foreign Policy.*
New York, 1968.
URBAN, GEORGE, ed., *Stalinism.* London, 1982.
WADE, REX A., *The Russian Search for Peace.* Stanford, Cal.,
1969.

Index

About the Author

Walter Laqueur is Chairman of the Research Council, Center for Strategic and International Studies in Washington, University Professor at Georgetown University and co-director of the Institute of Contemporary History and Wiener Library in London. The founding editor of *Survey* (London, 1955–65), he is the co-editor and founder of the *Journal of Contemporary History, Washington Quarterly,* and the *Washington Papers.* His books include *Young Germany* (1962), *Russia and Germany* (1966), *Road to Jerusalem* (1969), *The Struggle for the Middle East* (1969), *Europe Since Hitler* (1970), *A History of Zionism* (1972), *Weimar* (1975), *Terrorism* (1977), and *The Terrible Secret* (1981). In 1969 he received the first Distinguished Writer's award from the Center for Strategic and International Studies.